The Multiple Worlds of Pynchon's *Mason & Dixon*

Studies in American Literature and Culture

The Multiple Worlds of Pynchon's *Mason & Dixon*

*Eighteenth-Century Contexts,
Postmodern Observations*

Edited by
Elizabeth Jane Wall Hinds

CAMDEN HOUSE

First published 2005
by Camden House

Camden House is an imprint of Boydell & Brewer Inc.
668 Mt. Hope Avenue, Rochester, NY 14620, USA
www.camden-house.com
and of Boydell & Brewer Limited
PO Box 9, Woodbridge, Suffolk IP12 3DF, UK
www.boydellandbrewer.com

ISBN: 1–57113–318–6

Library of Congress Cataloging-in-Publication Data

The multiple worlds of Pynchon's Mason & Dixon: eighteenth-century contexts, postmodern observations / edited by Elizabeth Jane Wall Hinds
    p. cm. — (Studies in American literature and culture)
Includes bibliographical references and index.
ISBN 1–57113–318–6 (acid-free paper)
    1. Pynchon, Thomas. Mason & Dixon. 2. Biographical fiction,
American—History and criticism. 3. Mason, Charles, 1728–1786—In
literature. 4. Postmodernism (Literature)—United States. 5. Literature
and history—United States. 6. Frontier and pioneer life in literature.
7. Dixon, Jeremiah—In literature. 8. Scientists in literature. I. Hinds,
Elizabeth Jane Wall, 1960– II. Title. III. Series.

PS3566.Y55M3736 2005
813'.54—dc22

                                                              2005014649

A catalogue record for this title is available from the British Library.

This publication is printed on acid-free paper.
Printed in the United States of America.

Contents

Enlightenment Microhistories

Preface

IN DECEMBER OF 1998, the Modern Language Association hosted, in San Francisco, its first session solely devoted to *Mason & Dixon,* which had just been released in 1997. Having fallen utterly under its spell, I co-wrote, with my colleague John Loftis, a paper for that session, and after our early morning MLA presentation, all of the presenters — Terry Reilly, Hans-Joachim Berressem, Frank Palmeri, John and I — went out for breakfast.

Trained as an eighteenth-century Americanist, I had spent some years alternating between studies of eighteenth-century subjects and, as a kind of palate cleanser, publications on postmodern cultural subjects like *Star Trek,* heavy metal music, and increasingly, on Thomas Pynchon's novels. So when *Mason & Dixon* was published, I was ecstatic. I thought surely this novel was for *me,* in some scholarly-mystical way — that I was uniquely suited to study it because of my clever, switch-hitting, eighteenth-century and postmodern research agenda. The MLA post-session breakfast turned out to be a real eye opener: everyone sitting at that table, we all learned, had had the same rather solipsistic thought. *All* of us were eighteenth-century specialists, and all had "dabbled" in Pynchon studies over the years. But there was not a dilettante among us; we brought to the table a wealth of cultural-historical knowledge that seemed specifically positioned to unpack the bizarre, real-unreal, historical-modern landscape of *Mason & Dixon.*

That breakfast cured me of my narcissism regarding *Mason & Dixon,* and put in its place a strong curiosity to hear what others had to say about its eighteenth-century contexts. These many years later, I'm pleased to have heard so much more, largely from the contributors to this volume — among them, I'm happy to say, Frank Palmeri, from the original breakfast group. This volume has been about three years in the collecting, and my greatest thanks go to the contributors for sticking it out with me through a cross-country move and the distractions and lacunae that come with department chairing. Reversing Mason and Dixon's route, I headed east, from Colorado to New York, and in the process, have begun, with this volume, to get back to the origin of things American.

Two institutions have provided support for this collection. The work began, conceptually, during a sabbatical leave from the University of Northern Colorado. My colleagues there, Tracey Sedinger, Joonok Huh, and Rosemary Hathaway helped me to keep my arguments honest and my prose far cleaner than it would otherwise be: I owe them a debt of gratitude for their tough readings and steady friendship. John Loftis, who never tires of ideas, helped provide me with focus, both during our co-production of the MLA paper and during the early versions of what would turn out to be the introduction to this volume. Thanks go to my students — in particular to Ken Hughes — who made the long and rollicking trip through *Mason & Dixon* with me.

Since 2003, SUNY Brockport has given me a solid foundation and a supportive home. I am also indebted to a terrific team of editors at Camden House. Mark Klemens has been unflaggingly encouraging, and Jim Walker has engaged in the kind of persistent, stimulating dialogue that all authors should have the great fortune of experiencing.

Note on Quotations from *Mason & Dixon*

M ASON & DIXON INCLUDES a great many ellipses in the original. To distinguish between Pynchon's ellipses and those added by authors of the essays to indicate where they have omitted text, the latter will be enclosed in brackets [. . .] — while Pynchon's original ellipses will appear with no brackets.

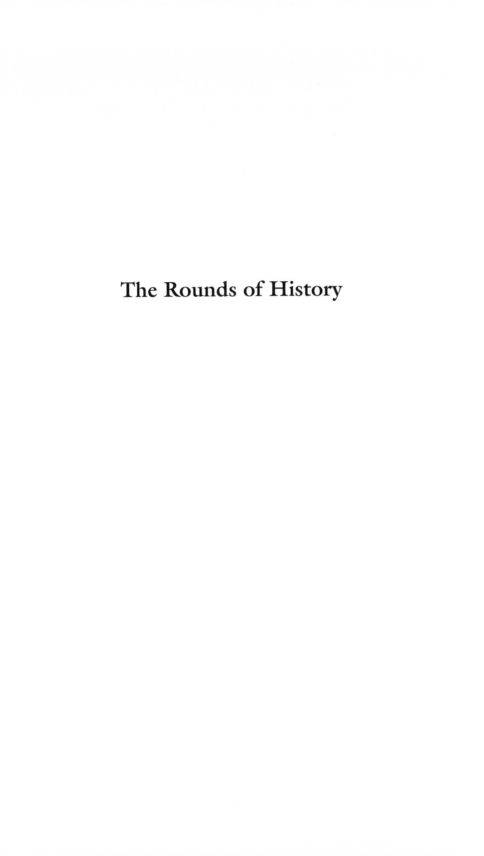

The Rounds of History

Introduction:
The Times of *Mason & Dixon*

Elizabeth Jane Wall Hinds

> *Happy are those ages when the starry sky is the map of all possible paths — ages whose paths are illuminated by the light of the stars. Everything in such ages is new and yet familiar, full of adventure and yet their own. The world is wide and yet it is like home, for the fire that burns in the soul is of the same essential nature as the stars.*
> — György Lukács, *The Theory of the Novel*

Making the Rounds of History

THOMAS PYNCHON'S 1997 *Mason & Dixon* is a novel obsessed with time. A "postmodern" novel, it reconstructs a historical period, the mid- to late-eighteenth century, with both an accuracy surpassing many *bona fide* histories and a disregard for the actual past seldom met with in a historical novel. Its play of and with histories, along with its determinedly late-twentieth-century timbre, makes time — and especially its passing — a constant focus. From first to last, from character Charles Mason's melancholia associated with his wife's passing, to the deep and broad concern with calendar reform in the novel, to the very fact of its being an "eighteenth-century" novel, *Mason & Dixon* layers time periods and temporal themes to produce an uncertainty of reading bordering on vertigo; finally, and from the first page, this constant thrust of time passing sets up a nostalgia that progresses and deepens at the same time the novel mocks the ludicrous idea of nostalgic sentimentality. It begins with a past so thoroughly passed that it is past perfect, and with a scene of childhood so nostalgically rendered as to be always already in the past:

> Snow-Balls have flown their Arcs, starr'd the Sides of Outbuildings, as of Cousins, carried Hats away into the brisk Wind off Delaware,— the Sleds are brought in and their Runners carefully dried and greased, shoes deposited in the back Hall, a stocking'd-foot Descent

made upon the great Kitchen, in a purposeful Dither since Morning,
punctuated by the ringing Lids of various Boilers and Stewing-Pots,
fragrant with Pie-Spices, peel'd Fruits, Suet, heated Sugar,— the
Children, having all upon the Fly, among rhythmic slaps of Batter
and Spoon, coax'd and stolen what they might, proceed, as upon each
afternoon all this snowy Advent, to a comfortable Room at the rear
of the House, years since given over to their carefree Assaults. (5)

Such complex temporality figures alongside spatial concepts that are
also multiply layered in this novel. A story about drawing a conceptual
line in space, *Mason & Dixon* uses the Line as literal and figurative spine
for a corpus spreading over the globe and across two centuries. The culmination of the early modern era, the eighteenth century as reproduced
here packs in historical events over a space if not quite global, then one at
least representing characters from every corner of the globe. Within these
layers of space and time, Pynchon offers a "thick description" of documented history, where we encounter among other things Symmes' hole,
Jenkin's ear, the Transit of Venus, Jesuits in Quebec, the Mason-Dixon
Line itself, and everywhere, everywhere, slavery — slaves in Cape Town,
slaves in Bencoolen, slaves in North America, slaves of every color and
caste.

This stuff of history Pynchon delivers straight, the inarguable records
passed down in cold fact and brought to life again with character and
narrative. But *Mason & Dixon* is more than a "historical novel": beyond
just the record of what *did* happen, it animates what *might* have happened. In a century most noted in the West for its rationalism and cool
scientific interests, it revivifies the fertility of imagination that could and
did produce, in historical fact, both widespread reform of weights and
measures *and* common sideshow-type exhibits featuring talking dogs, wax
automata, and Jacques de Vaucanson's mechanical duck. Indeed, like time
and space in *Mason & Dixon* — the vertiginous collapsing of time periods
and the geographical wandering that amounts to a kind of spacial entropy — the natural world, and with it, the physics on which nature depends, also exist in a kind of boundary state wherein categories of "kind"
are as likely to cross over — from animal to human or human to vegetable
or animal to machine — as to stay comfortably and predictably in place.
Mason & Dixon enacts, then, an unsettled boundary existence with respect to several narrative objects: time, space, and nature. In doing so, it
represents a cultural landscape both continuously developing from the
mid-eighteenth century to the late twentieth, and weirdly, almost super-
naturally, also working in reverse, as time, space, and nature seem to be
influenced *in* the eighteenth century *by* the twentieth. Such historiography is of particular interest in that it collapses two eras into a unique time-

space that can be described as a border phenomenon, a space neither eighteenth nor late-twentieth century but including both.

The essays in this volume explore these boundary conditions in *Mason & Dixon* to seek to define what amounts to anachronisms of time, space, and nature. They range from analyses of the novel's temporal and spatial structure, to explorations of consumption and its relationship to slavery, to the relationship of power to spatiality, temporality, cartography, and historicity in *Mason & Dixon,* and finally to microhistorical moments of the eighteenth century: Enlightenment treatments of insanity and the weavers' rebellion. Each makes its focus the linkage between eighteenth and twentieth centuries. With these emphases, each is thoroughly concerned, whether directly or indirectly, with history, the present, and the passing of time.

With its collapsing of time periods, the novel insists that the past two hundred years be seen as one long scene, that the difference between the centuries amounts to very little at least in that the rationalizing impulse of the weighing and measuring, scientific eighteenth century deserves, as we still deserve here in the postmodern era, a solid round of criticism. As we see the consequences of scientific rationalism turned to geographical effect in contemporary realities such as global warming, and in the spiritual and ethical poverty of consumerism "foreseen" in *Mason & Dixon;* and as we have the benefit of historical distance to view the long-term personal, political, and national consequences of slavery and "Indian removal" that *Mason & Dixon* "documents," the Enlightenment mandate to redesign the natural world in light of intellectual categories, the habit of design that produced the Mason-Dixon Line, comes to be regarded in this novel as both an early manifestation of and a backward-echoing of late-postmodern life. Pynchon's historiography links the actual with an imagined eighteenth century, with the imagined bearing a close resemblance to postmodern sensibility — the disregard for the planet on the one hand, and concern amounting to paranoia on the other, the thrill of speed, the glib and practical-joking interaction of characters, all motivating a plot the main outlines of which did in fact occur in the eighteenth century.

Beyond the "factual" history, what *Mason & Dixon* more elegantly delivers is a history re-imagined, an alternative to recorded history in the form of what might be called the paranormal: reading this novel is like a visit to Charles Willson Peale's museum, itself an eighteenth-century creation, with its oddities and "freaks of nature" just close enough to verifiable fact to *look* believable; we question the veracity of a Peale display only out of its uniformly odd context, just as we question Pynchon's quasi-supernatural characters and happenings — those border phenomena — only in retrospect and under the harsh light of the least imaginative scientific method. If Peale could offer as "natural science" an exhibit of a then-exotic, slightly unbelievable mongoose from Sumatra alongside its American Buffalo, Pynchon can easily conjure an eighteenth-century obsession with extremes of the natural world, the "science" that vivifies the mechanical, the "natural" that borders on and intersects with the supernatural.

This alternative history offers, for instance, the mid-century invention, Jacques de Vaucanson's duck, which (who?) in Pynchon's re-telling becomes inspirited with life. More than merely animated, the duck evolves to a degree that her speed eventually makes her invisible, from which position she can stalk and in her way court Chef Armand, with whom she is smitten. A perverse love indeed, for Armand is famous for his variations on roast *canard*. And so it goes in Pynchon's universe, where the factual comes to be — who can say at just what point, exactly? — outrageous. The duck's superanimate life is not the only case of physics verging on metaphysics in *Mason & Dixon*. We are to understand from Pynchon's telling that William Emerson, mathematician and author of a series of books on "Fluxions," was Jeremiah Dixon's teacher; more, that Emerson routinely taught his pupils to fly. Emerson's historicity lays a groundwork of fact for this story: since he did exist, maybe he *did* teach his pupils something like flight, or at least its dynamics. But it would have been highly unlikely for Emerson to have been Dixon's teacher, for he was too ornery to keep a teaching post. While Emerson did have a few students early in his career, he lost them because of his bad temper and his life-long refusal to join the Royal Society.

Stranger and stranger become the connections between the actual eighteenth century and Pynchon's exaggeration of it. Timothy Tox, Pynchon's fictional national poet, author of the frequently quoted *The Line,* certainly bears close enough resemblance to Joel Barlow, poet of the doggerel *Columbiad* to make one wonder just how much Pynchon is inventing. The supernatural exists side by side with the natural to produce these border phenomena; such narrative interchanges operate in the same way that Jésus Arrabal, a character from *The Crying of Lot 49*, describes as "magic": "another world's intrusion into this one" (*Lot 49* 88). And indeed, the "magical" in *Mason & Dixon,* the presence of conversing ghosts and werewolves, a Jenkin's ear that listens, a Benjamin Franklin who never sleeps, all these oddities do not amount to an entirely made-up eighteenth century and seldom participate in the outright supernatural; it was in fact part of the recorded Anglo-American scientific scene to look into the farthest reaches of scientific possibility, to welcome the bizarre as *evidence* of the rational. One recurring character, the Learned English Dog, best verbalizes the happy coexistence of these "rational" and "irrational" universes. Questioned by Mason, who wonders that a dog (who prefers the name "Fang" to his proper "LED") can talk at all, he responds with a shrug: "'Tis the Age of Reason, rff?" (22).

History in *Mason & Dixon* is where small, pointedly insignificant lives of individuals meet global, long-lastingly important events such as the building of the Line and the Transit of Venus. If history is Pynchon's subject, the objects of his history are Charles Mason and Jeremiah Dixon, eponymous characters caught up in what appears to be an overdetermined machine of history, so ineffectual are their desires and plans. Dixon, a mere surveyor, hasn't a clue why he's been hired to work with astronomer Mason, and vice versa, but for Dixon, the adventure is worth the trip; Mason, a personality so "Melancholick" his recently deceased wife regularly called him Mopery, has much more at stake in the trip. But for all their palpable characterization, even Mason and Dixon themselves sense that the machine of time, of the Royal Society, of powers beyond their ability to know, much less control — the web of influence itself — is the main character of their paranoid plot: in short, they are themselves secondary. Meeting Captain Zhang, a Chinese runaway from the Jesuit recruiting machine in Quebec, Dixon is informed that "*We* [Zhang and his nefarious alter-ego, Zarpazo] happen to be the principal Personae here, not you two! Nor has your Line any Primacy in this, being rather a Stage-Setting. . . ." Dixon barely flinches: "Well, it's no worse than Copernicus, is it. . . ? The Center of it all, moving someplace else like thah'. . . ? Better not mention this to Mason" (545).

Mason & Dixon on the one hand domesticates its historical subjects — the Royal Society, their scientific interests, and their handymen Mason and Dixon — by giving them life and desires and quirks; yet on the other hand, it pictures an alien and alienating set of events not so much enacted by its characters as forced on them by channels of power all but invisible. Mason and Dixon, a couple of ordinary guys, persist through this novel with an innocence of power unimaginable except in a world as sprawling and a power structure as decentralized or at least as untraceable as any modern bureaucracy. The large world Mason and Dixon work in, beginning long before their assignment to America, in South Africa, and ending — in one of its endings — on a Mall on the Atlantic, holds encounters with a great number of powerful figures in history: a hemp-smoking Colonel George Washington, Samuel Johnson, Thomas Jefferson (identifiable only as a red-haired kid in, naturally, a bar), and most strangely, a Ben Franklin characterized as a pub-crawling insomniac who cooks up scientific projects like his namesake stove by day and runs bizarre electrical experiments with bar customers by night. Dixon, the night-dwelling thrill seeker, is of course the one to volunteer to be connected to Dr. Franklin's electrical machinery, and very nearly gets himself killed, so powerful is the voltage; his next thought, however, is going back for more. Mason's black moods prevent such thrill-seeking, but he does enjoy depressive states that bring him to a low enough ecstasy to hallucinate his dead wife and to converse with her, as well as to converse with Fang and Jenkin's ear.

While *Mason & Dixon* goes everywhere with the daily life of these ordinary folks, it also teases at the less-than-ordinary networks of power Mason and Dixon abide in. Employed by the Royal Society, neither has a clear picture of his place or their combined role in the organization. Questions proliferate, the answers to which cultivate suspicion rather than explanation: why did the RS hire a mere surveyor to assist Mason in the first place for the Transit of Venus work in South Africa, and then later for the work of cutting their eight-yard-wide "Visto" between Pennsylvania and Maryland? Why does the first ship they're on — the *Seahorse* — get ordered toward Bencoolen in spite of impending sure battle with the French ship *l'Grand*? This early episode is enough to make the two, for all their differences of character, paranoid enough to co-author a letter to the RS, believing in their hearts that "They knew the French had Bencoolen,— what else did they know? That's what I'd like to know" (41); the "They" of Pynchon's *Gravity's Rainbow* has reappeared, then, even more dispersed, more global and more untraceably in control.

Pulling the strings of Mason and Dixon's plot might well be the British East India Company as easily as the RS; we likewise meet Illuminati and American proto-Revolutionaries, not to mention the ubiquitous "Sino-Jesuit" connection appearing in the intermingled plots of *Mason & Dixon* and its interpolated novel *The Ghastly Fop*. In South Africa Dixon asks, "Whom are we working for, Mason?" "I rather thought, one day," Mason answers, "you would be the one to tell me" (347). Looking for patterns of experience to explain their role, Mason and Dixon are not only self-identified as "secondary" characters in their own drama, but they are also sure that "Men of Science . . . may be but the simple Tools of others, with no more idea of what they are about, than a Hammer knows of a House" (669).

As history, *Mason & Dixon* rejects any conception of the past as "grand narrative," as a linear chain of cause-and-effect to be reconstructed and narrated whole or from a single or authoritative point of view. The networks of power in this novel are too dispersed, too shadowy for such explanation. History here is not just the "rational" and the "irrational" sciences of the eighteenth-century Anglo-American world; it is instead a web of influence, a set of parallel lines that, if they ever meet at all, meet only at the always-receding horizon; in this history, *"everything is connected"* (*GR* 703). Such rhizomic, interlocking webs of causality, as historical method, are best served by *Mason & Dixon's* device of anachronism, more present here even than in his earlier novels. If the linkage between Pynchon's two eighteenth centuries — the actual and the imagined, what did happen and what might have happened — is strange and complex, *Mason & Dixon*'s coupling of the eighteenth and the twentieth centuries is equally disjunctive. The novel's time obsession is largely dramatized by a constant interplay of these real and imagined, past and present "presences."

Anachronism Now and Then

More than just recording, Pynchon revises history and its processes with its border phenomenon of anachronism, which positions the narrative neither in the eighteenth nor the late-twentieth centuries, but precariously at the intersection of the two. With its running subject of calendar reform, *Mason & Dixon* processes anachronism at several levels of plot and style to recast the eighteenth century in postmodern terms. This temporal matrix demonstrates the eighteenth-century "roots" of late-twentieth-century culture, but more than that, it reconstructs an eighteenth century "made" in the late twentieth, the result of which is to combine the ideologies of each century irretrievably into the other. It is through its many styles of anachronism that *Mason & Dixon* re-creates the several cultures of the eighteenth century and joins them with the late modern world.

The 1752 calendar reform in England was one of many products of Enlightenment science, designed — like the Mason-Dixon Line itself — to "correct" perceived flaws in nature and culture. Pynchon's Mason is obsessed with the "lost" days, which the novels' narrator, the Rev[d] Wicks Cherrycoke, calls "a chronologick Wound" (555). One aspect of Mason's obsessing is his denial that he himself experienced the "correction" of the calendar: while the calendar jumped ahead from 2 to 14 September and everyone else went ahead with it, Mason contends that he remained behind, living through the intercalary days in a vortex of time. He uses the time to go to the Bodleian, to try to read from hidden documents and to look for Astronomer Royal Bradley. During these "days," it is always night, and the ubiquitous full moon, rabid bats, and wild dogs make of Oxford a Gotham City — an anachronistic reference to the twentieth-century Batman phenomenon wrapped inside the larger temporal subject of calendar-reform. Ever since this episode in Mason's past, his movements have occurred on eleven-day cycles as he seems even biologically affected by the temporal event.

The "correction" and maintenance of time resounds throughout *Mason & Dixon*, with its interest in the calendar but also in the main characters' job of recording exact astronomical transit times, using more and more accurate (and historically accurate) timepieces. The calendar reform was only one of a number of eighteenth-century movements designed to standardize weight and measures, including, for instance, the experiments leading to Boyle's law of gases; each was designed as progressive scientific reform, but all were not without political and cultural causes and consequences of the kind that *Mason & Dixon* explores in its revision of history. The new Gregorian calendar had been in effect since 1582 on the Continent but the English resisted passing the calendar reform bill until 1750; the actual "correction" took place in 1752. Parliament resisted the change *because* it was associated with Continental interests, or what Puritan John Wallis called a "latent Popish Interest" (quoted in Poole, 109). The reform had, in somewhat "Popish" fact, been successful in Europe because it was sold as reconciling Easter with astronomical actuality. But the Enlightenment values of so-called scientific facts and "corrections" of the natural world had taken deep enough root in England by 1750 to overcome "Popish" paranoia, as perception of time itself had come to be experienced more rationalistically during the Enlightenment. Svetlana Boym describes this change:

> From the seventeenth to the nineteenth century, the representation of time itself changed; it moved away from allegorical human figures — an old man, a blind youth holding an hour-glass, a woman with bared breasts representing Fate — to the impersonal language of numbers: railroad schedules, the bottom line of progress. Time was no longer shifting sand; time was money. (9)

Mason & Dixon has Dixon express an awareness of the difference between scientific and a more pre-modern sense of time: "To hus must all days run alike, the same number of identical Seconds, each proceeding in but one Direction, irreclaimable. . ." (27).

And time, as Boym points out, came to be seen as irrevocably unidirectional (xv). Once past, it is heartbreakingly gone. Pynchon's Mason is the conduit for *Mason & Dixon*'s time-concerns — he "began to quiz himself insomniac" over what the calendar reform might mean (191) — but the novel itself, too, participates in Mason's refusal to accept the lost eleven days as a meaningless, calendar-only issue, as all of its attention to temporal matters keeps the issue in constant focus. Time as recorded here is occasionally non-consecutive; it can perform in even stranger chronologies than simply in reverse or in flashback or in parallel timeline (all of which do take place), in spite of, or perhaps as resistance to, its historical era's association with "scientific," linear chronology. One episode perfectly exemplifies its torturing of time and its recorders. Dixon, given a watch by his teacher, Emerson, constantly worries about it. It is a unique timepiece, evocative of the historical John Harrison's W4, the clock that solved the problem of measuring longitude at sea (Sobel), in that it keeps uniform time using perpetual motion. That it breaks the law of conservation of energy disturbs both Emerson (who claims not to believe in perpetual motion) and Dixon. Pondering the fact of the gift, Dixon considers that "If this Watch be a message, why, it does not seem a kind one" (318). It becomes a burden to Dixon, until one day when R.C., a land surveyor in the Line-building team, gives into his growing fetishism of the watch and eats it. When asked why he didn't hide the watch instead, he only responds: "There wasn't Time" (322).

Anachronisms throughout *Mason & Dixon* itself make a fetish of time, and more: they invariably link the eighteenth and late-twentieth centuries represented there. Like Mason's experience of calendar reform, the pervasive anachronisms fold together two discreet eras, creating at the juncture a "seam" that both connects and reveals the fact of disconnection. One of the novel's ubiquitous puns best verbalizes the phenomenon: "Suture Self, as the Medical Students like to say," says Dixon (20). A suture, revealing both a wound and its closure, visually represents the site of anachronism, where two time periods are equalized at the "fold." This narrative maneuver erases history's reality of before-and-after to create not chronology but synchronicity. *Mason & Dixon* joins eighteenth- and twentieth-century culture to disrupt our historiographic expectations, expectations developed in the Enlightenment itself, during which era Edward Gibbon-style "history" came to be synonymous with strictly chronological "grand narrative." Such linear, connected history was of a piece with Enlightenment scientific rationalism, all of which comes under attack, historiography included, as *Mason & Dixon* suggests "that the Enlightenment hope for overall rationalization via simplistic classifications and drawing arbitrary lines and false boundaries has proved counterproductive" (Lalo, 37). *Mason & Dixon* creates a counter-Enlightenment narratology to comment on the political and cultural biases that motivated calendar "correction" *and* the Mason-Dixon Line.

Anachronism, then, is more than a narrative habit: it amounts to a critique of rationalism by a great many players in the Enlightenment scientific drama: Gibbon himself, Linnaeus, and Newton all make appearances, not to mention the ubiquitous Royal Society and its powerful members. Were he not rendered so eccentric, Ben Franklin would be aligned with these forces — one can only say "forces of evil" — as well. Critical anachronism takes several forms, such as in the naming of characters — Cherrycoke, R.C., Pig-Belly Bodine — and in the phrasing of characters: Cherrycoke is advised, as he begins his journey, to avoid smoking dope, though if it must be smoked, "do not inhale" (10). Some characters come straight out of the twentieth century, like a squinting, puffing Popeye-like character who bellows, "I am that which I am" (486), or Mrs. Eggslap, a visitation from the modern world of country and western music, who declares, "Sometimes . . . 'tis hard, to be a Woman" (621).

More widespread twentieth-century cultural phenomena make regular appearances as well. Every new location, no matter how remote, offers Starbucks-style coffeehouses, and the characters engage in coffee gourmandizing equal to that of the 1990s. Most importantly, the novel establishes, through the character of Captain Zhang and a Chinese-Jesuit conspiracy headquartered in Quebec, a global communications network. A system of pulleys and levers that uses the stars to flash messages in the night sky, it is more than a physical mechanism. Emerson names it during a paranoid rant: "what your line-running Mate Boscovich also wants [is a] number of Jesuit Observatories, flung as a Web, all over the World it seems" (223).

The Sino-Jesuit satellite — an ur-World-Wide-Web — does more in *Mason & Dixon* than evoke the late twentieth century: it reroutes both history and historiography, undermining chronology with the anachronism, and furthermore, in this particular instance, executing a kind of communication-as-web in a postmodern, nonlinear performance of history as rhizome — of oblique connections whose causes and consequences remain as indeterminate at the end of the novel as at the beginning. In this web of time appears a running joke about *feng shui* in *Mason & Dixon,* a joke with serious thematic and narrative echoes. This 1990s environment-design fad was also an ancient art, so from the outset the concept is anachronistic — in both forward and reverse. Captain Zhang, *feng shui* practitioner, thus brings to the novel both ancient and New Age mysticism with a practice parallel to the surveyor's and astronomer's arts in their goal of aligning environment with human needs. The difference is that *feng shui,* unlike the Mason-Dixon Line, as represented by Zhang, conforms to and aligns human environments with natural boundaries. Of the Line, Zhang says at first sight and on first meeting Mason and Dixon and the survey party, "Terrible *Feng Shui* here. Worst I ever saw. You two crazy?" (542). *Feng Shui* "honor[s] the Dragon or *Shan* within" the earth, while the unnatural, right-angled Line "acts as a Conduit for what we call *Sha,* or, as they say in Spanish California, Bad Energy" (542). The postmodern, New Age anachronism of language finishes out the conceptual anachronism of the book's historiographical method — a critique of eighteenth-century action expressed in a language of history that itself resists eighteenth-century historiography.

The Zhang plot leads into *Mason & Dixon*'s most bizarre temporal vortex, which, as much as anything else in the novel, unsettles the very concept of linear narrative or historical chronology. Zhang first appears in a plot that springs up with no introduction and without relation to the *Mason & Dixon* plot. Chapter 53 initiates an American Indian Captivity Narrative, wherein Eliza Fields, who has been captured and taken to the Jesuit College in French Quebec to serve the Chinese also serving there, suddenly becomes the novel's main character; it appears here as if the Revd Cherrycoke is no longer the narrator at this point. The following chapter is in first person, completing narrative transformation into the interpolation. Here, Eliza escapes with Zhang to head south again, though not toward her home. Ethelmer and Tenebrae, characters in an outer, Cherrycoke-narrating frame, then suddenly appear, revealing that they are reading about Eliza and Zhang in an issue of *The Ghastly Fop,* a serialized novel appearing, like the coffeehouses, absolutely everywhere in the main *Mason & Dixon* plot: nearly every character, including the tough day laborers out on the Line, reads and discusses this serial.

Earlier in the interpolation, however, Cherrycoke has made a parenthetical comment, which suggests he was present at, even if he is not the narrator of, this plot. Yet it would be ontologically impossible for him to have been present in that story since he is an actor in the outer frames. Stranger still, in chapter 54, Eliza and Zhang meet up with the party on the Line, at which point the interpolation jumps ontological levels, from novel-within-the-novel to the main novel, without benefit of explanation or legitimizing circumstance. Like a Möbius strip, the narrative turns inside out to meet up with another side of itself, and in so doing, it sidesteps the normal paths of temporality and spatiality. Regular narrative implodes when these two plots become one, disrupting both time-as-narrative and fictive time-as-lived. Fredric Jameson's description of postmodern manipulation of history approaches, though it does not entirely explain, this kind of narrative:

> [T]he postmodern "historical novel," with all its false chronologies and made-up chronicles and genealogies, constitute(s) a referential use of fiction to free ourselves from the irrevocability of the "facts" of the history manuals and to institute a simultaneity of multiple worlds. (182–83)

Pynchon's novel, however, fictionalizes less than it *layers* a postmodern sensibility onto a near-factual eighteenth century, creating something beyond the postmodern. Aptly, narrator Cherrycoke, in one of his extra-novelistic writings folded into the *Mason & Dixon* story, *Christ and History,* most accurately explains this historiography:

> History is not Chronology, for that is left to lawyers,— nor is it Remembrance, for Remembrance belongs to the People. History can as little pretend to the Veracity of the one, as claim the Power of the other,— her Practitioners, to survive, must soon learn the arts of the quidnunc, spy, and Taproom Wit,— that there may ever continue more than one life-line back into a Past we risk, each day, losing our forebears in forever,— not a Chain of single Links, for one broken Link could lose us All,— rather, a great disorderly Tangle of

Lines, long and short, weak and strong, vanishing into the Mnemonick Deep, with only their Destination in common. (349)

The obsessive centralizing of time in *Mason & Dixon* looks a lot like
nostalgia. Indeed, Charles Mason, in many respects the novel's center of
consciousness, is a desperate nostalgic. Suicidally depressed over the death
of his wife, he takes every occasion to "revisit" the time of their life together; through dreams, memories, or "visitations" she makes to him in
what amount to waking visions. With its persistent attention to the
past — and especially to a past constantly refracted through the lens of its
1990s present — *Mason & Dixon* itself is a prime candidate for nostalgic
representation of past time. As Boym describes it, "Nostalgia is a longing
for a home that no longer exists or *has never existed*" (xiii, emphasis
added). With its anachronisms, the novel executes a time that never existed, for all of its accurate historical representations. But more than that,
it appears nostalgic due to its particular quality of yearning for "home," a
home which is not "a place, but actually [a] yearning for a different time"
(Boym xv). The novel's peculiar blend of past and present necessarily
compares the two periods, with the former sometimes appearing to offer a
richer experience, something closer to "home" than the present of the
1990s, though the latter was indeed a logical extension of the earlier. To
some degree, the sense of nostalgia comes from the sense of "rebellion
against the modern idea of time, the time of history and progress" (Boym
xv), and inasmuch as the eighteenth-century setting of *Mason & Dixon*
was less associated with "history and progress" than the 1990s, it now
and then offers a pre-modern sense of time.

However, the fact that slavery and other atrocities also take center
stage in this novel, and given the novel's technique of thrusting the late
twentieth century back into the eighteenth, the earlier period is not, finally, offered as either a beginning or as a pre-beginning — a time before
a current, corrupt period. As Dennis Lensing points out in his article col-
lected here, while Jameson might conceptualize postmodernism, and
therefore books like *Mason & Dixon*, as nostalgic due to their pastiche of
styles which both idealize and dehistoricize the past, *Mason & Dixon* itself
"transcend[s] the limitations diagnosed by Jameson" and therefore tran-
scends postmodernism itself. "Pynchon . . . choose[s] to *enact* nostalgia
in order to parody its emptiness, or rather, in order to satirize its ineffectuality. Thus, [it] transcend[s] the merely nostalgic in order to perform
precisely the historical," Lensing concludes (183).

Still, the America of *Mason & Dixon* is inflected with a utopianism
associated with nostalgia: it is at times a land of possibility and promise
that can only exist in the past as it so clearly does not in the present. The
giant vegetables encountered by Mason and Dixon in a landscape so fer-

tile as to be taken as a kind of hallucination are represented as singularly New World, utopian phenomena, for example. Section Two, entitled "America," begins with Mason and Dixon arriving at the shore near Philadelphia, where they first hear, and then see, the New World — a world already quite buzzing with human population but still rendered as "primitive":

> From the shore they will hear Milkmaids quarreling and cowbells a-clank, and dogs, and Babies old and new,— Hammers upon Nails, Wives upon Husbands, the ring of Pot-lids, the jingling of Draft-chains, a rifle-shot from a stretch of woods, lengthily crackling tree to tree and across the water . . . An animal will come to a headland, and stand, regarding them with narrowly set Eyes that glow a Moment. Its Face slowly turning as they pass. America. (258)

"America" is an idea, of course, as well as a place, but the place itself is clearly presented as, if not what once was — nostalgically — then as what might have been. The longing for the "might have been" amounts to nostalgia for the *future,* placed in a past that had promise of becoming something other than what we knew, in the 1990s, to have resulted from that past. The *sense* of nostalgia comes from a "temporal irreversibility" (Boym xvi) born of the modern, railroad-schedule kind of time; as time cannot be reversed, even the promise of the past cannot, the novel insists, return. Home, then, is a long lost idea, and to revisit a factual eighteenth-century America, however inflected by Pynchon's fictionalizing, is to apprehend that home simply doesn't exist.

The most frequently quoted passage from *Mason & Dixon* bears quoting again to make this point about both nostalgia and its critique, "America" and *its* critique, and the palpable sense of longing for "home" that never existed in the "triangulation" of these views one from the other:

> Does Britannia, when she sleeps, dream? Is America her dream?— in which all that cannot pass in the metropolitan Wakefulness is allow'd Expression away in the restless Slumber of these Provinces, and on West-ward, wherever 'tis not yet mapp'd, nor written down, nor ever, by the majority of Mankind, seen,— serving as a very Rubbish-Tip for subjunctive Hopes, for all that *may yet be true,*— Earthly Paradise, Fountain of Youth, Realms of Prester John, Christ's King-dom, ever behind the sunset, safe till the next Territory to the West be seen and recorded, measur'd and tied in, back into the Net-Work of Points already known, that slowly triangulates its Way into the Continent, changing all from subjunctive to declarative, reducing Possibilities to Simplicities that serve the ends of Governments,— winning away from the realm of the Sacred, its Borderlands one by

one, and assuming them unto the bare mortal World that is our home, and our Despair. (345)

Postmodern Observations

To read *Mason & Dixon* is to engage not only with history but also, and perhaps more urgently, to engage with historiography. Since the first reviews in 1997, readers have been driven to assess and name the peculiar blend of eighteenth- and late-twentieth-century facts, fictions, and sensibilities that the novel foregrounds so compulsively. In struggling to label Pynchon's historiographical method, many critics and reviewers focus on slavery and Native American atrocities as the thematic centers of *Mason & Dixon*, though these subjects are also interwoven with historiography as rendered here: twentieth- and eighteenth-century attitudes are layered onto the growing realization of Mason and Dixon that they are complicit in both slavery and "Indian removal." As a result, the protagonists grow more 1990s than early modern in their ideas, complicating the texture and method of *Mason & Dixon*'s historiography.

Rick Moody, for example, writing in the *Atlantic Monthly*, pinpoints the connections between the narrative manner and political matter of the novel:

> The kind of truth that we often encounter in Pynchon [is] not simply what it means, finally, to be American — kith and kin of slaveholders and abolitionists, racists and liberals, the powerful and the powerless, the dispossessed and the rapacious, the oppressed and the oppressors — but that the boundary lines that have been surveyed to separate our American dichotomies, the boundaries of rhetoric and philosophy, are arbitrary, tentative, unwritten in human nature. (110)

In an early response to *Mason & Dixon*, Charles Clerc works to establish historical data and to document the ways that Pynchon elaborates on a basic structure of historical fact. Just how the novel incorporates fiction into its facts is the subject of this reading. "While their dealings with the Vroom family, are of course fabricated, there's no questioning the 'odd behavior . . . going on all over the World . . . in Latin, in Chinese, in Polish, in Silence,— upon Roof-Tops and Mountain Peaks, out of Bedchamber windows that summer on the 5th and 6th of June as observers prepare for the TOV [Transit of Venus].' The scientific process is explained concisely" (58). Another nice example of Clerc's teasing fact from fiction appears in his analysis of the Harland household:

> On January 8, 1764, Mason wrote in his *Journal:* "Fixed on the house of Mr. John Harland's (about 31 miles West of Philadelphia)

to bring our Instruments to." From that simple entry, Pynchon has crafted a lovely comic exchange:

"Ye'll not wreck my Vegetable Patch," Mrs. Harland informs them.

"We are forbidden, good Woman, as a term of our Contract and Commission, to harm Gardens and Orchards. We'll set up in a safe place,— pay ye fair rent, of course."

"Welcome one and all," cries Mr. Harland.

Mrs. Harland remains less than enthusiastic. She wants to know why they've settled on her place. Dixon gives her a complicated evasive answer. She claims rightly that they might as well have chosen the Tumbling's farm. The truth now emerges in Dixon's yes-but response: "Mr. Tumbling fir'd his Rifle at us." (59)

Among other facts about the novel, the protagonists' "main progress in America follows the Mason and Dixon *Journal* [reprinted in Clerc's book] rather faithfully" (54), and so, "for all its playfulness, its many twists and turns, the novel remains at heart historical" (55), meaning that it is factual "at heart."

More complex readings of Pynchon's historical method surfaced early on in the criticism as well. Douglas Keesey points out that "the way it was" in *Mason & Dixon* exists alongside "what could have been" and "might yet be," and further, that the "mixture of history and comedy" (170) is the means to such blended history, "a key route to other pasts and futures — an alternative history" (171). Recent readings of the novel's historiography build to a richer understanding of the novel's complex time-space. Christy L. Burns reads *Mason & Dixon* as especially bound to its eighteenth-century ground by a historiographical method she terms "parallactic": using "the same method that Mason and Dixon employed to chart the transits of Venus and to draw their boundary line, applying parallax to a series of triangulated views, starting with Mason's and Dixon's attempts to assess the New World and eventually delivering a temporal form of parallax, a synchronization of the past with the present" (par. 1). In this parallactic method, "temporal or *historical* coordinates are the mappable difference, measurable via his synchronization of the 1760s charted alongside the 1990s. [Pynchon's] readers thus will interpret history as a dialogue between the differences and the uncanny similarities of that time's 'angle' and their own" (par. 3). Burns's "parallactic method" gives equal "weight" to eighteenth- and twentieth-century "angles" on issues such as slavery and its cultural aftermath, thickening the reading of history beyond the linear, chronological interpretations that concentrate on a twentieth-century culmination of Enlightenment processes.

More complex still are readings concerned with Pynchon's "backward echoing" historiography — those that accentuate the novel's late intervention in the early modern era. Vlatka Velcik says flatly that "Pynchon's novel portrays eighteenth-century America as a postmodern world in which private stories are indistinguishable from public history"; this "eighteenth century becomes indistinguishable from our own century" (42). Several essays in the Brooke Horvath and Irving Malin collection, *Pynchon & Mason & Dixon*, both credit and fault the novel for its primarily 1990s viewpoint. This volume, offering a fairly uniform view of Pynchon as an "old hippie" with singularly 1960s political attitudes, argues that the Revd Cherrycoke, one of the centers of consciousness of the novel, is a "trained minister with the soul of a hippie, a Job in tie-die," and that this narrator is reacting to an age "strikingly similar to the Eisenhower fifties" (Dewey, 119). Looking at *Mason & Dixon* as first and foremost a postmodern novel, using the eighteenth century to serve a late-twentieth-century point, these essays round out earlier interpretations which focus only on a forward-looking, sins-of-the-fathers-visited-on-the-present chronology, but they are equally unilateral in their readings of Pynchon's subject, taken here to be geographical and spatial rather than temporal. In counterpoint to Clerc's assertion of the basic factuality of *Mason & Dixon*'s narrative, the Horvath and Malin collection goes so far as to claim that fiction "corrupts" the facts of this history:

> Considering the constant barrage of anachronisms both minor and hilariously blatant. . . . Instead of the facts adding authenticity to the fantasy, the fantasy corrupts the facts and disrupts the whole retelling of history, infecting it with the uncertainty of fiction. (Foreman, 162)

With all this scholarly and critical attention to its historical method, it is clear that *Mason & Dixon* is what Linda Hutcheon termed "historiographic metafiction" (*A Poetics of Postmodern Fiction: History, Theory, Fiction*, 1988): by drawing attention to history's unknowable qualities and the historian's later interpretation of earlier events, historical metafiction "refuses the view that only history has a truth claim, both by questioning the ground of that claim in historiography and by asserting that both history and fiction are discourses" (93), in this view drawing on Hayden White's groundbreaking analysis of historiography in *The Content of the Form*. While historical metafiction does aptly name a quality of attention drawn to history as discourse, it does not go so far as to finally parse a book like *Mason & Dixon*, whose particular form of metahistory not only layers historical periods in both backward- and forward-looking causality, and not only draws constant metahistorical attention to that layering with its anachronisms, but which also uses its "parallactic" doubling of views to make an ethical point quite beyond the usual play of most postmodern fiction. This point — and its deep association with Pynchon's historical method — is what Frank Palmeri elegantly describes as "other than postmodern," a "new structure of thought and expression" ("Other than Postmodern" par. 1) that moves away from "the representation of extreme paranoia, toward a vision of local ethico-political possibilities" (par. 5) by shifting away from the individual to a more diffuse set of subjects — two, or even three protagonists, counting Cherrycoke, for instance, all of whom are self-admittedly not the main characters — and a less "human" kind of concern.

While Palmeri writes that the "late postmodern . . . is committed to recuperating the liberal individual," as is the case with the heroic saviors of *The X-Files* and *The Matrix* who battle against dehumanizing human-machine hybrids, "other than postmodern" texts "decline to idealize the unmixed human self"; rather than "encouraging a private consumer self," in its centering of ethical behavior in animal-human, human-machine, and animal machine hybrids *Mason & Dixon* challenges "such privatizing subjectification" (par. 38). Pynchon's diffusion of historical point of view undergirds this kind of post-identity performance. More than simple layering of two distinct periods, *Mason & Dixon*, in fusing the two, reinforces the absence of "beginning" or "end" to both the crimes and the humanity that are "America": "Pynchon represents the world of the 1760s and of the eighteenth century generally as *already* largely shaped by shadowy transnational institutions" (par. 29, emphasis added).

Parallactic, historical metafiction, other than postmodern — or what Boym would term, in her analysis of nostalgic texts, "off-modern," *Mason & Dixon* enacts a history neither linear nor nonlinear, both circular and drawn in a straight line. I would call it "parahistory," for one era resides *beside* the other, perhaps in parallel lines but at any rate in a set of spreading, overlapping causes and consequences that belies both the notion of "fact" and the notion of "fiction." As Justin Scott Coe writes, "Dialectic may not be the correct term . . . [because] the worlds are increasingly commingled to the extent that it is hard in most passages to tell the difference between the real historical experience of Mason and Dixon, and the various fantastic worlds that swirl at their side" (par. 9). Inasmuch as *Mason & Dixon* is nostalgic, its complex nostalgia exists in the past that was not a beginning *and* in a present that is not an end, when we still must try to recuperate something of humanity in full knowledge that even the past, though it *might have been* otherwise, formed the ground for a corrupt present. Scott Coe writes that *Mason & Dixon* "takes up this eighteenth century yearning for both history and 'futurity'" (par. 2). Just what futurity holds, whether it is the future of the eighteenth century or the future of the present day, is the subject of *Mason & Dixon*.

* * * * *

These essays represent a second wave of *Mason & Dixon* scholarship, one that keeps in view the complex linkages — linear and nonlinear, nostalgic and ironic, "other than postmodern," paramodern, postmodern, and early modern — that its historiography offers. The first section, including the Introduction, offers essays on time and history. "'The Space that may not be seen': The Form of Historicity in *Mason & Dixon*," takes on historiography and the intricacies of Pynchon's temporalization of narrative form. Mitchum Huehls here argues that the narrativity of *Mason & Dixon* is constituted by a complicated commingling of moments and durations, a commingling responsible for the specific *form* of the interface between the eighteenth and twentieth centuries. The novel temporalizes its form by creating a scene in which an unnamed narrator narrates the narrator Cherrycoke's exemplary narration of Dixon's narratives; there are four stories, three frames, and even more from time to time in *Mason & Dixon*. Such layers of narrative perspective deploy a temporalized form to render the novel a performance of historicity itself. As Emerson's gift-watch to Dixon measures time and, never needing to be wound, *is* time itself, *Mason & Dixon* measures history and *is* historicity itself. Narrating only from a particular moment produces history without historicity, while narrating from within the temporal passing of duration produces historicity without history; the first offers overdetermined content without form, while the second offers form without meaning. Huehls maintains in his essay in this volume that an expansive understanding of the "moment" allows Pynchon to unite the moment-ness of narration (narrative perspective) with the duration of both the event being narrated and the event of narration.

The second section of the volume, "Consumption Then and Now," includes two essays on slavery and trade, and the connection between slavery and trade, consumption. Consumption is treated in its several aspects in these two essays, from buying of goods to trade within a global market to the preparation and eating of food as performance of class. Brian Thill, in "The Sweetness of Immorality: *Mason & Dixon* and the American Sins of Consumption," makes a particularly relevant case about the preternatural resemblance of our own age of global commerce, with its capacity both to draw together and also to undermine the differences among local cultures, and an early version of globalization in the eighteenth century. Thill argues that central to the environment of heated political debate in *Mason & Dixon* is the system of global commerce that was becoming an integral part of the economies of the colonies as well as the other continents with which they conducted business, be it in tobacco, sugar, or slaves. Pynchon demonstrates throughout *Mason & Dixon* the extent to which not only tradable goods but also the members of a laboring class themselves became in the eighteenth century the most recognizable representative objects of the emerging global market. At the same time, Pynchon demonstrates how the eighteenth-century "debris of global Traffick" (*M&D*, 259) bears an uncanny resemblance to our own modern era, whether it be in the chat-room sensibility of Janvier's bar or the Starbucks-grade menu at the All-Nations Coffee House, where coffees from distant lands are served by girls whose "whimsical" (*M&D*, 299) costumes allegorize and criticize the extent to which, both then and now, the global economy connects cultures via commerce while repressing, transforming, or appropriating those cultures on which this commerce depends.

In "Consumption on the Frontier: Food and Sacrament in *Mason & Dixon*," Colin Clarke positions food as a symbolic repository of thematic drama in this novel. Just as the smell and flavor of cooked sheep seep into the walls and so become a constant underlying presence in *Mason & Dixon*'s fictive Vroom household, so too does food reappear in the novel as a whole as a subtle reminder of the political and social forces governing the lives of the main characters; in so doing, Pynchon's treatment of food suggests the overlap between the eighteenth and twentieth centuries. Food in *Mason & Dixon* is inevitably connected to the frontier, and so becomes part of that boundary, yet another line in a novel driven by lines, between the exotic and the everyday, the "savage" and the "civilized," and the earthly and the mystical. Food divides the classes (Mason's wine vs. Dixon's beer, elitist epicures vs. the practical sandwich-eaters), defines the frontier (European tradition vs. the exotic), and draws attention to the global commerce of both the eighteenth and twentieth centuries. Consumption is deeply connected with slavery as a means of production and colonialism as a political and economic gesture, in a land in which food can be a dietary necessity, a form of legal tender, or a religious sacrament.

The "Space and Power" section includes two essays about the connections between "place" and imperial power in the eighteenth century. In "'America was the only place. . .': American Exceptionalism and the Geographic Politics of Pynchon's *Mason & Dixon*," Pedro García-Caro claims that racial relations and their part in the formation of an independent American identity form a prominent theme in *Mason & Dixon*, problematizing in its representation a number of debates about the ideological import of other texts by Pynchon. History is critically reinscribed in *Mason & Dixon*, which underscores the inconsistencies between discourses and practices at the moment of formation of the U.S. as a nation. Pynchon's political and intellectual stance reaches out for a metaphor of the destruction of human difference in the apparently harmless scientific enterprises of observing the Transit of Venus or building the Mason-Dixon Line. The direction of the Line criticizes the westward movement of the Anglo-Saxon Empire as it is drawn, and it is also an indictment of the social relations prevalent before and after the American Revolution. In this critique, *Mason & Dixon* denounces imperial practices in a late-twentieth-century survey of the structures of power, foregrounding the relation between space and power in both the past and the present as central themes in the novel.

Dennis Lensing focuses on the trope of longitude, central to both *Mason & Dixon* and Umberto Eco's *The Island of the Day Before*, to examine the ways in which the two works interrogate notions of spatiality, temporality, cartography, and historicity, all of which are central to most accounts of postmodernism; the study of the novels together lend a heightened understanding of *Mason & Dixon*. Lensing argues that these two novels resist many of Fredric Jameson's characterizations of postmodern literature: they gesture beyond commonly theorized ahistoricity towards a multiplicity of radical and usable pasts. In doing so, Pynchon achieves a first step to that which Jameson generally considers an impossibility in late capitalism: the rehabilitation of cognitive mapping in the postmodern subject. Indeed, in such rehabilitation, *Mason & Dixon* achieves an ethical core central to the "other than postmodern."

Finally, "Enlightenment Microhistories" studies in fine detail three particular cultural phenomena in the eighteenth century. First, in "Haunting and Hunting: Bodily Resurrection and the Occupation of History in Thomas Pynchon's *Mason & Dixon*," Justin M. Scott Coe examines the ways in which *Mason & Dixon* enacts the idea and possibly the reality of physical resurrection. Enlightenment readings of Christianity — in particular, Calvin's conception of the "ascent to Christ" — has Pynchon collapsing the distinction between nostalgia and history through this novel's serious preoccupation with the influence of religion on history and history's preoccupation with futurity. Second is an essay on the eighteenth-century scientific discourses and practices surrounding "insanity" and *Mason & Dixon*'s incorporation of those historical practices into an American narrative tradition. "'Our Madmen, Our Paranoid': Enlightened Communities and the Mental State in *Mason & Dixon*" highlights the importance to *Mason & Dixon* of the interface between eighteenth- and twentieth-century perceptions of insanity. Exploring several instances of insanity and other abnormal mental states, Ian Copestake makes a case for the inadvertently redemptive status of madness in the Age of Reason, the irony of that redemption, and its processes in both eighteenth and twentieth centuries. This work reflects on Pynchon's awareness of the resonances between historical and fictional notions of insanity and its treatment, and the imposition this awareness represents, relating them to a specifically American tradition of fictive idealism and resistance through fiction.

The final essay offers a deeply historical account of General Wolfe and the weavers' strike of 1756 and Pynchon's revision of that incident. Frank Palmeri demonstrates here that in *Mason & Dixon,* as in his other novels, Thomas Pynchon combines strict fidelity to previously forgotten historical records with conjectural or fantastic narratives which nevertheless contribute to a moral, political, or epistemological point. Charles Mason was born in a small town a few miles from Stroud, known in the eighteenth century as "a sort of capital of the clothing villages" in Gloucestershire. As Pynchon imagines it, both his wife's father and mother came from families of weavers. Oppression of weavers by clothiers figures significantly at a number of points in the novel, especially when Mason recalls the autumn of 1756, when several thousand striking weavers marched through the streets of Stroud and forced some clothiers to jump out of a second-floor window before they agreed to a wage increase for the workers. To see that no outrages were committed, soldiers of the Twentieth Infantry were dispatched to Stroud under the command of Col. James Wolfe, the future hero of Quebec. Palmeri's research at the British Library has confirmed the accuracy of all the details of this account, except for the occupation of Rebekah Mason's ancestors and the contempt that Pynchon's Wolfe exhibits toward the weavers.

"General Wolfe and the Weavers: Re-envisioning History in Pynchon's *Mason & Dixon*" contends that the conjunction of the weavers' strike with Wolfe's presence in Mason's hometown within ten years of his working on the Line, historically, parallels some of the principal concerns in novel, namely slavery and Braddock's hatred of American Indians. Thus Pynchon characteristically builds on a ground of almost forgotten but incontestable fact a narrative that makes prominent use of counterfactual or fabricated elements, in order to convey the underside of official history — truths about the past that have long been suppressed, erased, or ignored.

Each of the essays in this volume focuses primarily on eighteenth-century culture, though all recognize, and in many cases directly explore, the late-twentieth-century creation of the novel and its latter-day position on the historical moment of the setting. The essays offer fresh thinking about Pynchon's work, not only due to the subject-matter — Pynchon's most recent novel — but also because the authors take up the curious linkages and slippages between eighteenth and twentieth centuries in studies as concerned with culture as with the literary text. The collection explores several methodologies of Cultural Studies and American Studies in their approach to the eighteenth century, the twentieth century, and the ties that bind the two, whether the causal chain is seen to be "forward," as in the "natural" progress of history or "backward," as practiced in a late-twentieth-century version of the eighteenth century. As such, these essays move beyond earlier studies of Pynchon and *Mason & Dixon,* to look as closely at the cultural contexts as at the inner workings of the novel itself. The historical and historiographical interests represented here, taken together, provide a set of layered "maps" of temporal relationship which, in parallactic fashion, adds up to the several "worlds" of *Mason & Dixon*.

1: "The Space that may not be seen": The Form of Historicity in *Mason & Dixon*

Mitchum Huehls

> *So if I draw a boundary line that is not yet to say*
> *what I am drawing it for.*
> — Ludwig Wittgenstein,
> *Philosophical Investigations*

AT THE CONCLUSION OF *Mason & Dixon*'s thirty-second chapter, Jeremiah Dixon receives a letter from his long-time mentor, William Emerson, who has entrusted Dixon with a watch of perpetual motion that never requires winding. Dixon has written to Emerson to report that the watch was swallowed by R.C., a member of the surveying party, and Emerson's reply bears the challenging post-script, "Time is the Space that may not be seen. —" (326). This essay reads *Mason & Dixon* as a literary attempt, not to render time visible, but to produce meaning from time itself. As such, Thomas Pynchon incorporates temporality into the narrative's production, not only writing about the historical interface between the eighteenth and twentieth centuries, but also performing the historicity of that interface. To make meaning from time's perpetual motion, Pynchon employs a temporally parallactic narrative form (different narrators deliver the story from ostensibly different moments in time)[1] that effects, for the reader, a semblance of experiential time. These narrative tricks superimpose linear and cyclical models of time into one textual form, and they allow Pynchon to write about time without sacrificing, by spatializing, time's temporality or history's historicity.

Chapter 32 narrates the story of the perpetual motion watch, one of many quasi-real artifacts that could be treated as a metaphor for the novel itself. Although perpetual motion directly affronts Newton's Law of the Conservation of Energy, it nevertheless resonates with a basic understanding of temporalized human experience (including the experience of reading) as motion.[2] Until we die, we produce meaning and gain knowledge in the midst of life's "motion," yet the form of time's passage resists incorporation into the content of that knowledge. Pynchon's aim in *Mason*

& Dixon involves producing a meaningful narrative that can accommodate just such an on-the-fly model of coming into knowledge.

Emerson explains the watch's function to Dixon like this: "[w]ith the proper deployment of Spring Constants and Magnetickal Gating, Power may be borrow'd, as needed, against repayment dates deferrable indefinitely" (317). The watch borrows against the future to run perpetually in the present, thereby creating disequilibrium between the power put into the watch and the energy it expends; in short, it runs on credit. Instead of indexing the dissipation of energy to the fact that energy will be expended linearly over time (which would be the assumption of Newton's law), now the driving force of every present moment of energy expenditure derives from a deferral of the future based on the guarantee that there will always be more future to be had. The watch no longer measures time; rather, time now runs the watch. As its own engine, the watch runs on a strange economy in which it incurs and settles debts in terms of itself. But the debt settled must remain perpetually incongruent to the debt incurred because the failure of equivalent return and full repayment produce its perpetual motion.

Thus, time moves forward by looping back on itself without ever perfectly returning to itself — an imperfect cycle generates its linearity. The recursive structure (the gesture toward exchange superimposed on the pure forwardness of perpetual motion) makes meaning possible in the midst of so much motion. Without at least pretending to a certain dynamic of exchange, time could not be permitted meaningful content; it would be only formal motion with nothing to move. But perpetual motion also mitigates access to clear meaning, a problem exemplified by Dixon's multiple attempts throughout the chapter to discern the meaning of the watch's message. For instance, when Emerson first entrusts him with the watch, Dixon feels like he is being told something, but the narrator tells us that Dixon's history with Emerson "has been one of many such Messages, not necessarily clear or even verbal, which Dixon keeps failing to understand" (318). Treating the watch as a "message," Dixon thus goes to great lengths to interpret what "it might be confiding to him" (319). He even dreams of Emerson presenting him with a sheaf of legal papers "emboss'd with some intricate Seal, which if not read properly will bring consequences Dixon cannot voice." In the dream, Emerson is "reading [Dixon's] Thoughts," and "the Watch wishes to speak, but it only struggles, with the paralyz'd voice of the troubl'd Dreamer. Nonetheless, Dixon's Salvation lies in understanding the Message." Only in the daylight does he begin to hear the watch saying: "When you accept me into your life [. . .] you will accept me . . . into your stomach" (320–21). Although the message remains muddled as long as no one internalizes the watch, its internalization will obviate its ability to speak and make meaning. This is the paradox of producing meaning from perpetual motion: the watch's meaningful message can only be delivered once that message is unreceivable, and as long as the message is receivable, it will be inadequately given.

This paradox presents unsatisfactory options: producing meaningful content requires ignoring the formal fact of time's motion, while gaining knowledge of that motion requires silence about its content. If we treat the watch as a figure for Pynchon's own attempt to make meaning in his novel, then the message of the watch's mini-narrative implies the need to approach the tension between meaning and time formally. That is, the watch is both time and the form of time, a model of signification that can be performed but not named, written but not written about. As such, our investigation of Pynchon's novel about the watch's meaning cannot focus on what Pynchon writes about (this would land us in the same paradox that Dixon encounters in trying to understand what the watch means), but on how he writes.

In *Mason & Dixon*, Pynchon wiggles his way through this paradox by reimagining the instant as the constitutive component of time, its motion, and its meaning. In the midst of Dixon's anxiety over what the watch means, the instant asserts itself at two critical junctures, each time in relation to R.C., the man who ultimately internalizes the watch: "From the Instant he sees the Watch, the *Mens Rea* is upon him. He covets it" (321). And when the members of the party speculate about why he ate the watch, he describes his compromised position as having to make the choice "the Moment presented." "I had less than one of the Creature's Ticks to decide," he states (323). Despite its perpetual motion, the watch initially seems to rupture time and stand outside it. For example, when his cohorts question, "Shouldn't you've set it down someplace, 'stead of swallerin' it?," R.C. literalizes the instant's ostensible negation of time by retorting, "There wasn't Time" (322).

On closer inspection, however, the moment of choice, purportedly instantaneous and without time, actually contains two versions of time, both instant and duration, and functions more like the pure, empty form of time itself. After R.C. asks, "What were my choices?," the narrator intercedes, explaining that the watch "was either bewitch'd, by Country Women in the middle of the night,— Fire, monthly Blood, Names of Power,— or perfected, as might any Watch be, over years, small bit by bit, to its present mechanickal State, by Men, in work-Shops, and in the Day-time. That was the sexual Choice the Moment presented,— between those two sorts of Magic" (323). This description is odd. First, if the choice presents itself in a Moment, from where does the time to choose between two things come?[3] Some smaller unit of measure subdivides the present moment and permits the formulation of choice, while simultaneously rendering that choice a non-choice (i.e. the narrator, not R.C., elaborates the choices; R.C. merely asks his question in rhetorical defense of his action, not in any actual assertion of two choices). Even weirder, this choice, contained in a moment, itself contains both a moment and more than a moment — time as both instant and duration. The narrator claims that the moment presented a "sexual Choice" between women who cast a spell, instantly instilling the watch with its powers of perpetuity, and men who have performed the same feat "over years" and "bit by bit." To sum up, a choice between two things presents itself in an instant that is logically only one, and that instant not only contains a choice of two, but a choice of two comprised of one (the Country Women's curse) and more than one (the Men's work-Shop labor).

How does an instant, both infinitely large (to the extent that it contains more than one thing to be chosen in that instant) and infinitely small (to the extent that it slices a cross-section from time), affect the watch's message and its production of meaning? As the narrator's explication of R.C.'s choice implies, the paradox between the content and form of the watch's temporally constituted message leaves the reference of "Choice" unclear.[4] The narrator's explanation entails an attempt to fill the emptied temporal form (emptied by the rhetoric of R.C.'s question) with content. But to the extent that the narrator does not even include "watch swallowing" on his curious list of possible choices, the narrative content seems nonsensical. The nonsensibility of the narrator's attempt to attach referents to "choices?" demonstrates the difficulties that attend the production of meaning in terms of time (in this case, the instant). Even if we focus on the narrator's recharacterization of R.C.'s choice as a "sexual Choice," whether swallowing the watch means he chose the magic of country women or that of the men in their work-shop remains entirely opaque.

The problem posed by the relation among meaning, time, and motion thematically dominates *Mason & Dixon*. As travelers to a new land, Mason, Dixon, and their surveying party confront a territory and a nation growing so rapidly that meaning is constantly contested. In America, what happens next still depends on what came before, but history moves too quickly for anyone to determine what the past means. On the level of content, the paradox requires sacrificing some component of the subject's perspective, a sacrifice that yields incommensurability between either an event and its history, an object and its representation, or space and its temporality.[5] For example, as part of their surveying instruction, Emerson teaches his students to fly, a lesson intended to instruct them about "the great Invariance whereby, aloft, one gains exactitude of Length and Breadth, only to lose much of the land's Relievo, or Dimension of Height,— whilst back at ground level [. . .] one regains bodily the realities of up and down, only to lose any but a rough sense of the other two Dimensions, now all about one" (504–5). The moment that one's perspective becomes comprehensive, the observed becomes unreal, its truth only ever "truth-like." Either we can totally and perfectly know something utterly unreal, or we can partially know the truly real.

The Rev[d] Wicks Cherrycoke, the novel's principle narrator, articulates this contradiction in representational terms while meditating on consubstantiation and transubstantiation, concepts which find their political analog in speculations about the government's representation of its citizenry, a prime concern for Americans during Mason and Dixon's tenure in the country. Cherrycoke and the citizenry worry about the extent to which symbolic embodiment adequately subsumes what it intends to represent. In terms of governmental policy, transubstantiation seems woefully inadequate: "this giggling Rout of poxy half-wits [Parliament], *embody* us? Embody *us*? America but some fairy Emanation, without substance, that hath pass'd, by Miracle, into *them*." Although these pre-revolutionary complaints express the colonists' desire for representation to entail a more material presence than Parliament seems to offer, Mason quickly points out the possible failures of a consubstantial model: "whatever they [Parliament] may *represent*, yet do they remain, dismayingly, Humans as well" (404).

Just as an aerial perspective sacrifices the fact of temporality for knowledge, Pynchon's text implies that both theological and political representation require a similar sacrifice of time — this discussion about political representation eventually identifies the temporalization of the represented object as the principle impediment to its representation. The occasion for this realization comes as one of Mason's interlocutors in the discussion inflammatorily (or so it seems to Mason) calls for organized resistance to the "Tyranny" of the Stamp Act. Cherrycoke narrates Mason's response:

> Mason expects shock'd murmurs at this — that there are none shocks him even more gravely, allowing him a brief, careening glimpse at how far and fast all this may be moving — something styling itself "America," coming into being, ripening, like a Tree-ful of Cherries in a good summer, almost as one stands and watches — something no one in London, however plac'd in the Web of Privilege, however up-to-the-minute, seems to know much about. What is happening? (406)

Here, the perpetuity of "coming into being" foils both the transubstantial and the consubstantial models of representative government. The material reality named America not only has space and breadth (it moves "far"), but it also has a temporality (it moves "fast," and relations to it are de-

fined as "up-to-the-minute"). As Bourdieu might say, America is "real activity as such," and anyone trying to figure out what kind of government
can "represent" that fact must do so from "within" that real activity.
Thus, trapped in archaic representational models, London will never gain
access to a subject position that can adequately grasp the action of America, and instead they can only ever ask "What is happening?" (another
rhetorical question).[6] Significantly, this paragraph does offer an alternative
perspective that might, in fact, be able to determine the representational
status of the pure happening of America: Mason's "brief, careening
glimpse." Echoing the expanded instant of R.C.'s watch consumption,
this glimpse is born from grave shock, yet another example of a pregnant
instant, a moment infinitely large in its subdivisibility.

Mason's encounter with these political revolutionaries occurs while in
New York, as he and Dixon have taken separate trips prior to surveying
the great westward line. Although not precisely simultaneous with Mason's "careening glimpse," Cherrycoke also narrates Dixon's concurrent
trip to Virginia where he meets Thomas Jefferson at a tavern, thereby ex-
posing Dixon to "the unmediated newness of History a-transpiring." The
moment in the tavern finds the men exchanging politicized toasts. Not
wanting to step on any politicos' toes (the exact opposite approach from
Mason's toe-stepping in New York), Dixon raises his glass "To the pursuit of Happiness," a phrase in which the young Jefferson delights, asking
Dixon if he might "use [it] sometime" (395). Here we receive our own
careening glimpse of the making of History, happening in a moment that
gives birth to the notion of endless possibility (the pursuit of happiness)
that has driven the perpetual expansion of America for over two centuries.
Both the illimitable horizon and the object of history (as the phrase ultimately finds itself inscribed in the Declaration of Independence) are produced out of the moment of history's happening.

In general, however, perpetual motion's intercession between observer and observed creates problems throughout the novel, most often
taking the form of objects that can only be seen when they stop moving.
This is the case with a mechanical duck that develops emotions and a Jewish golem that walks through the forests of Western Pennsylvania, two
machines constructed to mimic life so perfectly that they become living
despite remaining invisible while in motion (376, 486). "[C]ertain stars in
Chinese Astrology," which lose their invisibility once they come to rest,
also share this condition, and in an alternative ending to the story, Mason
and Dixon acquire this property as well: "The under-lying Condition of
their Lives is quickly establish'd as the Need to keep a [. . .] fix'd Motion,— Westering. Whenever they do stop moving [. . .] they lose their
Invisibility, and revert to the indignity of being observ'd and available
again for earthly purposes" (707). And again, motion in these instances

functions as time. The narrative implies, for instance, that time's acquisition of "additional Properties" permits the duck and the Jewish golem to acquire their life-like properties (379). And elsewhere, the duck's ability to oscillate between visibility and invisibility is explained variously by time no longer mattering to the duck, time passing in some different way for the duck, and by the duck's ability to move in and out of "the Stream of Time" whenever she wants (637).

Perpetual motion forces the observer to rely on the instant, but the instant stabilizes time only when treated as a withdrawal from time, a rupture that sacrifices time's formal properties to better observe its content. This assumption about the instant informs Mason and Dixon's observation of the Transit of Venus in Capetown, the first assignment they share. They are charged with assisting in determining the solar parallax, defined by Cherrycoke to his listeners as "[t]he size of the Earth, in seconds of Arc, as seen by an observer upon the surface of the Sun" (96). The observation involves measuring four distinct moments of Venus's transit across the sun: the moment when Venus first makes contact with the sun, the moment it enters the circle of the sun, the moment it touches the other edge of the sun's circle, and the moment it disengages from the sun.[7] As we might surmise from the above discussion of instantaneity, however, the instant proves less reliable than was hoped. Dixon's recorded times of the four instants "are two to four seconds ahead of Mason's," which is not to say that Mason's measurements are the correct set (98). Like the months preceding the event of the transit that "crept unnaturally" and the months following which "hasten by miraculously," Mason and Dixon might both be incorrect, with the only true measurement of the event occurring within the expansive temporality of the instant itself.

An unavoidable pun on the word "seconds" suggests the inevitable incommensurability resulting from any attempt to measure or make meaning from motion. Mason explains that calculating the parallax involves reducing the measurements to "a simple number of Seconds, and tenths of a Second, of Arc" — a spatial measure born of their temporal measurement of four instants (93). The incongruity derives from the fact that spatial seconds are discretely limited by a circle's 360 degrees while temporal seconds, ticking forward into an open-ended future, are not similarly bound. A Jesuit, warning Dixon of the "Cult of Feng Shui," amusingly makes the same point when he tells of the Sinoists' attempt, "in willful denial of God's Disposition of Time and Space," to give circles 365 degrees so that each degree would coincide with a calendar day (229). Because time is not a calendar in the same way that the Earth is round, indexing space to time, and vice versa, never yields representational congruency.

This essay investigates how Pynchon formally copes with this specifically temporal paradox of representation. Or, if producing meaning temporally is the text's thematic problem, what is Pynchon's literary answer to the paradox? Can narrative produce its meaning while inhabiting an aleatoric temporality of the pure happening of event-ness? Can text achieve the kind of perpetual motion exhibited by the mystical watch?[8] Drawing on the thematic discussions above, we can conclude that motion's compromise of meaningful observation requires that the narrator and his narration take the fact of this motion into account. If a stable narrative perspective sacrifices the time and motion of the observed, then a narrator might stabilize his relation to the event simply by mirroring the motion of the observed. But several decades separate Cherrycoke and his narrative while over two centuries separate Pynchon from his. Alternatively, a narrator might interrupt action with commentary, ignoring the challenges of narrative multi-tasking.[9] In general, Pynchon temporalizes narrative meaning more elegantly. Recognizing that narrative cannot internalize the perpetual motion of its content in the same way that R.C. can eat a watch and that observer and observed are always in motion in very different spaces and times, Pynchon casts his narrative form into its own perpetual motion, never really bothering to mirror the perpetual motion of the narration's object or content. Without getting caught up in transparently recreating or performing the specific motion that constitutes the narrative content, the simultaneity of the text's perpetual and not-at-all homologous motions creates the effect of a singularized perpetuity, evocative of our lived experience of time as motion. And on a larger scale, history finds its historicity.

* * * * *

Instead of finding motion in time's linear irreversibility, *Mason & Dixon*'s ingenuity comes from locating it in the pregnant space of an instant expansive enough to "contain" both instant and duration. By expanding the moment and treating the instant as another version of time instead of as an affront to time, Pynchon imagines a structure of mutual invagination — durations comprised of instants containing durations and instants, etc. This structure applies not only to the relation between instant and duration, but also to the relation between textual content and form. That is, Pynchon's work rethinks not only the temporality of instantaneity, but also the meaning of textual content: content expands sufficiently to contain and to be constituted by its performance. Textual content and form are neither identical nor mutually exclusive. Rather, they are mutually invaginated and mutually productive — each delivers both, and their commingling produces meaning.[10]

This structure allows Pynchon to pack narratives within narratives like interlocking Chinese boxes. The Revd Wicks Cherrycoke functions as the story's primary narrator, but he provides just one of many temporalized narrative frames. The conclusion of chapter 32, for example, quickly runs through several narrative instants in the course of one page:

> "You wish'd release from your Promise," Mason reminds him [Dixon]. "Think of R.C. as *Force Majeure.*"
>
> The Letter, in reply, proves to be from Mrs. Emerson. "When he receiv'd your News, Mr. Emerson was quite transform'd, and whooping with high amusement, attempted whilst in his Workroom to dance a sort of Jig, by error stepping upon a wheel'd Apparatus that was there, the result being that he has taken to his Bed, there, inches from my Quill, he nevertheless wishes me to say, 'Felicitations, Fool, for it hath work'd to Perfection.'
>
> "I trust that in a subsequent Letter, my Husband will explain what this means."
>
> There is a Post-Script in Emerson's self-school'd hand, exclamatory, ending upon a long Quill-crunching Stop. "Time is the Space that may not be seen. —"
>
> ('Pon which the Rev^d cannot refrain from commenting, "He means, that out of Mercy, we are blind as to Time,— for we could not bear to contemplate what lies at its heart.")

In addition to narrating the dialogue between Mason and Dixon, Cherrycoke also tells us of the letter, within which Mrs. Emerson becomes a narrator of her husband's misfortune. Within her narration, Emerson's voice comes through in her citation of his speech ("Felicitations, Fool, for it hath work'd to Perfection"), and he appears more materially when he appends, in his own hand, the not-so-clarifying explanation that time is the space that cannot be seen. This commentary on his wife's commentary ("I trust that in a subsequent letter [. . .]") on his commentary ("Felicitations, Fool [. . .]"), all quoted by Cherrycoke despite the fact that he never saw the letter, receives a final commentary from Cherrycoke ("He means, that [. . .]"). At this point, however, a larger-order narrator steps in parenthetically to narrate and comment upon Cherrycoke's commentary on the letter (326).

The parentheses enclosing the final paragraph of the chapter point back to the beginning of the chapter where another set of parentheses also narrates Cherrycoke's narration:

> If Mason's elaborate Tales are a way for him to be true to the sorrows of his own history (the Revd Cherrycoke presently resumes), a way of keeping them safe, and never betraying them, in particular

those belonging to Rebekah,— then Dixon's Tales [. . .] seem to arise from simple practical matiness . . .

"Directly before the Falmouth Packet sail'd" he begins, one night as they wait for a Star, "William Emerson presented me with a small mysterious Package . . ."

"'Twill not be an easy journey,—" quoth he, "there'll be days when the Compasses run quaquaversally wild, boxing themselves, and you, into Perplexity [. . .]." (316–17)

While some other narrator parenthetically narrates Cherrycoke's narration, Cherrycoke's narration of Dixon's narration (beginning in the second quoted paragraph) takes a standard form — Cherrycoke speaks and "he" refers to Dixon. Thus this earlier message from Cherrycoke to his frame-tale listeners, informing them that the ensuing will be an example of the type of story that Dixon enjoyed narrating to Mason, frames the story about the deferred arrival of the watch's message. And Cherrycoke's narration of Dixon's narration about the watch's "narration" of its message is itself narrated (parenthetically) by an unidentified narrator who signals Cherrycoke's resumption of his story. In other words, an unnamed narrator narrates the narrator Cherrycoke's exemplary narration of Dixon's narrative about the message of a watch that never stops running.

But what temporal effect does this Chinese-boxed narrative structure have? The re-beginning of Cherrycoke's story ("Cherrycoke presently resumes") contains the beginning of Dixon's typical story ("he begins"), as narrated by Cherrycoke. These two narrative "beginnings," appearing in consecutive paragraphs, function like a Klein bottle in which the entrance is always both entrance and exit — the beginning always resumes itself. The singularity of the textual surface unifies the otherwise distinct temporal moments at which these multiple narrations occur (first the watch's/ Emerson's, then Dixon's, then Cherrycoke's, then the unnamed narrator's, then Pynchon's authorship). That is, the logically necessary chronology of the narrative moments creates a linear duration of straight, measurable time that historicizes the story we read. But the singularized moment of the experience of reading subsumes this chronology, instituting a 180-degree twisting and looping of this apparent duration, thereby effecting a time infinitely subdivisible in a narrative instant (this simultaneously circular and linear structure mirrors that which allows the watch to run on credit).[11]

Instead of stretching forward into the unknown vastness of infinite possibility, the narrative and its temporal non-coincidence derive from the infinite subdivisibility of the instant, a subdivision performed by each new act of narration. Transferred to the Mason-Dixon Line, an image easily conceived as a metaphor of Pynchon's text, we should recognize that the line divides vertically as well as horizontally. The line moves forward inexorably, flowing on in perpetual motion, but it also divides every moment along the way, rendering all moments infinitely large. By dividing the space between the line's end and its eventual terminus in half, Zeno would tell us that the line must stretch on forever into the infinite possibility of the future. The line is also vertically asymptotic, however, functioning as that infinitely subdivisible space which ensures that two entities will never converge into one — Pennsylvania and Maryland, like Mason and Dixon or like Emerson sitting "inches from [Mrs. Emerson's] Quill," can converge forever without ever uniting. A brief sketch of the temporal structure of the narrative in chapter 32 will further illuminate exactly how these infinitely subdivisible instants temporalize narrative meaning to produce the form of history's historicity.

The pure temporal form of the watch's perpetual motion subsumes and constitutes what seem to be four distinct narrative moments in time (the time of the events surrounding the watch, the time of Dixon's narration to Mason, the time of Cherrycoke's narration to his audience, and the time of the unnamed narrator's narration of Cherrycoke). These four narrative moments and perspectives are not linked together into a chronological narrative with a temporal duration; instead, the watch's perpetual motion functions as the temporal form of the chapter itself — each moment of narrative perspective exists as just one of an infinite number of subdivisions of the pure form of the watch's time. The watch even acts as a transition-piece between these apparently different temporal moments: "the Watch ticks complexly on" moves the narrative from the moment of direct dialogue between Mason and Dixon to the time of Cherrycoke's speculative narration, and "as the days of ceaseless pulsation pass one by one" moves us from the conclusion of the watch-eating fiasco to some point in the future after R.C. has been living with the watch for a while (320, 324). Instead of what appear to be narrative iterations that stretch out over time, the narrative actually offers different temporal positions subsumed under time itself; this singular collection of narrative moments both transpires over a duration of time and occurs in the simultaneity of the moment (the same effect that occurs for R.C. whose "Choice" in the moment contains both instantaneity and duration).

We can identify this effect in several curious moments in the chapter. First, Cherrycoke tells us that "he [Dixon] begins" his story, but it remains entirely unclear where Dixon's story ends; instead, we only find different narrative times all forming part of the same story (e.g. the time of Dixon's beginning is also that of Cherrycoke's resumption). Thus, immediately after Cherrycoke signals the beginning of Dixon's story, we read Dixon's voice: "''Twill not be an easy journey,—' quoth he" (318). Just as Dixon assumes the narrative mantle, however, Cherrycoke quickly reappears with "Emerson told him," a line in which "him" names Dixon.

Eventually, this oscillation of narrative voice gives way to pure dialogue, making it impossible to know if we are reading Dixon's narration to Mason or Cherrycoke's narration of that narration. More complicatedly, an equivocation on the word "Now," in the first line of the paragraph after the dialogue between Dixon and Emerson (the moment that would ostensibly mark the end of Dixon's narration), blurs the jump out of Dixon's narration and into Cherrycoke's: "Now what seems odd to Dixon, is that ten years ago [. . .]" (318). Although clearly narrated by Cherrycoke, "Now" could refer to the present time of Dixon's dialogue with Emerson, to the present time of Dixon's narration of this story to Mason, or it could simply be a conjunction, lacking all temporal reference and meaning something like, "in view of the fact that [. . .]."

Another curious narrative quirk that effectively unites these multiple narrative instants into one (conflating past and present, present and future) involves Cherrycoke's tendency to ventriloquize the speech of his story's characters. In two different instances, his ventriloquization follows a rhetorical question. First, as we have already seen, when R.C. asks about his choices, his directly quoted words are followed by Cherrycoke's narration: "'What were my Choices?' R.C. nearly breathless." Here, Cherrycoke's words intervene while we wait for R.C. to catch his breath, after which point he will presumably continue to defend himself with more than just a rhetorical question. But instead of R.C.'s words, we read the description of the two choices, narrated by Cherrycoke but sounding exactly like a continuation of R.C.'s speech. The phrasing and syntax are seamless, but the *non sequitur* choices make the disjunction glaring. A second ventriloquization occurs in the paragraph succeeding R.C.'s watch consumption. Mr. Barnes, another member of the party, notes that they are in "The Wedge," a space left over from some imprecise surveying of Maryland's eastern border with Delaware (the two borders, much like all other pairs in the novel, fail to unite into one contiguous border). Barnes asks rhetorically, "Has anyone consider'd where we are?," and the narrator again fills in the openness of the rhetorical question by explaining, this time with quotation marks even though the words do not belong to Barnes, "All know that he means, 'where just at the Tangent Point, strange lights appear at Night [. . .]'" (323).

On one level, Cherrycoke's oscillation between direct and indirect discourse and his conspicuous absence from the majority of the events he narrates are entirely unremarkable, explained away by pointing to omniscient narration as a literary device. On another level, however, the point warrants consideration because Cherrycoke is also resoundingly non-omniscient (his absence from an event often serves as an excuse for his inability to narrate that event) and the direct dialogue that populates his narration purports to a precision that his absence directly contradicts.

Once we realize that Cherrycoke was not yet a member of the surveying party during chapter 32's events, this oscillation between direct quotations and narrative commentary becomes utterly perplexing and perhaps only explainable by the temporal conflation that such fuzziness effects.

While the above instances of ventriloquy demonstrate the intrusion of the narrative present into the past present of the narrated events, the paragraph after Cherrycoke ventriloquizes Barnes adds another temporal moment, perhaps sometime in the twentieth century. This paragraph, narrated without quotation marks by either Cherrycoke or the larger-order narrator, elaborates the history of the Wedge and concludes that the confusing demarcations there "present to Lawyers enough Litigation upon matters of Property within the Wedge, to becoach-and-six a small Pack of them, one generation upon another, yea unto the year 1900, and beyond" (323–24). Simply put, the inclusion of "1900, and beyond" makes the "present" of the passage impossible to determine. The paragraph's present could be in the past with Mr. Barnes, in Cherrycoke's present 1786 narration, or in a future moment some time after 1900. The introduction of 1900 equally suggests either that Cherrycoke is speculating (or exaggerating) from 1786 into the future or that some other narrator, presumably the larger-order narrator writing in the historical present tense, has taken over Cherrycoke's narration to provide an even larger historical perspective on the Wedge. The inability to determine who narrates when creates the effect of multiple narrations at multiple times, all subsumed by the singularity of their reading. Cherrycoke simultaneously inhabits the roles of limited and omniscient narrator, oscillating between a simultaneity of knowledge and non-knowledge that constitutes (by conflating) the temporalities of the narrative. Moreover, this temporalization of narrative accommodates content and form, leaving content susceptible to the vicissitudes of time's form and motion without precluding the production of meaningful content.

Cherrycoke begins his entire narrative with the caveat: "I was not there when they met,— or, not in the usual Way. I later heard from them how they remember'd meeting. I tried to record, in what I then projected as a sort of *Spiritual Day-Book*, what I could remember of what they said,— tho' 'twas too often abridg'd by the Day's Fatigue" (14). What does Cherrycoke mean by "not in the usual Way"? The answer appears in a later scene in which Mason explains who was chosen to inhabit the 11 days that the 1752 calendar reform removed from the calendar. Referring to the time of Mason's explanation, the larger-order narrator parenthetically states that Cherrycoke "was there in but a representational sense, ghostly as an imperfect narrative to be told in futurity" (195). Even when absent, Cherrycoke was always present, but he was not sufficiently present to avoid having the larger-order narrator swoop in and parenthetically narrate the fact of his absence. On a textual level, however, the event's expansive instant already contains the future transformation of that event into narrative (just like Cherrycoke has already "projected" the representational existence of his *Spiritual Day Book*).[12]

Supporting the notion that an event's narration always accompanies its occurrence, the larger-order narrator also manifests an always-already, "representational" presence in the frame tale. As the narrator of Cherrycoke's narration, he must inhabit a narrative instant somewhere in the chronological future, but the absence of information regarding his narrative position (so often parenthetical and always in the frame tale) suggests a conflation of his ostensible futurity with the present moment of Cherrycoke's narrative. For instance, when Mason encounters Dr. Samuel Johnson and Boswell in a pub, Mason nostalgically tells Boswell, "I had my Boswell once [. . .] Preacher nam'd Cherrycoke. Scribbling ev'rything down, just like you." Then Mason has the meta thought, "Sir. Have you [. . .] ever . . . had one yourself? [. . .] a Boswell, Sir,— I mean, of your own" (747). Indeed, Mason's curiosity begs the question of whether Cherrycoke has a Cherrycoke, and to the extent that his narration is so frequently narrated, the answer seems to be yes. The suggestion that Cherrycoke might literally have someone following him around like he follows Mason and Dixon introduces the possibility that the larger-order narrator and Cherrycoke exist in the same place and time. At the very least, this would seem to be the case in a "representational sense."

Cherrycoke's Cherrycoke appears most frequently in the frame tale, but various instances in which Cherrycoke appears in the third person in his own narrative (i.e. not in the parenthetical narrative of the larger-order narrator where we are used to seeing Cherrycoke in the third person) suggest the larger-order narrator's representational presence throughout. In one instance, Cherrycoke appears in the third person in his narrative description of Mason's journal. Mason writes, "Should I seek the counsel, God help me, of the cherubick Pest, Cherrycoke? He will take down ev'ry Word he can remember" (434). In this case, Cherrycoke's third-person appearance is plausible if he had access to Mason's journals (we do not know if he did or not); but the same slip into the third-person also occurs elsewhere: in quotation marks, Mason says to a ghost seeking a chaplain, "Of course. Our Reverend Cherrycoke," absent quotations, while in counsel with the ghost, we read, "The Rev^d cannot help having a fast look over at the Visto . . ." and, "The Rev^d runs thro' the possibilities" (537); when all three meet on the ship to Capetown, Cherrycoke appears as "the Rev^d" (35); and when they are all snowbound at an inn prior to surveying the Line, Cherrycoke appears as "young Cherrycoke" and "the Rev^d" (384–85). Although this short sampling of slips into the third person could simply represent Cherrycoke narrating himself in the third person much like Henry Adams does in *The Education of Henry Adams*, they also suggest the at-least representational co-presence of Cherrycoke and Cherrycoke's Cherrycoke, a coincidence that seems to occur only when Cherrycoke is physically present for the described events. In other words, Cherrycoke adeptly narrates those events for which he was only present in a "representational sense," while those events for which he is most present (including the frame tale) require that his own Cherrycoke intervene to handle the narration for him.

Also uniting a multiplicity of times under the singularity of their representation, Cherrycoke's narrative often drags the future back into the present, creating a temporal co-presence that figures the future as a sub-division of the present rather than as an extension of it.[13] For instance, speculation about how an event will be narrated in the future preemp-tively subdivides that event's present happening: "Afterward, none in the Household will be able to agree which was which" (98); "Whenever she tells the story after that, she will put in . . ." (368); "Mason and Dixon, happening to be lost at nightfall (as they will later tell it) . . ." (412); "Mr. LeSpark, as he will come to tell the Tale" (430); "a mischievous glint in her eyes that . . . others will later all recall" (446); ". . . the choice not to dispute oftentimes sets free minutes, indeed hours [. . .]; Neither appreci-ates this at the time" (461); and "Later, not all will agree on what they have seen" (485). Again we see the future's possibility deprived of its ex-tension and instead contained within the present moment of the event as "imperfect narration."[14]

Not only are the times of the event being narrated, of Cherrycoke's narration, and of Cherrycoke's Cherrycoke's narration, all mutually sub-sumptive like a Klein bottle, but also the texts that populate these various narrative times invaginate each other as well. For instance, the *Ghastly Fop* text appears throughout Cherrycoke's narrative: St. Helena's population, ax-men out on the Line, Mason, and Mason's son back in England all read the text. Even in the frame tale, Ethelmer and his younger cousin Tenebrae steal away from Cherrycoke's narrative to read the lesbian sec-tions of the text. As readers of *Mason & Dixon*, however, we only dis-cover that Ethelmer and Tenebrae are reading the *Ghastly Fop* after we have read a significant portion of it seamlessly inserted into Cherrycoke's story and the text of *Mason & Dixon*. That is, only after we have read deep into the story of Eliza, Zhang, and their Jesuit enemies does the nar-rative telescope out, forcing us to realize that what we have just been reading is only the *Ghastly Fop* text as it is being read by Ethelmer and Tenebrae in the frame tale. But later, when Zhang and Eliza run into the surveying party, the two narratives converge, not only narratively, but also temporally, since the action at the moment of the textual collision is con-tinuous. Despite being a logical impossibility, when the *Ghastly Fop*'s characters and narrative action intersect with the time of the surveying, the time of Cherrycoke's 1786 narration, *and* the time of our own reading, all three times are effectively rendered concurrent — the instant expands and all (readers included) can move freely and meaningfully in it. The simultaneous looping and linearity of these texts has an effect similar to that experienced by the people chosen to populate the 11 days removed from the calendar: they inhabit a non-elapsing temporality, a kind of perpetually moving non-motion or a simultaneity of instant and duration.

* * * * *

A representational sensibility and a good book would thus seem indispensable for treating temporality as an expanded and infinitely subdivisible instant. During their stay at the inn, when discussion turns to implements like levers and pulleys that "multiply the apparent forces, often unto disproportionate results," Cherrycoke literalizes this point about textual power when he offers "the printed Book," with its "thin layers of pattern'd Ink, alternating with other thin layers of compress'd paper, stack'd often by the Hundreds," as an example of one such implement (390). Cherrycoke here cites the book's singular multiplicity, the way its multiple pages form all one surface, as the property that causes its inside to be disproportionately larger (and thus more powerful) than its outside. This fractalization of space takes various forms throughout Pynchon's own book: an historical uprising between local Indian leadership and the East India Company resulted in the Black Hole of Calcutta, a miniscule cell in which 146 Europeans were purportedly imprisoned (109); James's Town, the city in St. Helena where Mason makes some observations, appears "small in secular Dimensions . . . yet entering, ye discover its true Extent — which proves Mazy as an European City . . . no end of corners yet to be turn'd. 'Tis Loaves and Fishes . . . and Philosophy has no answer" (126); Cherrycoke tells of traveling in a coach, "a late invention of the Jesuits, being, to speak bluntly, a Conveyance, wherein the inside is quite noticeably larger than the outside, though the fact cannot be appreciated until one is inside" (354); and one night after getting lost in their return from observing, Mason and Dixon stumble across "a cabin, hardly more than a shed" that upon entering reveals "more room inside than could possibly be contained in the sorrowing ruin they believ'd they were entering" (412). To make these wholly spatial images germane to time we should return to one final description of Cherrycoke's magical carriage ride. After describing the infinite subdivisibility of the space internal to the carriage, Cherrycoke speculates about the coach's relation to time and eternity:

"What machine is it," young Cherrycoke later bade himself good-night, "that bears us along so relentlessly? We go rattling thro' another Day — another Year — as thro' an empty Town without a Name, in the Midnight . . . Long before the Destination, moreover, shall this Machine come abruptly to a Stop . . . gather'd dense with Fear, shall we open the Door to confer with the Driver, to discover that there is no Driver, . . . no Horses, . . . only the machine, fading as we stand, and a Prairie of desperate Immensity. . . ." (361)

In short, the carriage, with its supra-dimensionality, runs like Time itself, ostensibly measuring distance and duration while actually subsumed by the expansiveness of the pure form of infinitely subdivisible Time.[15]

The narrative techniques discussed above in the second section of the essay combine to drive the text's perpetual motion — what I would call the *form* of historicity or the experience of time. The text's parallactic narrative form superimposes linear and cyclical structures, resulting in a form predicated on its own imperfect return. Within the novel, imperfect return physically results in a host of alternative "spaces" functioning more like conditions of being that people inhabit in perpetuity. These fantastical landscapes adhere to a model of time in which the infinite subdivisibility of a discrete territory (and not its pure openness to the future) produces the sense of life's motion. From the outside, the inhabitants of these spaces seem trapped, but they experience life inside these externally bound spaces as infinitely expansive: the liminality of the Bermuda-Triangle-like Wedge (324), the subjunctive status of those living on the inner surface of the Earth (740), the cyclical inhabitation of the eleven days that were removed from the calendar during the 1752 calendar reform (559), the five degrees that Zhang claims were removed from the measure of the circle (630), and any space larger inside than out, all manifest the failure of perfect return (630). If we include Pynchon's novel in this list of alternatively dimensioned spaces, then its own failure to return is directly responsible for the production of its narrative meaning. Within the story, this is precisely the case: Cherrycoke produces his story because he has failed to arrive on time to Mason's burial, and he perpetuates his narrative because the terms of his stay depend on his ability to keep the children entertained (6). And of course, the result is a 773-page novel told in the short time of an Advent — truly just a moment compared to the duration of time its telling would actually take. By beginning post-mortem, Cherrycoke's narrative avoids the inevitability of death's finalizing survey.

In what Cherrycoke describes as an alternative ending to his story, Mason and Dixon ultimately choose their own subjunctive, alternative space of perpetual motion — they become Lethe's ferrymen. A ferryman they meet earlier in the novel, Mr. Ice, models this late-in-life career choice. While ferrying them across a river, "[e]xactly at the middle of the river, for a moment . . . ," Mr. Ice tells the post-mortem story of his massacred family. Because "[t]he Ferryman's Grief is immune to Time — as if in Exchange for a sacrifice of earthly Freedom, to the Flow of this particular Stream" — time stops while he speaks (659). However, only time as linear duration stops; the ferry rests not outside of time but rather in the very midst of pure time, figured as the river flowing all around them. Mr. Ice neither defers his debts indefinitely nor forgets them so as to ignore the consequences of his actions. Instead, the condition of occupying this instant in the river and narrating his story from it functions as a narrative act of simultaneous giving and exchanging, an act that lives in perpetual motion and that derives its meaning from its unique relation to time. Similarly, as ferrymen in the novel's alternative ending, Mason and Dixon live on an island in the middle of the Atlantic where travelers between Europe and America can stop for a rest. There, we learn, "[t]hey are content to reside like Ferrymen or Bridge-keepers, ever in a Ubiquity of Flow, before a ceaseless Spectacle of Transition" (713).

But is the role of ferryman an ideal or a cop-out? Functioning like a shuttle in the middle of the river/ocean, does the ferryman get the best of both worlds (old and new, life and death), or is he trapped in a purgatory of subjunctivity?[16] *Mason & Dixon* reclaims the purgatoried status of the subjunctive ferryman and treats subjunctivity as a mode of being within time that nevertheless lacks the future's possibility. Why? Because in the New World, Manifest Destiny has already overdetermined the future, making violence and greed the order of the day.[17] Pynchon solves the paradox outlined at the beginning of this essay (how best to deliver a message in the midst of perpetual motion without sacrificing form to content or vice versa) by expanding the instant and reveling in its subjunctivity. The detailed discussion of narrative technique was intended to show how Pynchon achieves this effect formally. In a sense, all the narrators, existing in their specific moments of time, are like so many ferrymen telling their stories in the midst of time's river. Like the watch with perpetual motion, the ferryman defers repayment of his debt indefinitely because the very form of deferral produces the content of the debt's repayment, which is never paid in full, thus giving rise to more deferral which produces new content, and so on. In this way, meaning is produced, stories are told, traumas are remembered, and all are born out of that "moment" in the middle of the river when time stands still, but only because one rests at its very heart.

Notes

[1] On "parallactic" form, see Cindy L. Burns, "Postmodern Historiography: Politics and the Parallactic Method in Thomas Pynchon's *Mason & Dixon.*"

[2] The same theme appears in *The Crying of Lot 49* when Oedipa Maas drives north to visit John Nefastis, inventor of the Nefastis Machine, which engages the fictitious Maxwell's Demon to sort and keep hot and cold molecules in perpetual motion, thereby contradicting the second law of thermodynamics. This law states that heat energy (as opposed to kinteic, potential, or electical energy, for instance) is a lower quality energy because it cannot be reversed into its original form. To violate this law would be to create a closed system which, despite not being able to draw energy from an outside source, would nevertheless remain in perpetual motion.

[3] Contemporary scientists measure the most quickly occurring events in attoseconds. One attosecond is a billionth of a billionth of a second. That means that 1,000,000,000,000,000,000 of them elapse over the course of one second. (There are only 2,366,820,000 seconds in a life spanning an average of 75 years, which means that there are 422,507,837 times more attoseconds in a second than there are seconds in a lifetime). See David Labrador, "From Instantaneous to Eternal."

[4] Puns achieve this same effect by meaning two things absolutely simultaneously. Specifically, in the moment of its event a pun contains both the simultaneity of meaning which characterizes it as a pun and the deferral of meaning that allows us to hear a pun first one way and then another. Not surprisingly, an aural pun on "Horology" instigates Emerson's introduction of the watch. He tells Dixon that the watch "will revolutionize the world of Horology," and Dixon responds, having heard "whore-ology," by asking if it "calculates when she's over-charging and by how much." Also, just after Dixon shows the watch to R.C., R.C. speculates as to whether the watch might earn the prize money that the Longitude Board is offering for standardizing the longitude. Dixon describes the Board as "tight-fisted," explaining that one must open their grip on the money with a "Prying-Bar." To which R.C. responds, "Must be why they call it 'Prize' money."

[5] In a sense, Mason and Dixon's journey positions them as anthropologists in the New World; the problem of time in producing anthropological meaning has deep roots in that discipline. Marcel Mauss, Claude Lévi-Strauss, and Michel de Certeau all address the problem, and Johannes Fabian's *Time and the Other: How Anthropology Makes its Object* organizes much of their work, arguing that "time is involved in any possible relationship between anthropological discourse and its referents" (28). Although somewhat short on practical solutions, Pierre Bourdieu strongly makes the same case in *The Logic of Practice* and *Outline of a Theory of Practice,* trans. Richard Nice 96, in which he shuns the "phenomenological reconstitution of lived experience" (4) and instead calls for the anthropological observer "to situate oneself *within* 'real activity as such,' i.e. in the practical relation to the world" (96).

[6] This question about happening resonates provocatively with Jean-François Lyotard's notion of the "Is it happening?," which he discusses in *The Differend: Phrases in Dispute*. The "Is it happening?" can be understood as the "content" of the gap created by a differend (defined as the incommensurability between phrases and discourses), a "content" that "represents" the silence caused by this incommensurability (181). The "Is it happening?" is a silent expectance, a feeling for a phrase and the effectivity of pure occurrence which nevertheless "is invincible to every will to gain time." Occurrence for Lyotard is that which must be judged and valued despite being neither a sign nor a piece of a story: "You can't make a political 'program' with it, but you can bear witness to it."

[7] The four key moments of the Transit mirror the structure of the chapter containing its description. The chapter begins in the frame tale, corresponding to the period before Venus's initial, external contact; the transit is then narrated in exemplary generalities, a narrative style corresponding to Venus's ingress into the sun; the narration of the actual event corresponds to "Venus now standing alone against the Face of the Sun" (97); the actual event then ends with a transitional section narrating Mason and Dixon's departure from Capetown which corresponds to Venus's egress out of the disc of the sun; and the chapter concludes back out in the frame tale, where it began, just like Venus now fully detached from the sun's disc.

[8] Although these representational paradoxes warrant a lengthy digression into Immanuel Kant's *Critique of Judgement*, specifically his discussion of the faculties of comprehension and apprehension as they relate to judgment of the sublime, Kant's ideas are too large for the limited space of this essay. See sections 25–27 on the mathematical sublime where Kant speaks to an irresolvable tension between comprehension, the faculty which bounds judgment into a graspable totality, and apprehension, the faculty that functions according to the infinite seriality of perception. Kant argues that comprehension subsumes apprehension in order to make meaningful sense out of a series of apprehended objects. G.W.F. Hegel's *The Phenomenology of Spirit*, however, revises Kant's partiality to reason, arguing that the initial moment of perception is an act of simultaneous comprehension and apprehension. The question of representing that simultaneous moment is what Pynchon, via Cherrycoke, seems interested in addressing in *Mason & Dixon*.

[9] Such interruption would be the literary response to Thomas Khun's important insight in *The Structure of Scientific Revolutions*, that science cannot simultaneously be done critically and reflexively.

[10] This conflated relation can be figured as a Klein bottle. Essentially a three-dimensional mobius strip, this shape, identified by the German mathematician Felix Klein, is formed by elongating a bottle's neck, passing the neck through the bottle's side, and joining its opening to a hole in the base. The effect is a one-sided surface without volume that nevertheless functions as a container (this explains what I mean when I say that the instant "contains" both the instant and duration). Thus, the bottle is both its own inside and outside, a singular surface with multiple properties.

I offer this model of "mutual invagination" as an alternative to deconstruction's more conventional approach of identifying constitutive paradoxes or the inextricable bond between two apparently oppositional terms; mutual invagination denotes a relation of singular multiplicity instead of mutual exclusion. "Singular multiplicity" invokes the image of the Klein bottle as a mode of deconstruction that need not name its paradoxes "impossibilities." In this model, the two terms (in this case, inside and outside) need not be negated. They are not deconstructed to the point that we can say that all insides are really just outsides and vice versa — to do so would be to ignore the fact that they successfully function as containers. Instead, the conceptual gravity of the terms must be retained because on some level, the bottle still has an inside and an outside, despite the fact that there is also no inside or outside at all.

[11] Drawing primarily on the work of Jacques Derrida and Emmanuel Levinas, Derek Attridge has recently been treating literature's singularity in terms of ethics. See, for instance, "Expecting the Unexpected in Coetzee's *Master of Petersburg* and Derrida's Recent Writings," *Applying: To Derrida,* and "Innovation, Literature, Ethics: Relating to the Other." Attridge carefully describes the experience of receiving literature in structural instead of psychological terms.

[12] Occasionally, Cherrycoke's cranky frame-tale listeners force him to abandon the "representational sense" of his narration. For instance, Cherrycoke alters his narrative after Uncle Lomax charges him with "Parsonickal interpolation" of others' words. Although initially defending his narration, Cherrycoke eventually concedes that his characters "withdrew out of my hearing, so that regretfully I quite miss'd the Information" (652).

[13] This effect is described when Mason tells Dixon that he had the privilege to enter the 11 days that were removed from the calendar. He says that those who jumped ahead 11 days became ghosts that haunted the 11 days not from the past, but from the future (560).

[14] E.J.W. Hinds's "Sari, Sorry, and the Vortex of History" discusses the role of anachronism in *Mason & Dixon;* thus I will not repeat the argument here. I would simply note that the anachronism allows Pynchon to enact the same structure of a future collapsed into a past present that Cherrycoke's narration employs. Hinds notes numerous anachronisms; of particular interest to me are the literary ones. To name just a few, *Mason & Dixon* alludes to *Gravity's Rainbow* (23), Dylan Thomas (28), "Billy Budd" (33), *Moby Dick* (292–93), *The Metamorphosis* (293), *Ulysses* (351), and *Tristram Shandy* (the only one of these texts not written after Cherrycoke's 1786 narration) (364).

[15] The lines that precede this speculation further reinforce this reading. In explaining why boundaries and surveying so inflame people, one of the vehicle's passenger's speaks of the initial moment of creation in which God separated the waters from the firmament, and "[a]ll else after that, in all History, is but Sub-Division" (361).

[16] Pynchon makes the tropological implication of this argument clear as images like the shuttle of a loom and the shuttling across the river intersect with images of the turning of the heavens around the star named *tropus.* Vehicles like the ferry and Cherrycoke's mysterious carriage metaphorize metaphor itself, thereby suggesting the integral role that language and the motion immanent to its produc-

tion of meaning (motion from the exchange between signifier and signified) play in accessing pure time's "Ubiquity of Flow."

[17] The Doctrine of Pre-Emptive Action articulated in the Bush administration's 2002 National Security Strategy provides a real-life example of this point. The logic of pre-emption, like that of Manifest Destiny, justifies violence in the present (against Native Americans, against Iraq) by overdetermining the future. Once the future becomes a "possibility," its events are already set in motion and thus require action now. For a thorough theorization of the dangers of possibility, see chapter 4, "Ideas and the Synthesis of Difference" in Gilles Deleuze's *Difference and Repetition*. Deleuze's concept of virtuality develops in partial reaction to the problems he identifies with the logic of possibility.

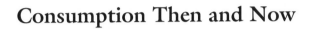

Consumption Then and Now

2: The Sweetness of Immorality: *Mason & Dixon* and the American Sins of Consumption

Brian Thill

NOWHERE IS THE COMPLEX NARRATIVE engagement with the position of the modern ethical subject in relation to the global commodity culture more profoundly drawn than in the works of Thomas Pynchon, and *Mason & Dixon* in particular stands as a narrative summa of his career-long interest in the historical dimensions of that position. This is not because the novel is more immediately concerned with the operations of a social ethic within the narrow dimensions of its plot and narrative (in fact, it is probably less concerned with such operations on that level than *Gravity's Rainbow* or *Vineland*), but because the problems of Pynchon's lifelong interest in the place of the radical, the humanitarian, the outsider, is here forced to contend with an emergent global market that will provide the fundamental base from which a wide array of colonial endeavors will be launched: the expansion of international trade, the entrenchment of chattel slavery as its privileged mode of production, and the often paradoxical relations of such a system to Enlightenment notions of reason, dignity, and freedom. It is with a sensibility grounded more in the appraisal of dramatic and literary conventions than in the demands of a historically meaningful social activism that many critics have approached the issue of how Pynchon seems to confront despicable historical institutions like slavery; the present analysis, then, endeavors to serve as a preliminary corrective to our critical tendency to sentimentalize Pynchon while glossing over his more deeply embedded conceptions of what constitutes moral sensibility, meaningful action, and agency in general in Mason and Dixon's era of expanding capital and our own. The omnipresence of slavery in the novel, then, constitutes only the most pressing historical example of how those various forms of agency inevitably come into conflict when situated alongside the historical forces Pynchon seeks to confront.

In what has already become one of the most frequently quoted scenes in *Mason & Dixon*, Pynchon produces his version of the apocryphal story of the historical Jeremiah Dixon's encounter with a Baltimore slave driver.

Having barely managed to keep his cool around the driver the night before at a local tavern, Dixon now witnesses the driver cracking his whip and cursing his unsold lot of slaves, and suddenly finds himself interceding:

> "That's enough." He stands between the Whip and the Slaves, with his Hat back and his hand out. Later he won't remember how. "I'll have that."
>
> "You'll have it to your Head, Friend, if you don't step out of my Way. These are mine,— I'll do as I damned well please with my Property." Townspeople pause to observe.
>
> Dixon, moving directly, seizes the Whip,— the owner comes after it,— Dixon places his Fist in the way of the oncoming Face,— the Driver cries out and stumbles away. Dixon follows, raising the Whip. "Turn around. I'll guess *you've* never felt this."
>
> "You broke my tooth!"
>
> "In a short while thah's not going to matter much, because in addition, I'm going to kill *you* . . .? Now be a man, face me, and make it easier, or must I rather work upon *you* from the Back, like a Beast, which will take longer, and certainly mean more discomfort for *you*." (698–99)

It has already become something of a commonplace for reviewers and critics of *Mason & Dixon* to single out Dixon's attack on the slave driver as the crucial narrative moment of righteous action in this long and dense novel — crucial because it seems to signal the culmination of Dixon's slowboiling rage in the face of chattel slavery everywhere that he and Mason travel, from the Dutch colony of South Africa to the pre-Revolutionary colonies of America. In fact, Dixon's intervention serves for many readers as the defining moment in his — and thus the novel's — moral response to the horrors of slavery. A small sampling of these should suffice for our critical purposes: Dixon, we are told, "enacts his Quaker abolitionism to the extent of risking life and limb in the Baltimore slave-market episode" (Strandberg 106); the thrashing he gives to the slave driver can be seen as "something redeeming" and "carries with it an air of moral censure" (Foreman 154); the novel's "most heroic moment is not the completion of the [Mason-Dixon] Line or its abandonment; it is Dixon, returning from his failed mission, striking down a slave trader" (Siegel 177); and so on. Most troubling of all is the following commentary on the scene: Dixon "rises to true heroism when he snatches the whip from a slave trader and flays the villain's hide, unable to abide the institution in South Africa — or Baltimore either. Especially not Baltimore" (Boyle 9). What is most disturbing about these readings is their positioning of this moment of violence as the zenith of the novel's activist ethic. In fact, Boyle (himself a novelist of historical fiction) completely misrepresents the scene by suggesting and even praising the idea that Dixon turns the tables and whips the slave driver — an event that never actually transpires in the narrative as Pynchon has written it. What is it about this particular brief scene that moves Pynchon's readers? Why is it that this moment functions for them as the apotheosis of social activism in the face of the ubiquitous slave economy in pre-Revolutionary America, even becoming so important to understanding the novel's approach to the problem of slavery that, paradoxically, that novelistic vision is radically distorted in the process of explication?

To locate a meaningful activist ethic in Dixon's rare moment of violence in Pynchon's vision of the eighteenth century's burgeoning global commodity culture, I would argue, is to read the novel's rare expressions of violence as privileged ethical moments and to further reify the suffering black body as the locus of those moments at the same time. This relentless attention to the slave driver episode as the site of the novel's endorsement of morally righteous and socially effective activism runs counter to the far more subtle and complex ethical issues Pynchon poses in all his works, but most especially in *Mason & Dixon,* where the greatest violence and true horror of the global market (like that of the Nazi machinery of death in *Gravity's Rainbow*) is rendered most powerfully as an almost-hidden force infecting elements of social life that many people cannot or will not recognize. Pynchon's development of this slave-driver scene and other relevant sections of the novel that deal in a variety of ways with the practice, spectacle, and ubiquity of slavery in the American colonies and beyond reveals the unheroic and ethically dubious nature of what transpires in that dramatic scene.

At the same time, the critical preoccupation with such moments of violence as the primary sites of identification with the oppressed suggests something about the way the horrors of slavery are made real and meaningful for us. This is a problematic area of criticism generally, but in the case of works such as *Mason & Dixon,* this is especially clear. In *Scenes of Subjection,* Saidiya Hartman persuasively argues for a critical analysis of the modes of empathic identification at work in narratives of physical violence against the bodies of slaves. As Hartman argues, there has been a disturbing tendency on the part of historical eyewitness accounts (from white spectators, predominantly) of violence perpetrated against slaves. In many cases, empathy emerges only after the account of cruel physical violence, as a result of which any understanding of the horrible institution of slavery comes only through the white narrator's ability to translate the spectacle of this violence into an imagined space wherein violence is committed against the white body. As a result, the spectator's identification with the pain suffered by the slave occurs only after the actual black body has been erased from the scene and supplanted by imagined white suffering. Hartman is also correct to recognize the repetition of this phenomenon of identification in contemporary critical attention: namely, the tendency of historians and critics to succumb to a strikingly similar means of identification and understanding of slavery. It has become all too common, Hartman finds, for us to look to those same moments of narrated violence to make vivid for ourselves the historical trauma of black suffering. Critics have been inexorably drawn to the narration of violent spectacle as a way to introduce and comprehend the horrors of slavery. But Hartman asks the compelling question: "Why is *pain* the conduit of identification?" (20). She offers the following explanation and, most importantly, its consequences:

> This question may seem to beg the obvious, given the violent domination and dishonor constitutive of enslavement, the acclaimed transformative capacities of pain in sentimental culture, the prevalence of public displays of suffering inclusive of the pageantry of the trade, the spectacle of punishment, circulating reports of slavery's horrors . . . all of which contributed to the idea that the feelings and consciousness of the enslaved were most available at this site. However, what I am trying to suggest is that if the scene of beating readily lends itself to identification with the enslaved, it does so at the risk of fixing and naturalizing this condition of pained embodiment and . . . increases the difficulty of beholding black suffering since the endeavor to bring pain close exploits the spectacle of the body in pain and oddly confirms the spectral character of suffering and the inability to witness the captive's pain. (7)

The positive critique implied herein is that there are any number of ways to see the violence and trauma of slavery that do not depend on the instinctive urge to look to that spectacle of bodily injury and suffering, and yet our continued fascination with such scenes of subjection signals something more — something other — than the empathy or call to action that such a spectacle is ostensibly meant to summon. I begin with Hartman to address the overwhelming tendency of Pynchon's critics to gravitate toward the slave-driver episode in their attempts to render visible the often-concealed ethical dimensions of Pynchon's novel. In this sense alone, it could be argued that the continued attraction to this scene and the reliance on it as a means of theorizing Pynchon's activist ethos has outlived its usefulness and exceeded its applicability to an analysis of the narrative. But there is in addition to our critical attraction to violence Pynchon's own deep rendering of slavery and the tangled ethics inherent in the emerging global marketplace of *Mason & Dixon* that displays a much less spectacular, but far more radical notion of abolitionist activism elsewhere. The activist impulse in the novel emerges not through physical violence, but through a radical unmasking of the interrelationship between the slave economy and the burgeoning consumption of new global commodities in America's formative pre-Revolutionary era. What we discover in *Mason & Dixon* is thus not merely an implied argument against violence as a viable activist strategy against an institution as pervasive as chattel slavery in the eighteenth century, but also a fundamental conjunction of that century and our own insofar as various global systems of commerce and consumption and the forces required to disrupt them are concerned. Such a conjunction, we find, is constitutive of any ethical dimension to be derived from the novel in particular and across the wider field of Pynchon's oeuvre.

* * * * *

Seldom noted is the fact that immediately after he confronts the slave driver, Dixon suffers a moment of moral panic in the midst of this seemingly heroic fit of action, centered around the question technically posed by the novel's narrator, the Reverend Wicks Cherrycoke, but also, we are to believe, emanating from Dixon's mind in the moment as well. Having seized the whip from the driver, who is now cowering on the ground in fear, and having handed over the keys to the slaves so that they might free themselves, Dixon in his rage pauses to consider his next move. Should he kill the driver, as he would like to? In his frustration Dixon wonders: "What's a man of conscience to do?" (699). If this seems an odd moment for such a crucial question to be asked — a moral or philosophical quandary intruding on the moment of violence — it is because Dixon already seems to recognize that his intervention, however noble in intention, is not likely to make much of a positive difference in the lives of these few slaves, much less in terms of the ubiquitous institution of slavery itself, which is what it seems he really wishes to confront. Although this moment has been interpreted by some as Dixon's "enacting" of his noble Quaker abolitionism, Pynchon is quick to deflate any heroic rendering of the moment, immediately undercutting it with doubt, ambiguity, and the taint of failure. There are indications of this in Dixon's unanswered questions and in the one brief moment of speech given to the slaves at the center of this scene. Having taken the driver's keys and freed the slaves, Dixon now seems completely unsure of what to do or how to act, while the slaves seem to recognize that, despite Dixon's good intentions, this will in all likelihood still end badly for them:

A not at all friendly crowd by now having form'd,—"And as we're in the middle of Town, here," the Africans advise him, "Sheriff's men'll be here any moment,— don't worry about us,— some will stay, some'll get away,— but you'd better go, right now."

Despite this sound Counsel, Dixon still greatly desires to kill the Driver, cringing there among the Waggon-Ruts. What's a man of Conscience to do? It is frustrating. His Voice breaks. "If I see *you* again, *you* are a dead man." He shakes the Whip at him. "And dead *you'll* be, ere *you* see again this Instrument of Shame. For it will lie in a Quaker Home, and never more be us'd."

"Don't bet the Meeting-House on that," snarls the Driver, scuttling away.

"Go back to Philadelphia," someone shouts at Dixon. (699)

At the moment that Dixon seems to be acting in the best interest of these slaves, the slaves themselves are quick to point out how liberation in broad daylight in eighteenth-century Baltimore will end much differently than Dixon might have hoped. The slave-driver's comment, and the shout from some bystander, makes it clear that Dixon has in reality done virtually nothing to further the cause of abolition; in fact, his violence seems only to have hardened the will of those who find nothing at all offensive or immoral about slavery. In this way, Pynchon takes the historical account of Dixon's assault on a Baltimore slave driver and transforms that action into a meditation on the limits of social and moral effectivity as it unavoidably comes into contact with the institutionalized racism of American history and its interconnections with the systems of global commerce.

This crisis of social or moral effectivity is a fundamental one in *Mason & Dixon*, as it has been in various ways for all of Pynchon's work. It is, furthermore, a crisis central to the narrativization of postmodernism in general, with its own hyperexpanded versions of the horrible institutions with which Enlightenment figures like Dixon would have been all too familiar. As such, we should not be surprised to find that such a crisis extends beyond the borders of this particular novel and into the wider realm of Pynchon's earlier works, fiction and nonfiction alike. In his discussion of *Gravity's Rainbow*, which shares much in common with *Mason & Dixon* as far as its humanist politics are concerned, Jeff Baker recognizes that it is the *effects* of action and the *results* gained by such action that are the most important issue for Pynchon, while at the same time being the aspect of action that Pynchon's characters are themselves seldom capable of reflecting on or recognizing (104). Likewise, Patrick McHugh's analysis *of Gravity's Rainbow* suggests that the question of cultural politics as Pynchon constructs it is how to resist unjust and oppressive sociopolitical structures by means of a counterforce without this resistance itself becoming just another form of complicity and perpetuation (6).

Much the same could be said of *Mason & Dixon*. If the machinery of big business and death in wartime Europe and beyond in *Gravity's Rainbow* can produce at least the hope of a Counterforce to combat it, so too can the horrible institution of slavery — itself yet another system of big business and death — necessitate a force designed to oppose and dismantle it. But as McHugh points out in the case of *Gravity's Rainbow*, Roger Mexico, like Tyrone Slothrop and other central characters in the novel, never manages to achieve the desired effects that the Counterforce was designed to produce. This brings us back to the questions that must be asked of Dixon's assault on the slave driver: How will it alter material reality? Can it ever be more than, as Roger Mexico would say, a mere "pissing on the rational arrangements" of the business of slavery? Pynchon suggests that this act too shall fail, regardless of its seemingly heroic nature. Part of the problem for characters like Dixon is that their actions are tainted by complicity with the system that they seem to oppose. Throughout his work, Pynchon has repeatedly turned to this notion of complicity with the systems of oppression as a crippling component of the activism that seeks to oppose and transform those systems. Some critics have talked about these ideas in Pynchon's earlier works, but few have read *Mason & Dixon* sufficiently in these terms. Jeff Baker has briefly extended the arguments about complicity and action from *Gravity's Rainbow* into an analysis of *Mason & Dixon*, but even here, not enough has been made of Pynchon's abiding concern with problems of activist integrity and effectiveness. With the exception of Dixon's confrontation with the slave-driver, Baker contends, Mason and Dixon alike "are every bit as complicit as any slaveholder in the novel, for they are willing to enjoy the benefits of the system while complaining about its horrible injustices." In Baker's view this is the lesson the reader is meant to learn from this novel. "If we don't leave this novel with at least a vague sense of uneasy guilt," he concludes, "then we haven't read it nearly as carefully as it has been written" (182–83). Like so many other readers of the novel, Baker is drawn inexorably to Dixon's episode with the slave driver, and here again this particular incident seems to be accorded some special status in terms of understanding not just Dixon's moral character but that of a Pynchonian ethical project.

But this crucial notion of moral complicity is read by Baker in such a way as to suggest that the scene with the slave-driver is somehow a rare or anomalous instance of a proper moral character in Dixon, thus deserving to be bracketed off from the damning claims of his complicity — a desired critical separation that only serves to reinforce our attraction to perceived violence, whether in the service of a legitimate cause or otherwise. At the same time, though, Baker points us to a response that certainly seems correct: Pynchon does indeed mean for us to recognize Mason and Dixon's complicity as an early version of our own, with the world of bustling commercial expansion in the American colonies meant to be recognizable in our own fully-formed culture of global commodities. While a vague sense of uneasy guilt is certainly a part of what Pynchon seems to be drawing out from us, there has traditionally been in some fashion or other in Pynchon's work some possibility of hope, potential "routes of Escape, pockets of Safety" (69) from slavery and its modern analogues as well as the social guilt that follows from it. In *Mason & Dixon,* the fundamental possibility Pynchon posits for eradicating the horrors of slavery is not an extension of violence, but rather a radical awareness of the extent to which oppressive systems like chattel slavery cannot be understood, much less fought against, without recognizing how such systems are inextricably linked with various modes of consumption. The "heroism" granted to Dixon's intervention on behalf of the suffering slaves will be more accurately granted to those who can find methods of resistance to the system through a sort of ethical consumerism, a political notion that we will discover is not yet another of Pynchon's anachronistic invasions on the "purity" of his historical referents, but is instead a concept with an extensive history. If there is a lament in this narrative, it is not so much that America and the rest of the global market was built on slavery, but that in Pynchon's time and our own we are still too often content to judge history rather than recognize its modern-day reconfigurations and reorganize our ethical lives accordingly.

* * * * *

It is with this set of concerns about ethical agency as it is forced to contend with a global system that a seldom-discussed aspect of Pynchon's fidelity to historical facts and conditions in the colonial period becomes central — namely, the relation of emerging patterns of conspicuous consumption in the colonies to the development of a branch of Quaker abolitionism linking its social cause to those same modes of consumption. By the time the historical Charles Mason and Jeremiah Dixon were making their way to the American colonies to begin surveying their Line, the growing amount and variety of imports were dramatically altering consumption patterns in Europe and its colonies. As François Crouzet notes, items that previously had been unaffordable for many consumers (such as cotton and sugar) or even unknown (such as coffee and cocoa) were becoming increasingly popular due to availability and falling prices in this period. Several types of colonial produce, he adds, were addictive, and their consumption was also stimulated by "the new forms or places of sociability that were associated with them (e.g. coffeehouses). Starting out as luxuries for the elite few, they spread downward in society, becoming necessities for ordinary people in the late eighteenth century" (52).

Coffeehouses were, in fact, becoming by the mid-seventeenth century politically important places of sociability in England and thereafter in the American colonies. Also known as "penny universities" or "seminaries of sedition" (Moseley 22), coffeehouses became not only a preferred site for raucous debate and progressive political discussion but also a space for the consumption of the exotic imported goods now so readily available through the expansion of the Atlantic trade system.[1] The world of this emerging class, with its "modern ideas," was of course dependent on the labor of chattel slavery, primarily in the Caribbean, which produced so many of the goods these coffeehouse dwellers consumed. These new businesses marketing themselves as places of social and political discourse were also at the forefront of the colonial establishments selling the new goods for "luxury consumption" such as the alcohol and sugar of the Atlantic islands (Andrews 4). This fact, combined with the new affordability for products like coffee, rum, and sugar in the colonies and elsewhere, is more than just a crucial historical context for *Mason & Dixon* (and one that is already all too familiar to us today, from the ethical vantage-point that hindsight provides), but one inextricably linked in Pynchon's work to the problems of social activism and its vision of a more ethical mode of living.

This interrelationship is rendered in a condensed and immediate form in the following scene at Mary Janvier's, one of the numerous coffeehouses in which Mason and Dixon find themselves. While the patrons drink coffee and plot revolution, Pynchon intrudes on the good-spirited revelry by invoking yet again the crisis of slavery. In this instance the slaves themselves and the violent conditions under which they labor are present not as physical bodies whose pain is immediately visible and undeniable, but as the rhetorical referent, as the enabling conditions of the coffeehouse environment itself:

> Conversing about politics, under such a *stimulus,* would have prov'd animated enough, without reckoning in as well the effects of drink, tobacco,— whose smoke one inhales here willy-nilly with every breath,— and sugar, to be found at every hand in lucent brown cones great and little, Ic'd Cupcakes by the platter-ful, all manner of punches and flips, pies of the locality, crullers, muffins, and custards,— no table that does not hold some sweet memento, for those it matters to, of the cane thickets, the chains, the cruel Sugar-Islands.
>
> "A sweetness of immorality and corruption," pronounces a Quaker gentleman of Philadelphia, "bought as it is with the lives of

African slaves, untallied black lives broken upon the greedy engines of the Barbadoes."

"Sir, we wish no one ill,— we are middling folk, our toil is as great as anyone's, and some days it helps to have a lick of molasses to look forward to, at the end of it."

"If we may refuse to write upon stamped paper, and for the tea of the East India Company find a tolerable *Succedaneum* in New-Jersey red root, might Philosophy not as well discover some Patriotic alternative to the vile crystals that eat into our souls as horribly as our teeth?" (329–30)

Like many of the men enjoying themselves in Janvier's, many of Pynchon's critics have not been lured in by the Quaker's noble plea, although the specter of slavery seems to be a recurring theme in one fashion or another in their analyses. We forget this scene and recall instead (sometimes imperfectly) that glorious moment when Dixon abandons his pacifist principles and gives the slave driver his comeuppance; and yet the desire driving the Quaker's plea for a humane consumerism is essentially identical to Dixon's moment of violence. In both cases, the continued fact of slavery is recognized as a disturbing, cruel aspect of their modern society, and both wish to see it abolished. Even so, there is nothing to suggest that Mason or Dixon (or anyone else present) comprehends the ideas voiced by this unnamed Quaker gentleman or can imagine some method of implementing them. Beyond the brief response from an anonymous toiler among the "middling folk," the Quaker's suggestions do not seem to spark any sort of meaningful debate or discussion. Mason and Dixon are at that same moment embroiled in an argument with a man skeptical of the surveyors' labor performed in the dark of night, but the message is lost in the noise. "Is it the innocent roasted Berry," asks the narrator, "that has put them all in such a surly humor? . . . No one else in the room is paying much notice, being each preoccupied by his own no less compelling drama" (329). The Quaker's proposal to eradicate the consumption of sugar and other items bought with the lives of slaves — and by doing so, the logic goes, to eradicate slavery as well by rendering it unprofitable — simply fades into the din, giving way instead to young men kicking and pummeling "some Enlightenment regarding the Topick of Virtual Representation" into each other, while another group of men urge "sodomitical offenses against the body of the Sovereign" (330).

Despite its marginalization within the ostensible sphere of public debate, Pynchon is careful to position the Quaker's call for a radical reimagining of each citizen's complicit place within the global system of slavery right in the middle of issues that have come to define (or serve as a convenient shorthand for) American revolutionary ideology: the crises of representation, the damnable forms of excessive colonial taxation, and the limits imposed by imperial relations of forced trade and commerce. By situating an abolitionary consumerism within this set of "Patriotic" crises, Pynchon foregrounds the ironic disconnect between the historical arguments being made in the colonial public sphere (here the new and fashionable coffeehouse) about British oppression and the relative silence about the even more oppressive conditions of chattel slavery, which itself fueled the political and rhetorical ferment of an ostensibly intolerable colonial life. More than just the anachronistic intrusion of a twentieth-century humanitarian sensibility (which itself is far quicker to pronounce judgment on the horrible institutions of the distant past than to recognize their modern analogues), the Quaker's plea is, like so much else in Pynchon's fictional worlds, profoundly rooted in historical fact. The position taken by the Quaker in the coffeehouse, beyond serving as an historical precursor of the radical humanism Pynchon has long considered the noblest and yet least successful project of the 1960s, invokes a whole history of Quaker abolitionist rhetoric that sought to approach the problem of slavery in a variety of unorthodox ways.

Pynchon seems to have found in the novel's Quakers something akin to what he found so attractive and socially necessary about the heretical Puritan William Slothrop in *Gravity's Rainbow;* they, like William, professed a love and concern for the preterite, the unfavored — a love that Pynchon, throughout his career, has considered an essential foundation for combating the oppressive They-systems with which his characters must contend. In *Gravity's Rainbow,* it was the military-industrial complex of the wartime West; in *Vineland,* the reinvigorated McCarthyism and cultural vapidness of Reagan-era America; here, the rapid expansion of the international networks of trade running on the "greedy engines" of the slave economy. Thus, Pynchon's incorporation of Quaker abolitionism serves two functions. First, it reinserts certain notions of humane consumerism into the historical fold, where in most cases they remained little more than peripheral arguments until the Civil War a century later (and the emergence of critical appraisals of postcolonial conditions two centuries later) once more forced such notions back into public consciousness. Second, it awakens the postmodern consciousness to its own equally tainted relationship to global systems of oppression that seldom reveal themselves so nakedly to us as they were revealed to Dixon in the broad daylight of Baltimore.

* * * * *

One of the few Quaker abolitionists directly mentioned in *Mason & Dixon* is George Fox, who as early as the 1670s had been witness to the savagery of chattel slavery in Barbados. There he converted several slave owners to the Quaker faith and met with slaves in order to preach God's message of man's equality, which, not surprisingly, soon led to a public outcry and the eventual passing of an Act in 1676 to bar slaves from attending meetings. It was not long before the governors of many Caribbean regions began to prohibit Quaker meetings altogether, impose fines on disobedient Quakers, and even keep them from landing ashore.[2] Fox and many other prominent Quaker abolitionists of the time may have believed slavery to be an intolerable institution, but most, like William Penn himself, were more apt to see slaves as "children of God" worthy of conversion rather than as anything resembling sociopolitical equals to whites. Their immediate concerns were thus with the horrible violence perpetrated against slaves and the "proper" handling of them, a non-violent benevolence and goodwill, best displayed through sympathy for their unfortunate plight, which could best be ended through eventual emancipation.

Though certainly not a radical critique of the institution of slavery, such a perspective was an important early part of the history of the grad-ual progression of Quaker abolitionism in the seventeenth and eigh-teenth centuries. Early in the novel, Jeremiah Dixon has cause to think on Fox's famous advice about the equality of men when he first joins up with Mason:

> Altho' Dixon is heading off to Sumatra with a member of the Church of England,— that is, the *Ancestor of Troubles,*— a stranger with whom he moreover but hours before was carousing *exactly like Sailors,* shameful to say, yet, erring upon the side of Conviviality, will he decide to follow Fox's Advice, and answer "that of God" in Mason, finding it soon enough with the Battle on all 'round them, when both face their equal chances of imminent Death. (38)

The reference here is to Fox's assertion that every person has direct access to God because there is "that of God" in every person.[3] From the perspective of Quaker doctrine, this was a fundamental belief guiding how Friends were to approach all social dealings, whether among themselves or with people of other religious, racial, and cultural backgrounds. But unlike Fox, and employing arguments apparently beyond Dixon's ken, certain radical Quaker abolitionists sought to tackle the problem of slavery in a manner more closely aligned with that espoused by the Quaker gentleman at Janvier's coffeehouse, and Pynchon draws on this historical referent in order to drive home his own notions of radical hu-manism. While the arguments against trafficking in slaves were still often based on principles of man's equality before God or, differently, as Christian compassion and charity toward the less fortunate, some figures in the Society of Friends recognized that a possible solution to the problem of widespread slavery involved a scathing criticism not merely of those who kidnapped, bought, sold, and beat slaves, but of all those many colonial consumers — Quakers and non-Quakers alike — who enjoyed the benefits of global commerce at the expense of their souls.

The Quaker gentleman offering his own contribution to the raging political debates in Janvier's is thus representative of a certain strand of Quaker doctrine, expounded by the likes of Benjamin Lay, Thomas Tryon and, decades later, John Woolman, all of whom directed their abolitionist anger toward the new colonial consumer. Lay, for example, was so radical a figure (even in the eyes of the relatively progressive members in the Society of Friends) that his fellow Quaker abolitionists repudiated him. Famous for his thundering orations decrying the evils of slavery, Lay had a flair for the dramatic: puncturing a bladder of blood at the 1738 Meeting in order to make vivid the suffering of slaves; kidnapping a Quaker child to illustrate the unspeakable grief and torment suffered by African families torn apart (Soderlund 16). But it was his linking of the continued presence of slavery with patterns of seemingly harmless consumption that would go over with even less success, although it would be taken up by others in the decades following Lay's exile to a lonely cave. For Lay, the Quaker belief in pacifism was at its base a hypocritical doctrine in that Quakers professed to eschew violence in the conduct of their everyday lives, but yet continued to purchase the men and women plundered from Africa, and by so doing, he insisted, the Quakers "justif[ied] their selling of them, and the War, by which they were or are obtained" (10). Quakers thus carried "a worse thing in the Heart" than those whose violent methods they ostensibly deplored: the "plainer contradiction" of a lifestyle based on a doctrine of nonviolence and the dignity of man but actually functioning by virtue of an entire system of violence that could only remain incompletely disguised or alienated from those aspects of life with which that system was inextricably linked. Rather than placing the full or even primary blame on the captors and sellers of slaves, Lay seeks to lay the burden of guilt upon the ignorant or callous consumer.

The notion of consumer complicity is reinforced in even more extensive terms in Thomas Tryon's "The Negro's Complaint of Their Hard Servitude," wherein the Quaker abolitionist employs the voice of a slave-selling African in order to make a similar but more complexly drawn claim about the international market economy in which slave labor figures as the key term:

> Nor let any Christian Tyrants . . . upbraid us, for if it be (as in truth it is) a most unnatural wickedness in our People to sell them, is it not upon the matter almost as bad in the Christians to buy them?

Nay, rather is not the chiefest Crime in them, since they are the
Tempters and Occasioners of it? for [*sic*] they allure our People to it,
by offering them several sorts of Goods which they find they have
most mind to? (83)

The allure that undergirds this line of inquiry is that of an emergent
consumerism taking place on multiple continents simultaneously, a force
driving the desire for goods in Africa as well as the colonial Atlantic.
Tryon's lament speaks to the tangled ethics that inhere in this period, as
well as in its narrativization in a historical fiction such as Pynchon's, in
which the contemporary reader is certainly meant to absorb all this as historical crisis while at the same time recognizing its contemporary relevance in the era of global capital. While the initial blame in certain strands
of Quaker abolitionism was often placed on the sellers and captors of
slaves, and thereafter on the buyers and owners of slaves, arguments like
Tryon's also marked the crucial shift from a criticism of the buying of
slaves themselves to a criticism of the consumption of the luxurious foreign products of their forced labor.

In this sense anachronism in Pynchon becomes less interesting than
its narrative opposite, which is a commitment to rendering the ethical
space between Mason and Dixon's culture of global consumerism and our
own almost indistinguishable. As such, Pynchon is able to exploit for his
ethical purposes the views expressed by cultural critics whose conception
of the relations between an oppressed labor force and consumer society
would be valid and recognizable to many social theorists today. Consider,
for example, such a rendition of the relation between slave labor and the
excesses it allows for those in a position to benefit from it:

> We rise early, and lie down late, and labour beyond our
> strength, whilst our luxurious Masters stretch themselves on their
> soft Beds and Couches, they drink Wine in overflowing Bowls, and
> set their Brains a-float without either *Rudder* or *Compass,* in an
> Ocean of other strong and various Drinks, even till they are Drunk,
> and vomit up their Shame and Filthiness [. . . .] They feast them-
> selves with the fattest Lambs, and variety of rich costly Foods, and
> live in all Uncleanness and Glutton [. . . .] They wantonly consume
> the Encrease and Product of our heavy Pains in Riot and Voluptu-
> ousness, in Superfluity, and all kind of extravagant Vitiousness [. . . .]
> they yet proceed to gorge themselves with Wine, various sorts of
> brave noble Fruits, Tarts, Sweet-Meats, and a thousand Novelties
> brought from forreign Regions of themselves, more than sufficient
> for a sober and temperate Meal [. . . .] (Tryon 122–24)

If there is a significant difference between such a conception of economic and social relations and any number of similar ones as they are

quite rightly expressed in our current global climate of lopsided relationships of trade, it is the extent to which these arguments have in the interim been largely secularized, the rhetoric of gluttony and temperance perhaps now more commonly rewritten as a sociopolitical failing: an ethical crisis for Pynchon, to be sure, but one that no longer needs any sort of appeal to divine authority for its rhetorical force. A large part of the indictment here is concerned with making clear not just the extent to which consumption of these "Novelties brought from forreign Regions" depends on slave labor, but with insisting that the incredible sloth and gluttony of the consuming public greatly exacerbates the problem and provides it with a widespread international base.

John Woolman would take up these ideas much later when he considered the consumption of alcohol and other substances to be an evil that could be traced to its source in the related sins of avarice and superfluity. As Jack Marietta has noted, these sinful desires required unnecessary labor in order to gratify them. "In his journal in 1769," Marietta adds, "Woolman noted the intimate link between rum and the slave trade. To consume the former was to patronize the latter" (107). Woolman would appeal to his audience not merely by pointing out the immorality of their patterns of consumption, but by attempting to use this modern form of sin as an opportunity for instilling the fear of God's ultimate judgment: "These are the people by whose labour the other inhabitants are in a great measure supported," he argued, "and many of them in the luxuries of life [. . . .] and for our conduct towards them, we must answer before Him who is no respecter of persons" (qtd. in Bowden 208). In this fashion, Quaker abolitionists sought to cement in the minds of their audience the notion that consumption of products bought with the labor and lives of slaves was more than just socially unacceptable; it was, in fact, a mortal sin answerable to a much higher authority. In this same vein, the narrator of *Mason & Dixon* himself, the Rev[d] Wicks Cherrycoke, offers a brief gloss on this very matter soon after his arms-dealing brother-in-law J. Wade LeSpark shares a brief story about selling iron to be made into the weapons that will primarily be used for exterminating Indians:

> "What is not visible in his rendering," journalizes the Rev'd to himself, later, "is the Negro Slavery, that goes on making such no doubt exquisite moments possible,— the inhuman ill-usage, the careless abundance of pain inflicted, the unpric'd Coercion necessary to yearly Profits beyond the projectings even of proud Satan. In the shadows where the Forge's glow does not reach, or out uncomforted beneath the vaporous daylight of Chesapeake, bent to the day's loads of Fuel from the vanishing Hardwood Groves nearby, or breathing in the mephitic Vapors of the bloomeries,— wordlessly and, as some

may believe, patiently, they bide everywhere, these undeclared secular terms in the Equations of Proprietary Happiness." (412)

Here, as elsewhere in the novel, Pynchon means for us to scrutinize in the same way that radicals like Lay had, ever conscious of moral hypocrisy. While Cherrycoke finds his brother-in-law's business morally reprehensible, it is not so repugnant that he refrains from enjoying the hospitality of his brother-in-law's home. For all Cherrycoke's sermonizing, the occasion for and the ability to narrate his tale of Charles Mason and Jeremiah Dixon depends on his ability to bide his time comfortably there in the LeSpark home. In fact, the entire narrative — the "history" of Mason and Dixon's adventures to which Wicks claims to have been witness — begins with the LeSpark children laying out an array of goodies for their Uncle Wicks: "a large Basket dedicated to Saccharomanic Appetites, piled to the Brim with fresh-fried Dough-Nuts roll'd in Sugar, glaz'd Chestnuts, Buns, Fritters, Crullers, Tarts. "What is this? Why, Lads, you read my mind" (7). In other words, while Cherrycoke acknowledges the "undeclared secular terms" that make LeSpark's business possible and profitable, he also turns out to be precisely that sort of consumer whom the Quaker gentleman (and the historical Quaker abolitionists on which he is based) finds most offensive to the antislavery cause. Ever the glutton, however, Cherrycoke does not see — or perhaps chooses not to see — his own complicity with the system of oppression he seems to find so horrible.

* * * * *

If Pynchon is determined to unmask simple gluttony and reliance on the labors of others for one's various indulgences, he remains less clear about how something as bold and transformative as the Quaker's plea for humane substitutions could be implemented and made practical and real. In the end, the incorporation of an ethical dimension in *Mason & Dixon* — a way out from under the sinful yoke of sloth and complicity — would appear to be exceedingly difficult for two reasons: the very fact that this complicity is seldom revealed to us in any compelling way (as in the Quaker's brief moment) and, perhaps more pressing, the overwhelming sense that such systems of production and consumption cannot exist in forms that do not depend on oppression and exploitation. On a deeper level, Pynchon marks the psychosocial state that emerges from this dual crisis as constitutive not just of postmodernity (his historical place and ours) but of its historical progenitors, including but not necessarily limited to the Enlightenment and its various projects of reorganizing subjectivity and the contours of human relations through commerce, political debate, and ethical understanding. What Fredric Jameson has identified as the problem of cognitive mapping — a process always in crisis that in his rendering is aligned with a late form of global capital — becomes in Pynchon's hands a fundamental principle of American life generally, whether from the vantage point of the postmodern 1990s or the 1790s. The epistemological problems this principle poses in turn produce problems of individual agency, which both Jameson and Pynchon analyze, particularly with respect to how problems of conceptualizing or achieving some meaningful form of agency are then translated into the realms of social and political life.

Published in 1993, when Pynchon was still in the process of writing *Mason & Dixon*, Pynchon's essay on "Sloth" finds him once more engaging with these very issues. In "Sloth," which appeared as his contribution to the *New York Times Book Review*'s series on the "Seven Deadly Sins," Pynchon examines how the enduring sins of avarice, gluttony, and sloth were linked together historically in a sort of immorality domino-effect. Like the unidentified Quaker gentleman in Janvier's, Pynchon believes that "the state of our souls" needs to become "once more a subject of serious concern" (57). He tracks the movement of sloth and its brotherhood of related sins from a spiritual to a secular condition, and links early America's "consolidating [of] itself as a Christian capitalist state" to this seemingly paradoxical turning-away from the spiritual, which by the eighteenth and nineteenth centuries had, in Pynchon's view, become secularized partly due to the new obsession with efficiency and productivity, which replaced a sacred ordering of the day with one based on the demands of economic expansion and success. The stand taken by Melville's Bartleby becomes for Pynchon a key literary moment in American literature, wherein sloth becomes an offense against the smooth running of capitalism. Bartleby's insistent refusal to do anything (uttered "right in the heart of robberbaron capitalism") signals yet another important moment of crisis for Pynchon:

> While his options go rapidly narrowing, his employer, a man of affairs and substance, is actually brought to question the assumptions of his own life by this miserable scrivener — this writer! — who, though among the lowest of the low in the bilges of capitalism, nevertheless refuses to go on interacting anymore with the daily order, thus bringing up the interesting question: Who is more guilty of Sloth, a person who collaborates with the root of all evil, accepting things-as-they-are in return for a paycheck and a hassle-free life, or one who does nothing, finally, but persist in sorrow? (3)

Pynchon means for us to recognize that Bartleby's type of sloth — doing nothing but persisting in sorrow — is in one sense noble, insofar as it manages to stake out a position against creeping capitalism, but is at the same time a position understood in moral terms as being ultimately a disastrous and largely ineffective sin. And yet the type of sloth of which Bartleby's boss is guilty — the slothfulness of all those who accept "things-as-they-are" in order to secure profits and to avoid the hassles of fighting those tendencies — is even more horrifying. Pynchon knows how Bartleby's story ends; and yet he sees in such a figure something redeeming, some refusal to participate (which is, of course, a violent transformation in the order of things) that holds out the possibility of some alternative to things-as-they-are.

This view of sloth as being less about laziness or other sins against productivity than about the collaboration with the evils of a corrupt system is clearly central to *Mason & Dixon*. Pynchon seeks to criticize those who would simply accept "things-as-they-are," such as the institution of chattel slavery in colonial America and beyond, while at the same time suggesting that (in the words of the slave driver to Dixon the night before their violent encounter) *"All* are in the Market" for slaves, whether they immediately recognize it or not (696). Sloth, then, like the other sins Pynchon identifies, has in our modern world become not an offense against God, as a personal failing that requires individual absolution, but a secular offense with clear social and political (and thus moral) consequences. The paranoia that manifests itself in his work as a recognition that everything is connected is here turned into a possibility for transformation. This is made even clearer when Pynchon elaborates on his definition of sloth by examining its role in more recent political affairs:

> In this century we have come to think of Sloth as primarily political, a failure of public will allowing the introduction of evil policies and the rise of evil regimes, the worldwide fascist ascendancy of the 1920's and 30's being perhaps Sloth's finest hour, though the Vietnam era and the Reagan-Bush years are not far behind. Fiction and nonfiction alike are full of characters who fail to do what they should because of the effort involved. How can we not recognize our world? Occasions for choosing good present themselves in public and private for us every day, and we pass them by. (3)

As we have already noted, the problem for so many of Pynchon's characters is that, for the most part, they are not nearly as adept at "recognizing" their world as they might like to be — or, as Pynchon seems to imply, as they need to be. Dixon's intervention on behalf of the abused slaves would seem to stand as one of Pynchon's own fictional examples of "occasions for choosing good," and yet we have already demonstrated the extent to which his moment of violence can accomplish little more than Bartleby's disengagement from labor. In both cases, the noble action is easily subsumed and evacuated of force by means of the capitalist system that immediately reconstitutes itself in the minor wake of a small gesture of social activism. In short, Dixon's violence and Bartleby's perfection of sloth make for good drama, but poor politics.

In *Mason & Dixon*, sloth itself is reinvigorated and reimagined as a boon to capitalism, as the emerging dimensions of the eighteenth-century market that Pynchon highlights (the international slave trade, hyper-consumption of non-essential goods) are precisely those that derive much of their force from a culture where demand for certain types of goods delivered in a particular fashion has far outstripped any commitment to fair conditions of labor or equitable distribution of resources. This turns out to be a constitutive feature of Pynchon's novels in general, perhaps most famously rendered in Pökler's last moments at Dora, where Pökler is finally able to see (*visibility* here is central, as in *Mason & Dixon*) the horrors of the Holocaust, horrors for which he shares a clear portion of the responsibility:

> All his vacuums, his labyrinths, had been the other side of this. While he lived, and drew marks on paper, this invisible kingdom had kept on, in the darkness outside . . . all this time . . . Pökler vomited. He cried some. The walls did not fall — no prison wall ever did, not from tears, not at this finding, on every pallet, in every cell, that the faces are ones he knows after all, and holds dear as himself, and cannot, then, let them return to that silence. . . . But what can he ever do about it? How can he ever keep them? Impotence, mirror-rotation of sorrow, works him terribly as runaway heartbeating, and with hardly any chances left him for good rage, or for turning. . . . (*GR* 432–33)

The scene ends with Pökler sitting beside a frail survivor of Camp Dora before he takes off his wedding ring and places it in her hand. "If she lived," we are told, "the ring would be good for a few meals, or a blanket, or a night indoors, or a ride home" (433). The scene is at once a relatively rare moment of sober melodrama in the novel and a scathing criticism of Pökler's — and, by extension, our own — lack of concern for the horrors being perpetrated right under our noses.

It is also, of course, the moment when the ostensible "invisibility" of genocide is made clearer in the narrative, and it should not escape our attention that this moment, like Dixon's with the slave driver, depends for much of its force on a combination of moral crises occasioned by the undeniable physicality of the suffering body. As well, there is the same moment of action perceived as being morally righteous and meaningful, and yet frustratingly small and incomplete; the same narrative movement away from the slapstick and the absurd and into an emotional depth (but one always bordering on sentimentalism) that serves for Pynchon as a neces-

sary mode of narrativizing modern empathy; the same sense of the epiphany as the revelation of some individual insight into a large social injustice
demanding action and recognition; the same sense of impotent frustration
and rage with no satisfactory outlet; and the same unanswered — and
perhaps unanswerable — questions about how to act and what to do in
this world. While it is clear that, as Jeff Baker and others have suggested,
we are meant to see our own modern complicity with systems of oppression in moments like this, what is much less clear is what should be done
about it. In both moments, complicity, frustration and impotence are all
intertwined. The frustration of those who are compelled to witness such
miserable conditions — in other moments emerging as anger, rage, confusion, and despair — manifests itself with such force precisely because
characters like Pökler and Dixon, much like the members of the doomed
Counterforce in *Gravity's Rainbow*, are either ignorant of or somehow
blind to the underlying cruelty and injustice that lurks just beneath the
surface. Pynchon's characters, like so many of his readers, come to depend
on such forms of witnessing in order to condense the heretofore-
inconceivable relation between such suffering and our own lives (what we
eat, how we make our living) into something local and visible enough to
elicit sympathy and some form of action that is noble in intention if relatively insignificant in the face of global systems of oppression.

Even when this crisis of recognition and action does not depend on
the suffering body in Pynchon, it must rely on its specter, on the body
and its materiality envisioned in their absence. Shortly after his confrontation with the slave-driver, Dixon realizes, in a rare moment of lucidity, his
and Mason's own relationship to slavery, and the complicity and guilt that
Pynchon insists go along with it:

> "Ev'ry day at the Cape, we lived with Slavery in our faces,—
> more of it at St. Helena,— and now here we are again, in another
> Colony, this time having drawn them a Line between their Slave-
> Keepers, and their Wage-Payers, as if doom'd to re-encounter thro'
> the World this public secret, this shameful Core. . . . Pretending it to
> be ever somewhere else [. . . .] the innocent of the world passing
> daily into the Hands of Slave-owners and Torturers, but oh, never in
> Holland, nor in England, that Garden of Fools . . .? Christ, Mason."
> "Christ, what? What did I do?"
> "Huz. Didn't we take the King's money, as here we're taking it
> again? whilst Slaves waited upon us, and we neither one objected, as
> little as we have here, in certain houses south of the Line,— Where
> does it end?" (692)[4]

Again the privileged register for such moments of ethical crisis is not
the assertion or declaration, but the lingering unanswered question. If

the suffering and death of millions in *Gravity's Rainbow* is the "invisible kingdom" Pökler somehow never manages to see until it is too late, the same is true of the institution of slavery in *Mason & Dixon*. As with Cherrycoke's gloss on LeSpark's tale, it is slavery that is "not visible in [t]his rendering," but it is precisely that which makes the enjoyment of a fully-formed commodity culture possible. In *Gravity's Rainbow* the indictment is the same: just before Pökler discovers the survivor at Dora, Pynchon connects the more overt cruelty of a character like Weissmann to Pökler's less obvious but equally destructive version. Pökler's engineering skill, and, by extension, his complete blindness to the horrors around him, were "the gift of Daedalus that allowed him to put as much labyrinth as required between himself and the inconveniences of caring" (428).

Dixon and his colonial contemporaries, like Pökler and his twentieth-century ones, have been able to develop a wide range of techniques for putting things between themselves and the inconveniences of caring. It thus becomes necessary to read such a conception alongside Pynchon's discussion of modern sloth, where this notion of "inconvenience" is intimately linked to slothfulness, or its utopian opposite: a reinvigorated ethical effort, and one that, because of the historical demands placed on it, must somehow attempt to conceptualize an act and its real-world ramifications in both a local and global context simultaneously. This is what is at stake in Pynchon's assertion that people "fail to do what they should because of the effort involved" ("Couch" 57). In his analysis of Pynchon's "solutions" to the widespread problems his characters confront, Peter Cooper touches on this issue in his discussion of the nature of caring in Pynchon's fiction:

> For Pynchon the inability to care, or to translate caring into behavior, means the inability to perform socially and politically significant action. Pynchon is optimistic in presenting the Counterforce as a possibility, even a dialectical necessity, but pessimistic in showing how consistently it flops. Collectively as well as singly, his characters just don't have the wherewithal to make available solutions work. (103)

This is also certainly true of *Mason & Dixon:* Pynchon's chief characters don't have the "wherewithal" to set things right; or, put somewhat differently, the eighteenth century already seems in Pynchon's hands to hamper all efforts at a satisfactory cognitive mapping. If, however, at least some of these colonial characters are cognizant (on some level, at least) of the horrors occurring "under their noses" and sufficiently distraught about it, we then must examine whether or not this sense of social impotence is constitutive of Pynchon's understanding of social effectivity in general.

Pynchon's formal strategies (densely packed information; a wealth of historical referents — some "faithfully" rendered, others manipulated for often comic ends, his unique mixture of humor and pathos) are themselves keys to a certain reading of his novels' ethical content. The very density of his novels, in submerging their moments of profoundest moral insight (i.e. the lone Quaker's pleas), come through as formal manifestations of an often reclusive postmodern moralism, wherein an attempt to extract some sort of ethical meaning must of necessity seek out and explore the interstices of his narrative, just as one who wishes to occupy a position somewhere outside of contemporary systems of oppression would have no choice but to look at every point beyond the obvious and simplistic ones. Pynchon seems to remain ambivalent about the possibility of this position even existing in any imaginable social order. If the net result of this exploration is that there may be little in *Mason & Dixon* to suggest that abolitionism via some sort of ethical consumerism could ever hope to prove socially effective, the Quaker gentleman's plea, as well as the narrator's own commentary on the inhumanity of slavery, appear too centrally and repeatedly to be easily dismissed. In close proximity to both the Quaker gentleman and Rev[d] Cherrycoke's diatribes against slavery we find another crucial moment in which Pynchon very clearly builds on his idea, evident throughout the novel, that an inability to see human suffering or to act meaningfully against it is constitutive of all cultural relations within the expanding colonial market, and not merely a problem that will go away once slavery is somehow eradicated. At the site of the recent massacre of Indians at Lancaster Town, Dixon finds himself once more confronted with an evil he can barely comprehend, much less combat:

> Having been a Quaker all his life, his Conscience early brought awake and not yet entirely fallen back to sleep, he now rides over to the Jail as to his Duty-Station [. . . .]
>
> He sees where blows with Rifle-Butts miss'd their Marks, and chipp'd the Walls. He sees blood in Corners never cleans'd. Thankful he is no longer a Child, else might he curse and weep, scattering his Anger to no Effect, Dixon now must be his own stern Uncle, and smack himself upon the Pate at any sign of unfocusing. What in the Holy Names are these people about? [. . . .]
>
> Nothing he had brought to it of his nearest comparison, Raby with its thatch'd and benevolent romance of serfdom, had at all prepar'd him for the iron Criminality of the Cape,— the publick Executions and Whippings, the open'd flesh, the welling blood, the beefy contented faces of those whites. . . . Yet is Dixon certain, as certain

as the lightness he feels now, lightness premonitory of Flying, that far worse happen'd here, to these poor People, as the blood flew and the Children cried,— that at the end no one understood what they said as they died. "I don't pray enough," Dixon subvocalizes, "and I can't get upon my Knees just now because too many are watching,— yet could I kneel, and would I pray, 'twould be to ask, respectfully, that this be made right, that the Murderers meet appropriate Fates, that I be spar'd the awkwardness of seeking them out myself and slaying as many as I may, before they overwhelm me. Much better if that be handl'd some other way, by someone a bit more credible. . . ." He feels no better for this Out-pouring. (347)

Such a scene (in which, unlike the slave-driver episode, the only "action" or drama takes place internally) is in certain respects the most succinct account Pynchon can provide of his own narrative ethos. In terms of delineating the problem of social activism in the era of global capital, this is the key moment prefiguring Dixon's assault on the slave driver, and yet it is a moment that never seems to be considered alongside of it in discussion of the novel's vision of effective activism. If there is a moment in this novel in which we are witness to Dixon "scattering his Anger to no Effect," it is his subsequent confrontation with the driver. In both instances, the moments end without any satisfactory resolution: the driver scuttles away to reclaim his human property, while here Dixon's capacity for anger and extreme violence makes him feel no better and make the world no fairer.

The fact that this moment at the massacre site also never moves beyond the imaginary ultimately speaks to Pynchon's increasing cynicism about the likelihood of profound social change emerging from any engaged humanism, no matter how noble in intention. Dixon's presence at the scene is real enough, as are his emotions; but by the time his anger about the horrors whose remnants are still visible here has been converted into some impulse to action, the narrative subtly but quickly moves into the subjunctive register ("Yet *could* I kneel, and *would* I pray, *'twould* be to ask, respectfully, that this be made right."). Not only does Dixon do nothing to seek revenge on the Paxton Boys or to otherwise avenge the deaths of the natives; he doesn't even quite manage to make this prayer an actual one. In the form he has cast it, it remains the wished-for wish, the prayer that is not quite prayed. What we discover in this moment and elsewhere in the novel is that the rhetoric of doomed violent heroism or a more humanistic consumerism (if there could be such a thing) in *Mason & Dixon* is counterpoised with retreats into individual or narratorial fantasy.

In Pynchon, the glimpse of the horror of slavery and other systems of oppression, and the recognition of one's powerlessness in the face of them, often leads into the seduction of fantasy in its various forms as a sort of last resort for social idealism, a retreat into fantasy that is often too enticing (for his characters, yes, but also for the author) to resist. The allure of fantasy as a mechanism for coping with slavery and its moral entanglements in the social and economic worlds in which Mason and Dixon find themselves emerges at several critical points in the novel, as when the two men are performing work in Cape Town. In the midst of the Vroom family's efforts to use their slaves to seduce Mason, we find Mason and Dixon entertaining prolonged discussions about slavery in South Africa before Mason (who had up to this point been as angered by what he'd seen of slavery as had Dixon) contemplates the limitless possibilities the luxury of slaves might present to someone in their humble profession:

> Slaves here commit suicide at a frightening Rate,— but so do the Whites, for no reason, or for a Reason ubiquitous and unaddress'd, which may bear Acquaintance but a Moment at a Time. Mason, as he comes to recognize the sorrowful Nakedness of the Arrangements here, grows morose, whilst Dixon makes a point of treating Slaves with the Courtesy he is never quite able to summon for their Masters.
>
> Yet they entertain prolong'd Phantasies upon the Topick. They take their Joy of it. "Astronomy in a Realm where Slavery prevails . . . ! Slaves holding candles to illuminate the ocular Threads, whilst others hold Mirrors, should we wish another Angle. One might lie, supine, Zenith-Star position, all Night, . . . being fann'd, fed, amus'd,— ev'ryone else oblig'd to remain upon their Feet, ever a-tip, to respond to a 'Gazer's least Velleity. Hahrrh!"
>
> "Mason, why thah' is dis-gusting . . . ?"
>
> "Come, come, and you're ever telling me to lighten up *my* Phiz? I have found it help, Dixon, to think of this place as another Planet whither we have journey'd, where these Dutch-speaking White natives are as alien to the civilization we know as the very strangest of Pygmies,—"
>
> "'Help'? It doesn't help, what are tha talking about . . .? Tha've a personal Interest here, thy Sentiments engag'd, for all I know." (69)

Mason's efforts to cope with the nightmare of slavery may lead him to fantasy, but as Dixon quickly indicates, such a fantasy is of little help to the slaves themselves or to those like Mason and Dixon, who feel at once appalled and powerless in the face of Dutch South Africa's ubiquitous culture of slavery. Of particular interest is how Mason's notion of astronomer-masters articulates a fantasy of both absolute sloth and luxury and a simultaneous fantasy of increased productivity. His idyllic vision of slavery points to the apparent paradox of slave labor, which seems (for Mason at least) to serve two functions simultaneously: as a substitute form of labor, providing the bodies and labor required for the tedious tasks one does not wish for oneself (or the luxurious pampering one wishes performed upon oneself); and as a supplemental or additional source of labor, ironically "freeing" the masters to perform the important scientific work they imagine doing if only they could get a little bit of slave help for themselves — slavery leading the charge to Enlightenment. The terms are important: Mason's image of a world in which slavery "prevails" suggests not only a world where the institution of slavery is widespread and common (which is essentially already the world he lives in), but where the concept and practice of enslaving fellow humans *wins out* — prevails — over other possible constructions of the social world. Mason envisions a world in which the violence and horror of slavery are erased, and yet a willing subservience and servitude somehow remain, an imagined version of the order of things that covers that which makes slavery so abominable. As Dixon shakes him from this reverie, Mason's defense provides an uncanny echo of the terms so central to Pynchon's essay on historical sins and their modern counterparts: "And I'm making no Effort, is that it, you're accusing me of Servility? Sloth? You're never about, how would you know how hard I'm working? Do not imagine me taking any more Joy of this, than you do" (70). Even Mason cannot sustain the fantasy he has created, for it is incapable of containing slavery into something convenient and manageable, unfettered by nagging questions of morality.

It is thus unsurprising that the only unproblematic and adequately resolved "encounter" Mason and Dixon have with slavery occurs in the subjunctive mode — in a subjunctive chapter, to be exact, as Reverend Cherrycoke narrates events that *could* have happened but within the actuality of the narrative did not happen. This other fantasy is not Mason's or Dixon's, precisely, but the narrator's, who we will recall professed feelings about the institution of slavery much the same as those of the Quaker gentleman at Janvier's. "Suppose that Mason and Dixon and their Line cross Ohio after all," he begins (706), and all of what follows — the encounters, the details, the observations — are things that did not in fact happen, although Cherrycoke soon drops the linguistic markers that make this clear. Here, in the chapter immediately following Dixon's very real encounter with the Baltimore slave driver, he and Mason extend their survey (only subjunctively, of course) further into the West:

> Right in the way of the Visto some evening at Supper-time will appear the Lights of some complete Village, down the middle of whose main street the Line will clearly run. Laws continuing upon one side,— Slaves, Tobacco, Tax Liabilities,— may cease to exist upon the other, obliging Sheriffs and posses to decide how serious they are

about wanting to cross Main Street. "Thanks, Gentlemen! Slaves
yesterday, free Men and Women today! You survey'd the Chains
right off 'em, with your own!" (708)

We are left to imagine that the imaginary slaves are freed effortlessly
into a new life of limitless possibility. This stands in sharp contrast to the
likely fates of those slaves freed in the middle of town in broad daylight
just a handful of pages before, where only a moment after Dixon inter-
venes, he hurries off, fearing for his own safety, leaving the escaped slaves
and the remaining ones to their fates, perhaps at the hands of what he described at Lancaster Town as "someone a bit more credible." In the moment of actual liberation, Dixon is unwilling or unable to conceive of the
essential meaninglessness — or at least the ineffectiveness — of his action;
and he certainly never stops to consider the likelihood of their being re-
captured and made to suffer even more for the additional trouble caused
by his ostensibly heroic gesture. In the realm of the subjunctive, however,
troublesome social issues like slavery and human cruelty are dealt with
easily. One moment the surveyors are freeing slaves; by the next sentence,
the slaves are forgotten, and the surveyors are already preoccupied with a
"strange tribal sect" worshipping the newly-discovered planet we will
come to know as Uranus, "the Career-maker each has dreamt of"
(708) — in other words, the dream of a moral universe giving way once
more to dreams of a successful insertion into the labor market.

If there are choices to be made in the world of *Mason & Dixon*, as
there were even for poor Bartleby, they would seem to be between the
doomed ineffective heroism of the small act of kindness and violence, the
radical reorganization of economic power based in the mass awakening of
the socially conscious consumer class, or the retreat into any of a number
of attractive, albeit temporary, fantasies. In a certain sense, though, the
small act of kindness (such as Dixon's intervention in Baltimore) is precisely that: it certainly has an immediate practical value, insofar as Dixon
prevents that particular beating to continue; and yet it is too small an act,
Pynchon seems to insist; it is ultimately too easily absorbed by its oppo-
nents and devalued to be of more than temporary comfort to anyone.
Likewise, the space of fantasy — particularly the fantasy of slavery, which
is in Pynchon's hands a mechanism of avoidance and coping above all
else — is an example of precisely that which he describes elsewhere as the
turning-away that is a fundamental symptom of sloth, "a loss of spiritual
determination that then feeds back on in to the process, soon enough
producing what is known as guilt or depression, eventually pushing us to
where will do anything, in the way of venial sin and bad judgment, to
avoid the discomfort" ("Couch" 3). Throughout *Mason & Dixon*,
Pynchon invokes a society wherein the avoidance of discomfort is in part a

product of a culture in which the readily available commodity has become too convenient a form of pacification. While the specific forms it takes may change rapidly in our new global era, that culture, he would add, is nothing new; in fact, it has been with us at least since men in colonial coffeehouses entertained fantasies of an independent America. There then exists in *Mason & Dixon* a figuring of the commodity (once a luxury, now appearing to us as the basest of "necessities") as an object for consumption that has, already in the emerging global market of the eighteenth century, become almost completely alienated from the conditions of its production — a distance between the ethically corrupt conditions of its provenance and the site of its consumption. This distance offers up the goods of global commerce as unencumbered objects on which the ostensibly political animal is fatted, rather than as what they should represent for us, then as now: signifiers of subjection.

Notes

[1] The historical account of these coffeehouses offered by Edward Bramah will sound familiar to readers of Pynchon's novel:

> The coffee houses had contributed a great deal to the social history of their time, and they saw the emergence of a new and influential class of men, men of moderate means, good education and modern ideas; men who learned that they could successfully oppose the will of the monarch, and even get rid of him and appoint a new one, that they could see the country governed according to their wishes, express their views freely in the Press, organize trade and revolutionize literature. These men needed meeting places and in the coffee houses they found them. (50)

Pynchon thus seems to have found the colonial coffeehouse useful as a site for both anachronistic irony and as an historically grounded place in which to stage the rhetoric of an alternative approach to social activism.

[2] The historical information in this section is culled from various sections of James Bowden's multivolume *The History of the Society of Friends in America* (London: Charles Gilpin, 1850–1854). For those interested, Bowden offers a wealth of additional historical information on the history of Quakerism and its ties to abolitionist movements in the colonial era.

[3] George Fox's epistle on finding "that of God" in every man, first written in 1656, is found in *The Journal of George Fox*, edited by John L. Nickalls (Cambridge: Cambridge UP, 1952), 263.

[4] This echoes any number of other similar moments of what we might call the epiphany of complicity in Pynchon's work: in *The Crying of Lot 49*, for example, in which Oedipa Maas, after confronting a swastika dealer, realizes that "[t]his is America, you live in it, you let it happen" (150); or in *Gravity's Rainbow*, as the problems of knowledge and action within the Counterforce reveal themselves: "We do know what's going on, and we let it go on" (713).

3: Consumption on the Frontier: Food and Sacrament in *Mason & Dixon*

Colin A. Clarke

STATIONED IN CAPE TOWN to observe the Transit of Venus, Charles Mason finds himself bemoaning the lack of variety to be found in Dutch Cape kitchens, a lack which has driven his partner Jeremiah Dixon to sample every available *ketjap* and Malay delicacy in hopes of avoiding "[t]he smell . . . of Mutton-fat vaporiz'd and recondens'd, again and again, working its way insidiously, over the years of cooking, into all walls, furniture, draperies . . ." (86). Just as this scent of cooked sheep seeps into the walls and so becomes a constant underlying presence in the Vroom household, so too does food continually reappear in *Mason & Dixon* as a subtle reminder of the political and social forces governing the lives of the main characters, and as suggestions of the overlap between the eighteenth and twentieth centuries. In *The Empire Writes Back,* Bill Ashcroft, Gareth Griffiths, and Helen Tiffin place language at the center of colonialism, claiming that "[o]ne of the main features of imperial oppression is the control over language" (7). For Ashcroft, Griffiths, and Tiffin, language becomes one of the primary sites of colonial struggle, as the restriction of language allows control over the processes of communication, granting colonists a permeating power over nearly every aspect of life in the colonies. As such, language becomes a key figure in any post-colonial expression, as the re-emergence of native voices, or the appropriation and subtle repositioning of the colonial voice, suggests the ways in which the colonized come to exercise some control over that which had been one of the primary means of their oppression, and signify difference from the colonial center (43). In *Mason & Dixon,* food becomes akin to a discursive practice, frequently framing the attempt by the colonizers to control the voice and culture of the native and imported Other.

Simultaneously, the desire for the exotic, in this case in the form of produce and drink, which as marketable products partially fuel the colonialist endeavor represented in this novel by the Dutch and British East India Companies, the British Royal Society, French Jesuits, and Clive of India, suggests an emergence of the post-colonial voice, as the forbidden foods of the colonized increasingly find their way onto Western tables from Cape Town to Philadelphia. Food in *Mason and Dixon* becomes emblematic of colonial control as well as post-colonial difference and revolution; it becomes the embodiment of the vast network of cultural signifiers and appropriations that frame the colonial and post-colonial discourse which permeates the novel, and it serves to undermine myths of cultural permanence and superiority. For every stop on Mason and Dixon's transit, food is an abundant example of cultural imperialism and cultural difference. It is precisely that abundance, the appearance of the exotic and the ordinary at every stop of Mason and Dixon's journey, which reflects the overlap in this novel between the eighteenth and twentieth centuries, an overlap which allows the reader to witness a post-colonial voice in the process of becoming post-colonial and at the same time recognize the echo of the imperialist voice it will become.[1] While each appearance of an exotic *ketjap* or Sumatran coffee illustrates the omnipresence of eighteenth-century colonialism, it also suggests twentieth-century globalization and American excess, as Pynchon draws a long and unwavering line, in a novel obsessed with lines, between the colonial imperialism of the eighteenth century and the cultural imperialism of the twentieth. Many of these factors ultimately converge on the frontier in America, a land identified by its propensity toward conspicuous consumption and (caffeine- and narcotic-fueled) revolution, a land in which food can be a dietary necessity, a form of legal tender, or a religious sacrament.

In Cape Town, Mason and Dixon's first station in the novel, food becomes a primary site of colonial control and native subversion. For Dixon, Cape Town offers immediate entrance into a peculiar culinary underworld, his propensities for which, along with his Quaker upbringing, earn him the suspicions of the local whites, who notice "his unconceal'd attraction to the Malays and the Black slaves,— their Food, their Appearance, their Music, and so, it must be obvious, their desires to be deliver'd out of oppression" (61). In this, Dixon is drawn to that which is forbidden, as strict curfews govern white interaction with the native and slave-born sections of the town. Those restrictions are born of a standard colonial response to native and slave populations: isolate and silence that which is inconsistent with or in opposition to the goals of the colonial government. While such restrictions are often aimed at restricting language and the means of communication, Pynchon creates a sort of culinary discourse, in which food itself becomes a signifier of power at the center of the authoritative colonial government in Cape Town. That which is foreign, exotic, or at all outside the norm of the Dutch kitchen, is dangerous and therefore to be avoided in an attempt to establish cultural and colonial hegemony. In that regard, food in Cape Town is treated by the colonizing power exactly as language or any other form of cultural expression and identity. The "cultural denigration" of native foods becomes a primary expression of cultural domination (Ashcroft et al. 9). The more the Cape Dutch restrict the currency of native culture, in this case food, the more they establish their own culinary traditions as part of the normative center. Although Dixon is aware of the abuse of the slaves, specifically in the case of slaves forced into prostitution, and the oppression of the marginalized native population by the colonists, the oppression he most keenly notes is the constant use of mutton as the center-piece of meals in the Vroom household, most often the hind parts of the sheep, which "[o]ver the course of its late owner's life . . . has grown not merely larger and more fatty, but also, having absorbed years of ovine Flatulence ever blowing by, to exhibit a distinct Taste, perhaps priz'd by *cognoscenti* somewhere, though where cannot readily be imagin'd" (79). This, coupled with Cornelius Vroom's volcanic attempts to cover the taste of the meals and the intrigues of the house with pipe smoke, and the Vroom women's flirtations with Mason and Dixon in an attempt to drive them into the bed of their domestic slave Austra, a name which closely links her to the subject and site of colonial dominion, spurs Mason and Dixon into the forbidden sections of Cape Town, in search of the exotic in all its forms. This includes "*Dagga,* cleaned, graded, ready for your flame," "[r]eal Dutch gin," "*ketjap,* arriv'd Express from Indo-China, [and] Pineapple, Pumplenose, Tamarind,— an hundred flavors, a thousand blends!" (77). These exotic consumables are available primarily in the areas of Cape Town to which travel is prohibited after certain hours, a curfew Dixon characteristically ignores. This prohibition is not a matter of puritanical attitudes on the part of the Cape Dutch — in their own bars and clubs the Cape Dutch are supplied with the wide varieties of narcotics, pornography, and prostitution for which contemporary Amsterdam is notorious — but a product of cultural and racial attitudes. Such items are dangerous because they fall outside the Dutch norm, and so present cultures, some indigenous and others imported with the slave trade, which the colony is designed to systematically restrict, oppress, and potentially eliminate. In fact, Cornelius Vroom "has forbidden his daughters to eat any of the native Cookery, particularly that of the Malay, in his belief that the Spices encourage Adolescents into 'Sin,' by which he means Lust that crosses racial barriers," the mixtures of spices symbolic of the mixing of the races, and so taboo (62). The restriction on food then comes to mirror the standard colonial restriction of language and governance of interaction between colonizer and colonized. In *Mason & Dixon,* such restrictions express the deep-seated fear of the colonists, and the rules they create become a sort of political smoke-screen, less effective at restricting the Other than it is at simply, and gratefully, blinding themselves from the truth. Cornelius, willfully obscured within the folds of his pipe smoke, is the typical Cape Dutchman, ignorant of the seething sexuality within his own household, and desperately trying to live under the pressure of an entire "dark" continent at his back in a city which is, as Pynchon puts it, "[t]emporally, as geographically, the End of the World" (78).

Food in Cape Town serves as one of the many lines in this novel, a line that separates cultures and races, a line which is meant to accentuate the division between enlightened and savage, owner and owned. In its great variety, however, in the near constant availability of *ketjaps* and spices, gin and *dagga*, Cape Town reflects its role as a colonial enterprise. Never an especially profitable settlement for the Dutch, Cape Town geographically served a need for the Dutch trading companies plying the route to the Indies, providing ships with a deep port and fresh water.[2] Having little economic potential of its own — the Dutch government wanted the settlers to focus their energies on agriculture, while the settlers tended to turn to the herding of cattle and sheep (Bennett 52) — Cape Town was primarily a place where ships stopped on their way to or from the East Indies, and where a variety of goods from Europe or Asia were exchanged. In *Mason & Dixon*, Cape Town is emblematic of the effect of the blossoming colonial trade of the eighteenth century, a trade so profitable and well-organized as to bring together in one place European alcohol and Asian produce, in a manner and variety strikingly similar to the supermarkets of the late twentieth century. Pynchon deftly underlines this connection in what amounts to a lurid commercial pitch for Heinz ketchup, a scene in which one of the Vroom daughters, observing Dixon struggling to extract *ketjap* from "its slender bottle," advises Dixon, "Strike her on the bottom . . . and perhaps she will behave" (79).

Yet the colonial trade which passes through Cape Town and leaves behind a residue of exotic and illicit consumables perhaps unequalled elsewhere in the novel, is fueled by slavery. The variety of products the ships bring to Cape Town from both the east and west is mirrored by the slaves brought to and through the colony, slaves who were historically imported from both the west and east coasts of Africa, and largely from the Malay Archipelago, with which the Dutch did extensive trade.[3] Although Mason and Dixon rather democratically defy curfew and venture into the sections of Cape Town populated by slaves and free Malays and Africans in search of "all the Spices armies us'd to kill for . . . shrimp paste, tamarinds, coriander and cumin, hot chilies, fish sauces, and fennel and fœnugreek, ginger and *lengkua*" (82), they are also culinary tourists on the prowl for one more undreamt-of delicacy, another combination of spices unheard of in London. The only voices issuing from the forbidden stalls in native Cape Town are hawking wares desired by adventuresome tourists and rebellious colonists like Dixon; the African and Malay voice is indistinguishable from the product it promotes, making the product itself representative of the voice the colonial laws seek to silence. The laws which restrict access to the non-European sections of Cape Town serve as a more subtle application of the oppressive systems around which the colony is structured. Essentially, these restrictive rules prevent the Malays, Africans, and other colonized residents of Cape Town from entering and so, as Cornelius fears, tainting the European culture and its representatives. In turn, however, the frequently-ignored restrictions placed on the Cape Dutch and their guests allow the colonizers to enter the exotic underworld of native, black-market Cape Town, and so exercise their rights as consumers as well as colonizers. In this regard, Mason and Dixon's forays into the forbidden sections of the town simply serve to expand the control of the colony they both view to be morally and politically suspect. If their compulsive quest for the exotic at all validates the foreign and forbidden items which they encounter, that validation is limited to the geographical areas to which the vendors are restricted, and in which such items need no validation. Yet Dixon's role as a carrier, a character who transports the forbidden, in the form of *ketjap*, to the Vroom household and far beyond, expresses the futility of the Cape Dutch's segregationist policies; the authoritative discourse of the colonial power, no matter how tightly it attempts to restrict communication, cannot completely isolate a culture, especially, as in this case, if there is a marketable product behind it. Although the power structure in the colony is largely maintained, the Cape Dutch attempts to preserve a mythical cultural purity are undone by the very system of trade and profit that drives them.

Dixon's almost obsessive quest for food is but one aspect of his excessive nature; that Mason joins him is simply evidence of his desire to escape the temptations of the Vroom household and to give penance for his temptation. Despite its connections with colonial trade and slavery, food in Cape Town also serves a spiritual function. The excess with which Cape Town is associated, the "unrelenting Vapor of debauchery" (78) in which it is enveloped, makes of Cape Town a sort of Sodom, with the Cape Dutch seizing everything, animal, vegetable, or mineral, that comes to them in expectation of the day when they are finally swallowed by the ocean or buried underneath Table Mountain. On the Vrooms' table, scenes of salvation are revealed with every spoonful, as the tableware is painted with "scenes of martyrdom" and "obscure moral instruction" (83); with each nearly inedible bite Mason and Dixon have revealed to them a salvation, or perhaps a fate, they would rather avoid. Their search for the delicacies of the Cape Malay kitchens is a cheap form of refuge from both the smoke-filled hell of the Vrooms' kitchen and the religious instruction depicted on their flatware. As the narrator, Revd Cherrycoke (much like the soft drink, Cherrycoke turns up everywhere in the novel) notes, the Malay food preferred by the astronomers is a kind of moral jumping-ship, a preference for the exotic that can be "magical in purpose and effect" (86). Mason and Dixon are culinary mutineers, in this case abandoning culture and race in favor of the exoticized Other, willing to accept the native culture not so much because of any inherent understanding of or sympathy for it, but rather through a desire to escape the restrictions and responsibilities of the colonial class. The exotic for them, which stands both within the power of the colonial government but also, through its "magical" components, well outside of any known rules of law, becomes a temporary salvation. This potential salvation is represented at the end of their stay when the mangoes they search out at the height of their ripeness, become, held aloft in Cherrycoke's hand, a host: "This Mango handles like flesh,— to peel it is to flay it,— to bite into it is to eat uncook'd Flesh . . ." (85). Cherrycoke notes the potentially uncomfortable connection between the Christian tradition of the host and cannibalism, relating the mango in this case to the salvation which Dixon, in his almost childlike innocence, does not feel compelled to seek, and which Mason, in his continual mourning over his dead wife, feels he does not deserve and so disavows. Yet perhaps the main difference between cannibalism and the salvation represented by the host in this novel is that between the raw and the cooked. The mango is pure exoticism, an accessible flesh and bone untainted by heat or combination with other ingredients. In their search for the exotic, the astronomers may very well be avoiding the transformation represented by cooking itself, in which the right ingredients at the proper temperatures create a wholly new substance. Cherrycoke translates that transformation into its religious analogue: "Lamb of God, Eucharist of bread,— what Mr. Mason could not bear, were the very odors of Blood-Sacrifice and Transsubstantiation, the constant element in all being the Oven, the Altar wherebefore his Father presided" (86). For Mason, given his conflicted history with his father (a baker), and his perpetual guilt and studied denial of salvation, the exotic foods of Cape Town offer refuge from the uncomfortable questions raised by the sometimes gruesome transformations perpetuated in the Vroom's kitchen. Dixon, in the standard contrast created between the two, is drawn by his appetite, his gleeful participation in the exotic and the new, and his refusal to have his enthusiasm dampened for long by even the sobering reminders that the larger colonial and religious powers which put such exoticism at his fingertips are supported by the system of slavery he was raised to abhor.

If Cape Town sits at the end of the world, nervously waiting for its inevitable demise, then James's Town on St. Helena, as Pynchon describes it, has at least one foot in "the Other World," as it clings to the hillside on which it is set, and its residents live in continual fear of the winds which scour it and the ocean which "appears to lie *above*" it (107). Like Cape Town, James's Town shows all the signs of the collision of cultures that commerce and colonialism bring, as the town is occasionally "an unlit riot of spices, pastry, fish and shellfish," in this case being put to particularly inventive use in dishes such as "Penguin Stuffatas and Sea-Bird Fricasées" (114). Such unlikely combinations have the flavor of frontier ingenuity, although certain dishes, such as "Brochette of Curried Albacore" (127) are much more evocative of a twentieth-century appetizer, Pynchon playing with the possibilities of such cultural and culinary collisions on an isolated island at the whims of nature and trade, and suggesting to the reader that the "Other World" in which St. Helena is partially placed is the reader's own world, as well as the Western world for which the island is but a brief, transitional layover. Though St. Helena shows all the signs of commerce witnessed in Cape Town, it also shows the scars of that commerce, as when Mason and his superior on the island, Maskelyne, venture into the interior and

> stand in the scent of an orange-grove,— as tourists elsewhere might stand and gape at some mighty cataract or chasm,— nose-gaping, rather, at a manifold of odor neither Englishman has ever encountered before. They have been searching for it all the long declining Day,— it is the last Orange-Grove upon the island,— a souvenir of a Paradise decrepit [. . .]. (134)

The trade that brings such exotic things to market in Cape Town and James's Town also brings those who destroy the natural beauty and abundance of those places, a decline associated, through its connection to a once-pure "Paradise," to the fall of mankind as well. Commerce is the evil in this garden; as Maskeleyne puts it, "[i]n thoughtless Greed, within a few pitiably brief Generations, have these People devastated a Garden in which, once, anything might grow" (135). Such destruction is typical of the changes wrought on colonies, especially those whose land can be put to purposes which serve the mercantilist needs of the colonizers, as exemplified by Mark Pendergrast's description of the large-scale deforestation undertaken in Brazil and other colonies to clear lands for increasingly large plantations (24). As in Cape Town, Mason is just an onlooker, a tourist preferring to enjoy what the local markets and taverns have to offer rather than reflect upon his own implicit guilt in that which supports such trade, not only as consumer, but as a man whose job it is to make such trade more efficient. Although Mason and Dixon frequently pause to consider which forces exactly, the British government, the Jesuits, or Clive of India himself, among others, are controlling their lives, they more often choose to suppress such uncomfortable questions with profuse amounts of food and drink. While Mason in St. Helena drowns his fears with gin, wine, and the occasional "Cock Ale" (a product of global commerce and frontier ingenuity if ever there was one, consisting of the victims of Malay cockfights squeezed dry with a "Chinese Duck Press" and mixed with "dried Fruit Bits in Mountain, or Málaga Wine" [120]), Dixon in Cape Town placates himself with *Soupkie*, gin with "unusual herbs in it," the roasted "Haunch of some Animal unfamiliar to Englishmen," "Opium, Hemp, and Cloves," all to the tune of the Philippino guitarist in his local tavern (148–49).

Unlike Cape Town, where the colonizing body establishes a rigid system to restrict cross-cultural interaction, James's Town embraces such hybridity, partially as a function of its frontier characteristics, and partially in response to the almost supernatural chaos that seems to haunt the island. This hybridity, which can present to the astronomers influences from Europe, China, and Southeast Asia in just one drink, inevitably raises questions for the characters about what forces in this world could be so powerful and permeating as to make such combinations not only possible, but also increasingly frequent. For Mason and Dixon, St. Helena, like Cape Town, becomes something of a working grand tour; and while hard questions are asked, the almost dizzying possibilities in response are best considered over a pint of ale, a glass of wine, or a cup of coffee, a substance which becomes almost omnipresent once the two return to England. Global commerce and its attendant slavery are everywhere in evidence in Cape Town and St. Helena; when the astronomers return to England and its traditional fare, the undercurrent of those forces remains, reminding readers of the effect colonialism had both home and abroad, but also suggesting the degree to which profitable items of trade affect the colonizers themselves through the repositioning of the colonial center. The emergence of the exotic in England reinforces the flexibility of the colonizing culture and its ability to appropriate the products upon which its commerce relies, but that flexibility also betrays the myth of cultural permanence and superiority which the colonizers themselves promote.

Throughout *Mason & Dixon*, food defines one's social and economic class. In Cape Town, this is done along racial lines and is achieved in part through the physical and cultural barriers imposed by the colonizer; almost all the food Dixon seeks is purchased from Malaysians or Africans. But food in Cape Town also separates people along class lines. While it might be considered acceptable for a sailor to venture into a Malaysian shop, as Cornelius Vroom warns his daughters, no respectable European would be seen in one. And of course, *how* one eats matters; Cornelius's wife Johanna is fed pomegranates by her slaves, a scene which unmistakably identifies her with the upper class, and underscores the degree to which the colonizing class has profited from colonial trade and slavery.

The domestic slaves in the Vroom household are representative of the much larger group of slaves on which the Vrooms' wealth rests, the colonizer being literally and figuratively fed by her slaves. In England, however, what and how much one consumes are the primary indicators of wealth and social status. One of the main factors in such an association is drink: in eighteenth-century England, wine was traditionally favored by the rich, ale by the working classes, and gin by nearly everyone.[4] In their first meeting in Portsmouth, Mason is immediately identified as a wine drinker, and so presumably of a higher class than Dixon, who prefers ale (18). This difference in taste and standing continues throughout the novel, although as more of Mason's background is revealed, it seems the difference between the two characters is one of ambition more than class. Their true social standing is frequently revealed by their continual concern over funds; unlike Maskelyne, who runs a heroic tab at his James's Town bar despite the limitations of his Royal Society stipend, Mason and Dixon do not have Clive of India, the wealthiest man in the British Empire at the time, to cover their debts. Returned to London after what is considered by all a successful trip to Cape Town and St. Helena, Mason and Dixon find themselves at a fine restaurant, but eating only "a Ploughman's Lunch of unintegrated Remnants of earlier meals" (183). While the upper classes in Britain seem to eat copious amounts of nearly everything, Mason and Dixon enjoy the occasional chop at a tavern, and are served "the remains of the Bloat Herring from Breakfast, directly adjoining upon the Plate an Ox-Tail from several Meals ago, and something that may once have been a Haggis [. . .]" (215–16). Given such fare, it is no wonder Dixon pursues the food in Cape Town so doggedly, and secures a recipe for *ketjap* before he leaves.

All is not so meager for the upper class. Before leaving for Cape Town, Mason recalls the "sugar-Loaves and assorted Biscuits, French Brandy in Coffee" typically available at meetings of the Royal Society, quite in keeping with the items increasingly available in England during the eighteenth century, primarily a product of just the sort of trade Mason and Dixon observed in South Africa. Even at *The Jolly Pitman*, Dixon's local tavern in the relative backwater of Durham, the patrons are able to combine dough, anchovies, Stilton, some of Dixon's *ketjap*, and the knowledge of a Jesuit who had spent a few months near Naples to create the first pizza made in Britain, suggesting that the most isolated parts of the empire were connected in ways before unlikely or unnoticed (324–36). Much of this is in keeping with trade tendencies during the eighteenth century. A wide variety of fruits was being made available through the Middle East, Africa, and Southern Europe, tobacco was being imported in great quantities from Maryland, Virginia, and the Carolinas, and from the East and West Indies came spices, tea, and perhaps greatest in use and popularity, sugar and coffee.[5] Such a range of foods, from all corners of the empire, further reveals the degree to which Britain and other colonial powers benefited from the products of their far-flung colonies, and appropriated foreign produce for their own profit.

Just as significantly, this bulging variety exposes the ways in which the culture of the colonized, in this case in the form of food, finds its way into the daily lives of the colonizers, and so introduces exactly the sort of hybridity that Cornelius Vroom found so troublesome. As a result, as food seeps into every corner of Mason and Dixon's travels, the reader becomes aware that the sort of authoritative discourse sought by the Dutch at Cape Town can never fully be achieved; that as these exotic products enter into common usage, the language and culture of the colonized become ingrained into Western life in precisely the way the Cape Dutch feared, appearing daily on tables in the form of ketchup, sugar, and coffee. Although those items come to be seen as luxuries and staples, they also reflect a subtle repositioning of the consuming culture, no longer able to maintain its older traditions as newer and more desirable commodities come to market. Although the peasant workers and slaves producing these items rarely benefit from the exchange, even such seemingly minor examples of hybridity suggest the diglossic nature of the discourse between the colonizer and colonized, and prefigure an emerging postcolonial voice as described by Ashcroft, Griffiths, and Tiffin (35–39).

While styles of food come and go in this novel, drink is the constant, and coffee above all. Wine and beer must sometimes be abandoned for corn-liquor, and Dixon even tries to procure a supply of laudanum for dry times, but coffee is ubiquitous, always available if not always properly brewed. The eighteenth-century thirst for coffee mirrors almost perfectly twentieth-century devotion to that drink, and the peculiarities of those devotees. As a beverage, coffee demands a certain attention, often particular to the individual drinker: in Cape Town, Mason attempts to deflect the attentions of the Vroom women by "glumly concentrat[ing] upon the Coffee and its Rituals" (66); in St. Helena, Maskelyne suspects that his coffee is being weakened and "adulterated with inferior Javas," while Mason finds St. Helena to offer "Coffee beyond compare,— from Bush to Oast unmediated!" (127, 132). London itself was peppered with coffee-houses, each often with its own political or professional identification; by one count, London had almost 3,000 coffee houses by 1700,[6] only fifty years after its first house opened at Oxford (Pendergrast 12). Over the course of the eighteenth century, the amount of coffee imported by the British East India Company increased by 110 percent to reach eight million pounds by 1801, an amount that might have been doubled by smuggling (Olsen 238). This underscores the British thirst for coffee, as well as the increasing availability of the drink to the populace at large.

These quantities suggest not only the vast capabilities of the British East and West India Companies and other profit-minded Europeans, but also the enormous amount of labor necessary to produce any product in such quantity. Coffee and tobacco are paired as the substances available to the greatest number of people in this novel, regardless of race, class, or nationality, and their modes of production are connected by colonialism and slavery. The Dutch instituted a quota system in Java, requiring Javanese peasants to produce a set amount of coffee, which they were then required to sell at the low price established by the Dutch East India Company.[7] To keep pace with the growing demand at home and throughout Europe, according to Gwen Campbell, the French imported slaves to work the orchards in their coffee-producing colonies, "estimat[ing] that each coffee planter required a minimum of twelve slaves" to undertake the labor required to maintain and harvest each crop (69). Furthermore, as Steven Topik and William Gervase Clarence-Smith write, most New World colonizers who turned to growing coffee followed the already-established and profitable example of the sugar industry, which depended almost solely on slave labor (7). Pendergrast observes that the slave labor system was integral to coffee production in the French colony of San Domingo (Haiti), which produced half of the world's coffee in the years preceding the slave revolt there which effectively ended coffee production in Haiti, a revolt fueled by the fact that the slaves were commonly "housed in windowless huts, underfed, and overworked" (Pendergrast 18). As a product which required considerable labor and which was primarily produced in the southern United States and parts of the Caribbean, tobacco was similarly a slave-dependant venture. It is fitting, then, that coffee and tobacco — and by association, slavery — should be central to Mason and Dixon's experience once they reach the shores of North America.

Although much of what Mason and Dixon encounter in the American colonies can be described as frontier life, the Philadelphia in which they land shows all the signs of an international center of trade:

> . . . all 'round them Sailors and Dockmen labor, nets lift and sway as if by themselves, bulging with casks of nails and jellied eels, British biscuit and buttons for your waistcoat, Tonicks, Colognes, golden Provolones. Upon the docks a mighty bustling proceeds . . . and underfoot lies all the debris of global Traffick, shreds of spices and teas and coffee-berries, splashes of Geneva gin and Queen-of-Hungary water, oranges and shaddocks fallen and squash'd, seeds that have sprouted between the cobblestones, Pills Balsamic and Universal, ground and scatter'd, down where the Flies convene, and the Spadger hops. (259)

The trade, activity, and refuse of this river-front scene is what one would expect from a city which, by the time Mason and Dixon arrived there, was second only to London among British cities in the empire.[8] In this regard, Philadelphia becomes the perfect introduction to the American colonies in this novel, in that the city is simultaneously a metropolitan center of the empire and a colonized body, effectively establishing the difficult colonizer/colonized duality which is at once blessing and curse to many of the American colonials; they crave the products and trade made available to them as British subjects, yet they chafe under the restrictions imposed by the colonial governors. This duality provides yet another connection to twentieth-century America, which can be identified as both post-colonial and cultural imperialist. To make such an overlap complete, were it not for the presence of wagons, wheelbarrows, and wandering livestock on the Philadelphia docks, one could easily mistake the scene for one which might occur in the twentieth century, a possibility further encouraged by the abundance of coffeehouses Mason and Dixon encounter in Philadelphia. When the two are first introduced to Ben Franklin, he invites them to his local coffeehouse, The Blue Jamaican; Dixon hears of another coffeehouse, The Flower-de-Luce, favored by his fellow surveyors; The Restless Bee is only a block and a half from their inn; and Mason and Dixon accompany Franklin to another coffeehouse, The All-Nations Coffee-House, where the waitresses "are costumed in whimsical versions of the native dress of each of the coffee-producing countries,— an Arabian girl, a Mexican girl, a Javanese girl, [and] a Sumatran girl as well . . ." (268, 298, 304, 299).

The overwhelming abundance of coffeehouses, in every neighborhood and on multiple corners throughout the city, becomes an obvious reference to twentieth-century trends in caffeine consumption and commentary on the expansion of Starbucks and other chains during the 1990s, as well as a reminder that coffee in the twentieth century is produced by workers who often receive almost as little profit from it as did the slaves and peasant workers of the eighteenth century.[9] The connection between the coffeehouses in *Mason & Dixon* and twentieth-century coffee culture is never more clear than when Dixon orders at The Flower-de-Luce: "Half and Half please, Mount Kenya Double-A, with Java Highland,— perhaps a slug o' boil'd Milk as well," a request that might very well be filled in any Center City Philadelphia coffee shop today (298). But far from being a solely upscale shop, The Flower-de-Luce has a range of clientele, all with the requisite interest in surveying and things magnetic, but from a variety of professional and social classes: "German Enthusiasts, Quack Physicians, Land-Surveyors, Iron-Prospectors, and Watch-Thieves . . ." (298). Unlike the British coffeehouse, which according to Botsford in many cases developed into a kind of private social club or devolved into a tavern or gaming house (121), the Philadelphia coffee houses have fewer social restrictions, reflecting the more democratic impulses of the clientele and so connecting coffee to the revolutionary sentiment Mason and Dixon sense throughout the colonies. In fact, as Sally Smith Booth and others have argued, coffee is in some ways inherently connected to the Revolution in that coffee drinking became increasingly popular as a response to British taxes on tea (202), although the increasing popularity of coffee was also a consequence of the fact that much of the coffee which was imported into the American colonies was grown in the Caribbean and Central and South America, and so was usually cheaper than tea (Pendergrast 15). In that respect, coffee, like many other substances in this novel, both undermines and supports the colonialist enterprise, as the American colonists seek to throw off the colonial oppression exemplified by the tea trade by turning to a substance which is equally connected with colonial oppression elsewhere.

More often in *Mason & Dixon*, however, coffee is the stimulant to revolution, a substance that spurs the colonists on in their dissatisfactions and their deep-into-the-night airing of grievances. As such, and as a reflection of the almost inescapable influence of Starbucks as a chain and trademark, it can be found nearly everywhere. It is present when Mason and Dixon step onto the docks in Philadelphia to be offered coffee "brew'd once, and then pour'd thro' its own Grounds again" (258) and, as yet another reminder of the broad influence of empire, it is present past the frontier, where Mason and Dixon journey in drawing their Line, and where its proper concoction becomes a matter of science and religion, and, like the Cape Town mango, it becomes a matter of spiritual import: ". . . why, aye, only the first Cup's any good, owing to Coffee's Sacramental nature, the Sacrament being Penance . . . whereby the remainder of the Pot, often dozens of cups deep, represents the Price for enjoying that first perfect Cup" (467). In caricatures of the type, Dixon becomes the annoying, early-morning lip-smacking coffee drinker, uttering exclamations like "Mm-*m m!* Best Jamoke west o' the Alleghenies!" after a gulp of burnt coffee, while Mason becomes the equally reprehensible aficionado, preferring tea to anything but the perfect cup of coffee (467). Mason's preference for tea mimics perhaps a classical debate between adherents of the two beverages, yet further underscores Dixon's willing participation in popular culture, and Mason's continued aspirations to higher British society, whether he is in London or deep in the American wilderness. In between the two points lies Mary Janvier's tavern, The Indian Queen, in Christiana Bridge, Maryland, where Mason and Dixon find a fine revolutionary fervor, enhanced by the "roasted Berry" which is brought to the tavern in sacks to meet the demands of the patrons, who not only drink it but seem to snort it as if it were cocaine, and to similar effect (329). At Janvier's, the coffee is accompanied by tremendous amounts of sugar, on every table, in the form of pastries, punches, and brown sugar cones, all of it, as a Quaker patron notes, "bought . . . with the lives of African slaves, untallied black lives broken upon the greedy engines of the Barbadoes" (329). This patron also notes the hypocrisy of a people striving to throw off the injustice of foreign control, in this case referring directly to the tea tariffs, while at the same time turning to products produced through even greater oppression. Such observations and the questions they raise seethe beneath the flow of talk and traffic in the barroom, and are suppressed largely through the "unchecked consumption of all these modern substances at the same time, a habit without historical precedent, upon these shores . . ." (330).

Through such conspicuous consumption, Pynchon connects this scene to the American culture of excess of the twentieth century, an excess which in the novel is made possible by oppression, and which helps the populace forget the uncomfortable implications of the excess itself. The layering of twentieth century over the eighteenth in this novel is thus partially achieved by this echo of consumption and excess, which is girded in both cases by issues of slavery and oppression. Mason and Dixon often represent the colonial power, the ever-present reminder in colony after colony — Cape Town, St. Helena, America — of the power structure of colonialism and the long arm of empire. The revolutionary temperament they find everywhere in America is that emerging post-colonial voice, expressing rebellion through a number of discourses, including a culinary discourse which becomes a literal rebellion in its rejection of tea. And yet, the revolutionaries themselves are budding colonialists, intent on increasing their lands and profits through trade or theft, an impulse which prefigures American cultural imperialism in the century during which the novel is written. And so the excess and consumption in the past of the novel and present of the novelist are equated; the former represents the presence of the colonial power in America as well as the appetite of the colonists, while the latter represents America as the colonizer. In this way, Pynchon deftly equates the two forms of imperialism, and shows how in both cases, whether as oppressed or oppressor, the American rationalizes oppression in favor of convenience. A few lone voices speak up here and there, as in Janvier's tavern, but they are drowned out, forgotten under the consumptive excess of the crowd, whether it is fueled by coffee, or, as is frequently the case, alcohol.

Coffee is found nearly everywhere in *Mason & Dixon*, and alcohol is its depressive conjoined twin, always about, and rarely put to rest for long. This is in part historical — even British visitors to America in the eighteenth century were astonished by the amounts of alcohol the colonists consumed, according to Elaine N. McIntosh (212) — and in part an illustration of the lengths to which Mason and Dixon (and a number of colonists) must go to make life on the frontier bearable, and enable them to still the questions that haunt them concerning their true purpose in America, what powers are behind their movements across the globe, and what might be out there in the wilderness just beyond the Line they are pursuing westward. But just as often, drink for Mason and Dixon is the cure to the boredom of long days and cloudy nights spent on the Line; it is the refuge of the lonely immigrant, the fatigued tourist, the companions weary of one another's company. While there seem to be taverns almost everywhere, Mason and Dixon's drinking is at times the opportunistic drinking of the frontiersman, acquiring jugs of corn whiskey whenever more refined substances are unavailable. In time, the party establishing the Line westward becomes something of a moving "suburbs dedicated to high (as some would say, low) living" fueled in part by corn whiskey (477); eventually, as the Line moves further westward than many are comfortable following, a series of distillers are established to keep the party adequately supplied (674). Such drinking is easier on Dixon, a man of less discriminating taste and greater appetite than Mason, who is less interested in all things grain-based to begin with, a tendency that is not without its danger on the American frontier. Although Mason drinks his claret for as long as it holds out, "the further West they go, the more distill'd Grains, and the fewer Wines, are to be found,— until at last even to mention Wine aloud is to be taken for a French spy" (642). Especially on the frontier, food retains its cultural resonances, even if it is founded as much on stereotype as fact. Similarly, despite the growing anti-colonialist sentiment in the novel, when given the chance, revolutionary and loyalist alike return to well-worn nationalist sympathies; even though, as the enemy of England, France is the natural ally of the colonial revolutionist, old habits and allegiances die hard. Indeed, while Pynchon plays on what was no doubt a difficult time of transitory allegiances, revolutionaries siding with a nation which they had fought against only a few years before, he reinforces the resonance between the eighteenth and twentieth centuries through this persistent American suspicion of the French. In turn, while the connections between class and drink remain in place, as their westward movement places them more securely in what is now the American Midwest, Mason and Dixon find themselves at the whim of a much later middle-American culture in which beer and whiskey reign supreme. On the much more sophisticated and effete Mid-Atlantic coast, which is also considerably closer to and dependant upon the center of colonial power and trade, wine is more readily available and socially acceptable, and the beer, in common twentieth-century American style, is "as under-hopp'd, as 'tis over-water'd" (272).

Such dilution is absent from the food Mason and Dixon find in America, no matter the region or the host. In addition to the trade in all things consumable on the Philadelphia docks, Mason and Dixon run into one "Graziana . . . a daughter of Naples" who suggestively hawks pizza (260). Such scenes offer stark contrast to the culinary episodes in England; one is reminded of the difficulty the patrons of The Jolly Pitman had in putting together the first British pizza, whereas in Philadelphia, perhaps in reference to the thriving twentieth-century Italian immigrant community there, traditional Neapolitan pies greet the traveler fresh off the boat. In *Mason & Dixon*, America is a culinary wonderland, bringing together the forces of international trade, immigrant traditions, and a rumored agricultural potential of mythical proportions to create an epicurean experience which far surpasses the main characters' indulgences in Cape Town, St. Helena, and England.

This conglomeration is never more apparent than in the Knockwood's inn, in which Mason and Dixon find themselves snowbound for days. The scene in the inn is perhaps stereotypically cheery: glasses raised in toasts, fiddles playing, smoke rising from pipes indoors and chimneys out, and as the snow deepens casks of brandy are tapped "daily" (364). And this scene strikes one as particularly *American;* Pynchon includes in the crowd wealthy travelers and "Gypsy Brick-Layers," provincial agents and "Tool-Mongers" (365); and while the different constituents tend to create their own spaces, seek their own rooms, or quarrel, the classes mix in this inn in a way which would have been strikingly uncommon in Cape Town or London. While such a mixture is unplanned — none can leave because of the snow — the formation of such a society due to necessity and geographical isolation sounds much like the American colonies themselves, and perhaps mirrors the mixing of cultures, language, and as is quickly revealed, culinary customs in this novel, a simultaneous sign of colonial power and the inability of that power to prevent the emergence of a distinctive post-colonial voice. The setting is exceptionally *fresh;* the tavern room Mason and Dixon enter "is yet too new for the scent of hops and malt to've quite worked in,— rather, fugitive odors of gums and resins, or smoke from pipes and fires, of horses upon the garments of the company, come and go" (366), in striking contrast to the Vrooms' house, which the scent of mutton had long ago permeated and made its own. Yet this is no social paradise, but rather a seemingly unsullied setting, in which old traditions and biases are reinforced or reformed according to whim, political design, or inebriation. This is made perfectly clear when the proprietor makes a passing reference to the "Sandwich," the newly invented dish which, maligned by many in the upper classes, seems to have found a following in America due to its portability and convenience; on their ride from Philadelphia to Mount Vernon, Virginia, Mason and

Dixon eat sandwiches and carelessly throw the refuse, plates and all, out the window, acting surprisingly like twentieth-century motorists (274). In embracing the sandwich, a British invention which comes to be seen largely as an American dish, the colonists have co-opted the tradition of the colonizers, have taken it as their own and adopted it to what becomes a particularly fast-paced and unrefined national way of life.

The degree to which the sandwich represents a decline from European epicurean standards is made clear in the inn, where the utterance of the word "sandwich" elicits a violent response from the defender of gastronomic art and *haute cuisine,* the inn's French chef, Armand: "Sondweech-uh! Sond-weech-uh! . . . To the Sacrament of the Eating, it is ever the grand Insult!" (366). The patrons, provoked to defend the land of the sandwich's origin despite their own frequently revolutionary tendencies, eventually succumb to old-fashioned name calling, referring to Armand as the "bloody little toad-eating foreigner" (367). Pynchon is able to combine the traditional hostility between the English and the French, and the more recent American tendency to ridicule European snobbery, in this case by rising to the defense of the sandwich, food of the masses. The sandwich itself is a fascinating signifier in the novel. On the one hand, as a British invention, its portability suggests the permeating influence of British colonialism, as the sandwich as an object becomes embedded in the American culture. At the same time, however, the very flexibility of the sandwich is suggestive of the ways in which a culturally specific object can be appropriated by the colonized; the American defense of the sandwich in the Knockwood's inn is perhaps less a defense of Britain than it is a defense of a yet-to-be-realized independence. Its ambiguity in this regard is perfect for the American colonists in the novel, who are at once both representatives of the colonial center and budding post-colonialists. To spite Armand, the colonists, through the voice of Squire Haligast, create of the sandwich their own sacrament, one decidedly different from the salvation of *haute cuisine* defended by Armand: "[. . .] the birth of the 'Sandwich,' at this exact moment in Christianity [. . .] Disks of secular Bread,— enclosing whilst concealing slices of real Flesh, yet a-sop with Blood, under the earthly guise of British Beef, all [. . .] Consubstantiate, thus . . . the Sandwich, Eucharist of this our Age" (367). So the discussion ends, and the reader is left with yet another instance of the overlap between food and salvation, in which all consumption can be transferred to some heightened symbolic purpose, so that each bite of a sandwich makes one more a confirmed child of both the eighteenth and twentieth centuries, and makes of food more than just a matter of sustenance, but an anchor to time, place, politics, nationality, and culture.

Despite the inn patrons' response to Armand's opinion of the sandwich, they find themselves relishing the food he creates, food which is
classically French in principal but which could also be termed, to use a
word popularized in late-twentieth century restaurants, *fusion,* in this case
between continental European and frontier American fare. Through this
fusion, Pynchon establishes the essentially heteroglossic nature of colonial
life,[10] which requires the colonists to adapt to what their land will yield
and combine it with that which is provided by the colonial power. In doing so, the colonists naturally develop their own food culture, a synthesis
of European tradition, foreign exports, and local availability, and thus establish cultural difference from the colonial power which they seek to cast
off politically. Yet the (re)formation of tradition is itself political; each alteration of some European standard, in this case the food which finds its
way to the colonists' plates, is a gesture of revolution and difference. The
colonists lay claim to the frontier "corruptions" of traditional dishes as a
gesture of autonomy. That such a fusion should occur on the frontier is of
course completely understandable; as Ashcroft, Griffths, and Tiffin claim,
as imperialism pushed the colonized to the margins, "[m]arginality thus
became an unprecedented source of creative energy" (12).

Armand's apprenticeship and eventual rise to the top of the French
culinary scene is based on traditional dishes: *pâtés, blanquette de veau,* and
one of his signature dishes, *canard avec aubergines en casserole* (374). Yet,
driven out of France by Vaucanson's mechanical duck, Armand chooses
Pennsylvania as his place of refuge in part because of its obscurity to him
and so, he hopes, to the duck as well, but also because of the rumors he
hears of America as a land of plenty, with "fertile lands, savage Women,
giant Vegetables . . . Marshlands seething with shell-fish, Buffalo-Herds
the size of Paris" (380). While much of that is myth, Armand, by virtue of
his chilled brain mousse, earns his way to Pennsylvania, where he finds his
"Miracle of Plenty," a new world offering epicurean possibilities which
make his exile bearable:

> On market days in New Castle or Philadelphia, my Heart yet soars as
> ever it has done, . . . like a dream . . . Have you ever wanted to cook
> *everything,*— the tomatoes, terrapins, peaches, rockfish, crabs, Indian
> Corn, Venison! Bear! Beaver! To create the Beaver *Bourguignon,*—
> who knows, perhaps even the . . . the Beaver *soufflé, non?* (383)

Such combinations can easily be interpreted as degradations of the original dishes, but can also be translated into a culinary and cultural independence, in which food becomes inherently the product of a peculiar
combination of social, political, and geographical convergences. Although
his food may symbolize this streak of independence in his customers,
Armand also represents the marriage of two worlds, a man with one foot

in the culinary history and traditions of Europe and another in the frontier possibilities and limitations of the New World, yet another instance of the emerging post-colonial voice in the novel. Armand is exemplary of the same duality which Pynchon establishes with the city of Philadelphia. As a character who defines high culinary culture in the novel, Armand can be seen as one of the "agents of cultural imperialism," while at the same time he represents exactly the sort of hybridity associated with the post-colonial voice; the dishes he creates in his exile become then not only an example of hybridity, but because of their basis in both the Old and New Worlds, underline the essential failure of the colonial effort to establish a "high" and "low" culture (Ashcroft et al. 210). The food Armand creates is either always both, or neither. For Armand, the limitations of America are opportunities, and his distaste for even the idea of the sandwich reflects his belief that America holds great potential, and that its citizens are squandering that potential for a meal of meat and cheese slapped together between bread. Armand's dishes smack of frontier necessity, but also evoke the fusion trends of the twentieth century; his beaver stew would be at home in eighteenth- or twentieth-century Appalachia, his braised pork liver with eggplant in eighteenth-century Paris or twentieth-century New York.

Watching him cook, Cherrycoke is again driven to consider the Eucharist, in this case, whether the bread and wine are simply symbolic renderings of the body and blood, or whether they are the actual body and blood transformed through "God's mercy, for otherwise we should be repell'd by the sight of real human Flesh and Blood, not to mention the prospect of eating it. Thus to God's attributes must be added the skills of master Chef, in so disguising a terrible reality" (386). Again, the narration leads to a confluence of food and belief, of sustenance and salvation, elevating food in the novel above the plane of physical necessity and into a spiritual realm. Cherrycoke demonstrates, most effectively, that food is what you make of it: to Mason and Dixon in Cape Town, it is both curse and refuge; to Armand in Pennsylvania, it is the embodiment of tradition and culture, and consolation for exile; for Cherrycoke, it is salvation itself, but with unsettling questions. If the bread and wine *are* the body and blood itself, that implies, in Cherrycoke's words, "some ultimate Carnality, some way of finally belonging to the doom'd World that cannot be undone" (386). And so, despite the spiritual heights to which he takes food, Cherrycoke ultimately returns it to the earthly plane, restoring food, or perhaps resigning it, to its accustomed role as corporeal necessity, a role which the average American colonist more than readily accepts.

On the whole, what is distinctive about food in the colonies is the joy with which the colonists partake in what is available to them, and the ex-

cess to which all are prone, an excess limited primarily to the upper classes
at the stopping points outside of North America on Mason and Dixon's
transit. At New Castle, Delaware, they find "piles of mysterious delectable
Mediterranean food, 'Sandwiches' made of entire Loaves stuff'd with fried
Sausages and green Peppers, eggplants, tomatoes, cheeses melted everywhere, fresh Melons mysteriously preserv'd thro' the Voyage, wines
whose grapes are descended from those that supplied Bacchus himself"
(338–39). Falling in with revolutionaries in Brooklyn, Mason feasts on a
tavern meal of chops, roasted potatoes, fish chowder, bread, sandwiches,
and wine (399, 404). In the first house actually divided by the Line, the
party is fed at a "Table with plates of sour-cherry fritters, Neat's-Tongue
Pies, a gigantick Indian Pudding, pitchers a-slosh with home-made Ci-
der" (446). One Christmas spent near the Line, the astronomers feast on
"popp'd Corn, green Tomato Mince Pies, pickl'd Oysters, Chestnut
Soup, and Kidney Pudding," Dixon gives Mason a silver Claret jug, and
all the children eat sweets (509–10). And, in a scene of special plenty during the last Spring spent on the Line, a barn-raising in Octarara, Pennsylvania, is celebrated with "Parsnip Fritters, breaded fried Sausage, Rhubarb
Dumplings, Souse and Horse-radish, Ham-and-Apple Schnitz und
Knepp, Hickory-Nut Cake and Shoofly Pies," as well as a pudding made
by Armand "loaded with Currants, candied Violets, dried apricots,
peaches, and cherries chopp'd fine with almonds and rejuvenated in
Raspberry Brandy;" there are also "Hams and Fowl, Custards and Tarts,
fried-Noodles and Opossum Alamodes . . ." a feast part French, part
German, and throughout distinctively American (637–38).

Perhaps nothing underscores the joyful excess of the colonies as well
as Mason and Dixon's visit with George Washington, during which Mar-
tha Washington, having caught the scent of the smoke from the home-
and slave-grown "new-cur'd Hemp" in their pipes, supplies them with
"an enormous Tray pil'd nearly beyond their Angles of Repose with Tarts,
Pop-overs, Ginger-bread Figures, fried Pies, stuff'd Doughnuts, and other
Units of Refreshment the Surveyors fail to recognize" (278, 280). The
cumulative effect of such excess is to establish an eighteenth-century
America prone to the same sorts of over-indulgence as the America of the
twentieth century. In addition, each feast at which Mason and Dixon find
themselves represents the vast fusion in the colonies of colonial standard
cuisine, traditional immigrant fare, and dishes influenced by the oppressed
slave and Native American classes. American cuisine in this novel becomes
a product of a network of appropriations, with each representative class
subsuming some element of the available culinary influences into its own
specific tradition. Such appropriations obviously work in multiple cur-
rents: the colonial power seeks to enforce its own traditions as central, yet
cannot entirely resist the sometimes subtle influx of outside traditions due

to necessity or commerce; the emerging post-colonial voice appropriates certain aspects of the central colonial power as a sign of difference, identity, and in this novel, rebellion; and finally, the "doubly marginalized" classes, the slave and Native American population, are represented in these feasts as well, suggesting the deep persistence of tradition, the fluid exchange of culture, and the presence of a third voice, silenced by law but fully present on the heteroglossic American frontier (Ashcroft et al. 142). This heteroglossia is made exceedingly clear through Pynchon's frequent employment of food, establishing America as Armand's "Miracle of Plenty," where, like the citizens of New Castle, travelers and residents alike descend into sleep well fed and watered, "drooling into and soaking Pillows" (339).

The forms those dreams take may very well parallel those of Mason and Dixon, who imagine the Line continuing far west, where it crosses "the Illinois, where they find renegade French living out a fantasy of the Bourbon Court, teaching the Indians . . . Wine-Growing, *Haut Cuisine* . . . ," their ever-westward progress and discoveries leading them to fame and, if desired, "Haggis! You want Haggis after Midnight, all you need do is pull upon a bell-cord, and hi-ho!" (707, 709). This dream of excess, this miracle of plenty is the America suggested in the eighteenth century but realized in the future, in the overlapping twentieth century in which the fictional Mason and Dixon characters are created. Mason and Dixon return to an England shaken by food riots, almost unfathomable after such scenes of plenty in the colonies, which continue, at the beginning of the novel and some twenty years after the Line has been drawn, to thrive, as the novel opens with boilers and stew pots, pie-spices, fruits, suet, coffee, cookies, "Philadelphia Pudding," and "a large Basket dedicated to Saccharomanic Appetites, piled to the Brim with fresh-fried Dough-Nuts roll'd in Sugar, glaz'd Chesnuts, Buns, Fritters, Crullers, Tarts" (5–7). Such is America after the Line, after the Revolution, and, given our narrator Cherrycoke, our plethora of Starbucks-inspired Philadelphia coffeehouses, and our fusion *haute cuisine,* well into the twentieth century. Yet what haunts this first scene of post-Revolution plenty in America, always apparent during Mason and Dixon's travels in Cape Town and St. Helena, is the specter of colonial power and slavery, subtly woven throughout the scenes in the colonies as well; these scenes of plenty come at a cost. The colonists tend to ignore those costs, preferring to revel in the excess rather than consider the domestic and foreign slaves who are the primary producers of an enormous portion of that which is consumed in the novel. Such willful ignorance seems inevitably connected to the twentieth century, in which America has been so very willing to overlook its own role as an imperialist power, and its own implicit guilt as a primary consumer of goods made by those who rarely share in the profits. That is the irony of the indulgent and self-important revolutionaries who haunt the colonial taverns and rail against British oppression. Although the colonists may be proclaiming cultural and political independence through the culinary linguistics of the novel, their willingness to do so with fare reliant upon the use of slave labor becomes a dark sign of things to come. As Cherrycoke frequently suggests to his companions, this food, the mango, the bread and wine, even perhaps the sandwich itself, offers salvation, yet it is the excess, the carnality with which it is consumed that seems to strip it of such possibilities, to reduce it to its worldly role, and so make it subject once again to the oppressive systems of colonialism and slavery which make such excess possible.

Notes

[1] See Ashcroft, Griffths, and Tiffin, 72.

[2] See Norman R. Bennett, *Africa and Europe: From Roman Times to the Present*, 51.

[3] For this history, see, for example, Sir Harry H. Jacobs, *A History of the Colonization of Africa by Alien Races*, 128.

[4] See Kirsten Olsen, *Daily Life in 18th Century England*, 238–39.

[5] See Jay Barrett Botsford, *English Society in the Eighteenth Century: As Influenced from Oversea*, 34–35, 56–57, 59–61.

[6] A. E. Richardson, *Georgian England: A Survey of Social Life, Trades, Industries and Art from 1700 to 1820*, 30.

[7] See M. R. Fernando, "Coffee Cultivation in Java, 1830–1917," 158–59.

[8] See, for example, William T. Parsons, *The Pennsylvania Dutch: A Persistent Minority*, 52.

[9] See Pendergrast, xvi, 330–31, 409–10, for a discussion of undercompensation of these workers.

[10] This heteroglossia, a standard quality of the frontier, is especially rich in *Mason & Dixon*, in which we find speakers of English, French, German, Swedish, Chinese, and a variety of Native American languages, on the Line; those languages mirror the culinary influences scattered throughout the novel.

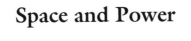

Space and Power

4: "America was the only place . . .": American Exceptionalism and the Geographic Politics of Pynchon's *Mason & Dixon*

Pedro García-Caro

> *But should [the poet] venture upon the dark story of their wrongs and wretchedness; should he tell how they were invaded, corrupted, despoiled, driven from their native abodes and the sepulchers of their fathers, hunted like wild beasts about the earth, and sent down with violence and butchery to the grave, posterity will either turn with horror and incredulity from the tale, or blush with indignation at the inhumanity of their forefathers.*
>
> — Washington Irving

IRVING OUTLINED THE TROUBLED, ambivalent attitudes toward the genocide committed against Native Americans by whites: incredulity — confirmed by a silence, which not always sounds condemnatory — or indignation — spoken through many acts of contrition — are only two, perhaps the most prevalent, of the many possible outlooks on the American Holocaust. Assuming the relentless impact of the Westward expansion of the country, Irving's prediction anticipates the destruction not only of the East Coast Indians, but of all the Native American peoples and their ways of life across the territory claimed by the United States in successive years: "They will vanish like a vapor from the face of the earth; their very history will be lost in forgetfulness" (361).[1] With a mixture of liberal nostalgia and historical fatalism, Washington Irving endorsed the prevailing myth of the "vanishing Indian," a theme that would pervade American culture into the twentieth century. The reverse trope of this historical fatalism — its photographic negative — is, of course, the grand narrative of Manifest Destiny: the American nation as a triumphant exception in a history of constant decline and depravation.

American exceptionality, a set of totemic narratives on which the politics of continental expansion and its associated ethnic cleansing, built from the time of its independence, is a complex and evolving group of myths about selfhood which range from Protestant millennialism to secular (pseudo)scientific theories about ethnic superiority. "Manifest Destiny" is but another phase in the evolution of the millenarian discourse that can be easily identified as the racial and religious justification of United States imperialism in the North American continent and elsewhere. It is one of the most powerful pieces in the ideological backbone of a certain "mainstream" definition of Americanness, and it provides American exceptionalism with a vigorous geographical agenda. America as the "consensual term" is thus the unchallenged space for a national "ideological consensus," as Sacvan Bercovitch's proposes (*Rites* 158).[2]

One of the main objects of study for Americanists is to inspect how these celebratory, omnipresent discourses of American nationalism, with their attendant silences, their erased flaws, and their implied expansionist agenda, rearrange historical materials in a teleological fashion. If Americanists — to paraphrase Amy Kaplan — aim to offer a critical remapping of America by looking at those "geographies that traverse and challenge [its official] borders," we need to avoid its recuperation as a spatial whole which, as Kaplan indicates, would present the danger "of reinstating a teleological lineal narrative of historical continuity, of viewing American history, even in its imperial dimensions, as a singular march [. . .]" (155). In that critical vein, the aim of this essay is to read Pynchon's *Mason & Dixon* as a critical interpretation of American colonial history and the ensuing national foundation of the United States, short-circuiting its recuperation into the grand narratives of the American nation.

As Etienne Balibar has maintained, the historical teleology of the nation is constituted upon "a narrative which attributes to these entities [nations] the continuity of a subject" (86). Balibar describes it as a twofold illusion. The first effect "consists in believing that the generations which succeed one another over centuries on a reasonably stable territory, under a reasonably univocal designation, have handed down to each other an invariant substance" (86). The "invariant substance" indicated by Balibar is the totemic essentialist cultural construct that confirms the apparent projection of any national identity into the future in the shape of a common destiny. This "destiny" is the second element of the dual impression as portrayed by Balibar: "[it] consists in believing that the process of development from which we select aspects retrospectively, so as to see ourselves as the culmination of that process, was the only one possible, that is, it represented a destiny" (86). Thus, the "illusion of national identity" is thoroughly linked to the symmetrical narrative figures of "project" and "destiny." In other words, there is a diachronic syntax of the nation, one that looks at history in search of the narratives of a particular subject whose invariant substance articulates those very narratives.

In its double axis, its Western projection, and its North-South divide, the Mason-Dixon Line embodies two main fault lines on which the historical narratives of the American nation have dwelled since before the time of its independence: two geographical axes and two subjugated groups, Native Americans and African slaves. These two geographical axes and their position in the formation of an independent American identity are prominently thematized in Pynchon's *Mason & Dixon*.[3] Destructive racial and cultural relations with Native Americans on one hand, and the fracture posed by two conflicting capitalist systems — Northern free-holding farming and industry versus Southern slave-holding plantation — on the other, contest the combined discourses of scientific progress and of enlightened freedom inscribed into the national consensus.

Pynchon sets out to debase the nationalist histories of American exceptionalism by pointing at the epistemic biases of the discourses of progress and science at the time of the Enlightenment, the intellectual context in which part of the British American colonies became an independent nation. I will explore here the ways Pynchon parodically uses historical materials and characters in order to reinscribe into the birth of the nation the cultural erasures and the epistemic violence involved in the narration of American exceptionalism. Pynchon's political intervention in a critical rewriting of history is aimed at showing the lack of national exceptionality in the American history of conquest and cultural homogenization.

The narrator in Pynchon's *Mason & Dixon* is the Rev[d] Cherrycoke; his voice replicates and parodies eighteenth-century English, asserts the need to see history, and the history of texts, not as a direct line — as lines are the real protagonist of that novel — but rather as an uncontrollable proliferation: "Not a Chain of single Links, for one broken link could lose us All,— rather, a great disorderly Tangle of Lines, long and short, weak and strong, vanishing into the Mnemonick Deep, with only their Destination in common." (349). Cherrycoke's chaotic "Tangle of Lines" is a fictional theory of history that advocates plurality of referent and multiple textual connections in the palimpsestic nature of the present text, or hypertext. Thus, the project of the novel is an incursion into some of those lines, a reading and a reworking of partial events in the history of the United States before its constitution as an independent nation, which seeks to refashion that history in a critical rather than an epic mode. Through a dense use of historical material, and through the use of parody, the novel confirms Pynchon's commitment to a reassessment of American history through fiction. Inconsistencies between discourses and practices at the time of the formation of the United States as a nation are underscored while the foundational narratives of the United States of America are critically reinscribed.

In *Mason & Dixon,* the material demarcation of the boundary between Maryland and Pennsylvania epitomizes the uncontrollability of the scientific process of mapping new territories: the Line gains a separate life from the two surveyors who trace it and who become increasingly concerned about the cultural and social effect of incorporating into the world map previously uncharted territories. The Line becomes a "great invisible Thing" (678), a monster of human ambition, not merely a boundary between neighboring provinces, but a way into the western Indian territories, "a tree-slaughtering Animal" which kills "ev'rything due west of it." Its real "intentions" beyond that are unknown to all. The newly charted territories become "known" and accessible to future colonizers, while the landmarks of previous societies are erased. At the same time, it is noted that the Line will serve also as the official separating incision between North and South during the Civil War one hundred years after it was marked out. As an index to the two mythical efforts articulating the nationalist images of Americanness throughout the nineteenth century, the conquest of the West and the Civil War, the Line stands at the center of American nationhood. The story itself begins at the very place of birth of the United States: Philadelphia, 1786, a few months before the U.S. Constitution was approved.

"I make an effort to keep to the Margins close as I may."

Faced with the horrors of slavery in the African colony of Cape Town, Jeremiah Dixon, the Quaker surveyor from Durham, reaffirms his marginality and his loathing of the practices of the East India Company. As elsewhere in the novel, ideas about the characters' marginal relation to the projects of the British Royal Society, the East India Company or the proprietors of Maryland and Pennsylvania, convey a sense of their irresolute participation in those projects. Their status as insiders/outsiders is a position in tune with other characters' perspectives in Pynchon's fiction, characters that parallel Pynchon's paradoxical marginality in the national canon of American literature. A suspicion about the location of Pynchon's marginal voice has been expressed often among critics of his work. The coincidence in time between the development of poststructuralist critical practices in the American academy with the early reactions to Pynchon's work, added to the lack of a physical authorial presence, has too often led to the surmise that the point about his novels is precisely the process of avoidance of an authorial voice. Pynchon was, and is to this date, elusive not only in real life — no photographs, no interviews — but also in a fiction opened up to many possible readings through the multiplicity of narrative voices.

My main concern is with the more formalist versions of these responses as they may be silencing one of the main textual features, namely Pynchon's critique in *Mason & Dixon* of the elimination of cultural differences by the homogenizing projects of enlightened modernity. In particular, the description of the novel as plot-less may be aimed at suppressing its politics. This process of political demotion in relation to *Mason & Dixon* is well illustrated in William Logan's article "Pynchon in the Poetic." The title gives away Logan's whole thesis: *Mason & Dixon* is "a poetic act" (424). What for some might be a point of agreement, the novel's excellence in metaphoric language, the dazzling sense of humor, the success of both pastiche and anachronism, turns under Logan's logic — or rather his lack of it — into a classification of the novel as a failure, which is a point that will surely provoke a strong cause for dissent. This is because Logan does not equate the language and the formal features of the novel to poetry as a form of praise of Pynchon's mastery, but rather as an excuse to indict its prose as hollow:

> Pynchon may have conceived *Mason & Dixon* as a supreme fiction, a poetic act freed of the slavery of plot and character; but conventions are cruel to those who betray them. As his stand-up comedy becomes merely a seven-hundred-page improvisation, the jokes grow hollow. Here Pynchon's poetics have seduced him: it hardly matters if most poems mean what they say. Poetry is the saying, but fiction (the drama, the action, the consequence, the regret) is the having said. (437)

The conclusion reached by Logan is consistent with his heavily formalist analysis of the novel. He accuses the characters' apparent "purposeful dither" of finally becoming "just dither" (433), failing to notice that the Line would *not* be finally completed, not because the "actions of the characters remain empty" (433), but precisely because of their final realization of the moral and cultural implications of the Line they are tracing. Logan's constant use of adjectives such as "empty," or "hollow" to refer to the novel and his affirmation that the novel's quasi-narcissistic texture is a product of the author's self-complacent attitude is one of the most explicit examples of a critic at the service of defusing a novel's voice through a mixture of praise and smear.

From a different angle, Pynchon's apparent marginality has been reviewed as part of the features that guarantee Pynchon's entry into the canon of American Literature. Michael Berubé's earlier *Marginal Forces/ Cultural Centers* connected Pynchon's seeming marginality with the process of canonization of the author himself, underlining the status of Pynchon's voice as a "consensus criticism of the consensus" (310).[4] This dissenting attitude from inside would be in tune with Bercovitch's characterization of mainstream American literature as enacting an internal disagreement which finally "serve[s] to sustain the culture" (*Jeremiad* 205).[5] It is in this sense that Pynchon's conflicting voice comes from the center itself and not from the margins. Pynchon can therefore be seen as "one more white man from the Northeast, writing big books about the Puritan origins of the American self" (309), as Berubé casts him at a certain point, and his concern for the margins, as in *Mason & Dixon*, might identify him with that future poet previewed by Irving who would finally "blush with indignation at the inhumanity of their forefathers."[6] And yet, the assumption that Pynchon is working inside the framework of the mainstream in terms of his access to the canonizing resorts of a white man from the Northeast with his background, cannot or at least should not be at the service of defusing his effort to dissent with the nationalist grand narrative of American exceptionalism.

In *Mason & Dixon*, Pynchon explores and critiques the destruction of human difference in the apparently harmless scientific enterprises of observing the Transit of Venus or tracing a line through the wilderness. Both historical and fictional characters do become aware of the implications of western expansion and of the cruelty and barbarity of its agents. As in *Gravity's Rainbow* and *The Crying of Lot 49*, the questing plot gives shape to the authorial preoccupation with the margins of society through a trip that takes the characters into a reality which challenges their complacent and trite lives. The direction westward of the Mason-Dixon Line criticizes the western movement of the Anglo-Saxon empire while it performs an indictment of the social relations prevalent before and after the American Revolution.

This inscription of Pynchon's text into a denunciation of imperial practices integrates it into a postcolonial critique of the structures of power, foregrounding the relation between space and power as the central theme in the novel.[7] Such a politicizing reading of *Mason & Dixon*, rather than ignoring the humorous and ambiguous aspects of the novel, its various registers, the accurately historical, the concisely anachronistic, Pynchon's mastery as regards the confluence of eighteenth-century styles of English and its parodic resonances in the twentieth and beyond, suggests a view of the text as a meeting point. In it, those stylistic features can be read not only as the signifiers of the political, but also as part of the signified, that is, part of the project of politically recuperating and re-enacting the past from the present time to which all historiography is committed.[8] A similar preoccupation with the epistemological problems of the interaction between history and fiction is expressed in the novel through the reutilization of historical material in a parodic mode. As Douglas Keesey points out in his survey of the first reviews on *Mason & Dixon*, the novel's carnivalization of history should be approached "with this assumption that comedy is *not* incompatible with history, but a key route to other pasts and futures — an alternative history" (171).[9] Parody is not a mere formal feature, Logan's "hollow jokes," but a political movement away from the "want of objectivity" studied by Hayden White, and which usually manifests itself as a "failure to narrativize reality adequately" (25). As the ethnocentric seriousness of enlightened science is questioned by private morals and practices, so are the ethnocentric discourses of objectivity by jokes and laughter.

In his *Postmodern Cartographies* Brian Jarvis regards space and its politicization as a constant element in the works of contemporary artists such as David Lynch or Toni Morrison. Published only a year after *Mason & Dixon*, Jarvis's book does not discuss Pynchon's most explicitly cartographical novel, yet its perceptive analysis of his earlier fiction proves to be useful as a framework for reading *Mason & Dixon*. In his analysis Jarvis perceives

> an acute geographical awareness in Pynchon's work from the outset, one which manifests itself not in "adestinality" or directionlessness, but in a continual movement *underground*, towards the critical contours of the postmodern landscape. Pynchon's fictions gravitate towards the contraries and contradictions of uneven development, towards the spaces occupied by the underclass and the disinherited and towards the omnipresence of forms of waste, which, potentially, may become oppositional objects once situated as anticommodities. (53)

In *Mason & Dixon*, Pynchon's "geographical awareness" is brought to the foreground. It demonstrates once more the author's commitment to that "continual movement underground" which Jarvis has identified in Pynchon's other fiction. In this case, the explicitly cartographical endeavor is also an encounter between Europeans and the pre-existing cultures whose geographical signposts they help erase. However much the fictional Mason and Dixon come to distrust the political motives behind their two expeditions, they were after all imperial bureaucrats at the service of the British Crown.[10] This contradiction allows us to look at the novel as an instance of postcolonial satire,[11] as it problematizes the contrast between the characters' moral beliefs and their scientific "westernizing" activities. Although it might be possible to claim that their metaphysical and moral beliefs are challenged by "Reason," it is their faith in progress that is ultimately shattered by their own actions and observations.

The Enlightenment as a liberating discourse has been an object of criticism on many occasions. Adorno and Horkheimer's *Dialectic of Enlightenment* identified such liberation with a process of cultural homogenization that is indeed the "line both of destruction and of civilization" (Adorno 92). Apart from this analogous image of the Enlightenment as a destructive civilizing line, Adorno and Horkheimer's criticism of the unifying logics of Enlightenment also coincides with the denunciation expressed in Pynchon's writings. His fictional condemnation of the destructive projects of European civilization in America concentrates also on the process of erasure of those other forms of knowledge which Adorno and Horkheimer see as the victims of Enlightenment's demythologizing action.

As an ideology, Enlightenment can be defined as a series of efforts to establish rational and standardized ways to study and manage nature and society, but with varying degrees of access to knowledge granted to a given population. Adorno and Horkheimer would add two main provisos to this definition. The first one relates to the idea that Enlightenment is a form of domination and that its search for knowledge is not an end in itself: "[W]hat men want to learn from nature is how to use it in order wholly to dominate it and other men" (4). The second proviso refers to the social hierarchies and the "access to knowledge" promoted by Enlightenment. For the Frankfurt scholars, Enlightenment becomes "wholesale deception of the masses" (42) as its mechanics seem to "liberate" while pursuing domination. Their conclusion that "today machinery disables men even as it nurtures them" (37) is close to Pynchon's paranoia about the technopolitical order that may or may not know where it is going.

In "Is It OK to be a Luddite?" Pynchon addressed the inevitable question of the political and economic implications of technological development.[12] Pynchon situates the movement from religious theology and faith through to the technological theology of Enlightenment in the eighteenth century:

> In ways more and less literal, folks in the 18th century believed that once upon a time all kinds of things had been possible which were no longer so. Giants, dragons, spells. The laws of nature had not been so strictly formulated back then. What had once been true working magic had, by the Age of Reason, degenerated into mere machinery. Blake's dark Satanic mills represented an old magic that, like Satan, had fallen from grace. As religion was being more and more secularized into Deism and nonbelief, the abiding human hunger for evidence of God and afterlife, for salvation — bodily resurrection, if possible — remained. The Methodist movement and the American Great Awakening were only two sectors on a broad front

of resistance to the Age of Reason, a front which included Radical-ism and Freemasonry as well as Luddites and the Gothic novel. Each in its way expressed the same profound unwillingness to give up elements of faith, however "irrational," to an emerging technopoliti-cal order that might or might not know what it was doing. (41)

In *Mason & Dixon*, the coexistence of "rational" and "pre-rational" be-liefs contributes to the characters' hesitation about the morality of Rea-son. The possible validity of "other reasons" to account for the world puts into perspective the ideological discourse of Reason. Pynchon's pre-occupation with the uses of contemporary technology for various political purposes can be clearly perceived in *Gravity's Rainbow* and in *V.*, where experiments with chemistry, conductist psychology, and rocketry com-modify the human body, inserting it in the machine. As in those two novels, in his evocation of the origins of Luddism, Pynchon openly establishes the social consequences of technologies, old and new, to certain economic practices. Although Pynchon seems to cherish the old "elements of faith," he does not seem to be promoting a return to religious beliefs or to mythical explanations of reality. Adorno and Horkheimer pointed out the ineffective "opposition" to Enlightenment from earlier forms of knowledge: "Whatever myths the resistance may appeal to, by virtue of the very fact that they become arguments in the process of opposition, they acknowledge the principle of dissolvent ra-tionality for which they reproach the Enlightenment. Enlightenment is totalitarian" (6).

In this article and in his novels, including *Mason & Dixon*, Pynchon explores the possibility of such an opposition to Enlightenment's domina-tion in the form of realization and conscience. In this sense, his political agenda may belong to another version of Enlightenment, Enlightenment inside Enlightenment: we need to know, to liberate ourselves, to get out of the immaturity of the Enlightenment itself. This is built on the tem-plate of Enlightenment's popular claim, delineated by Kant in his famous essay "Was ist Aufklärung?" Published in the *Berlinische Monatschrift* in 1784 as a response to that same question, Kant uses the metaphor of childhood, maturity, and development as progress of the rational mind to explain the process of Enlightenment as one that should "take man out of his immaturity" (54). Kant brings up to date the old motto *"Sapere aude"* as the paramount expression of the enlightened man's challenge.[13] The same motto may be applied to Pynchon's paranoia: "dear to know." In-stead of by reason, Pynchon's characters are motivated to know through paranoia, and their ultimate findings all direct them toward the conviction that they are being manipulated, that they are victims of a conspiracy, which is coincidentally, that of the technopolitical order that "might or might not know what it was doing." These insiders who do realize, and grow out of the immaturity of not knowing, become aware of the disenfranchisement of the non-modern, the "Preterite" of *Gravity's Rainbow* and the "Subjunctive" in *Mason & Dixon*. Their knowledge is a knowledge of the past, a nostalgia for a diversity that was destroyed and erased. The Enlightenment is a homogenizing project as the unification of times and measurements proves in *Mason & Dixon*, but in those other times that are lost, Pynchon's nostalgic moods find a form of fictional resistance to the relentless advance of *the* Line.

As a parody of the grand narratives of scientific achievements of the age of Enlightenment, the novel voices a disagreement with the established discourses about the history of social and racial relations in early American history, critiquing the construction of power groups and the history of the appropriation of knowledge. By doing so, it subverts both the triumphal narrative of the scientific achievement of tracing the Line between Maryland and Pennsylvania, and the nationalist narrative of progress and democracy underlining the accounts of the American revolutionary period.[14]

"... a Tale about America."

To most readers, *Mason & Dixon* will give the impression of an exceedingly complex text. Yet its complexity and the density of the historical material make it almost impossible to refer to the novel's structure without feeling that something is being left out. The novel is divided into seventy-eight chapters separated in three sections corresponding to the three main scientific activities carried out by Charles Mason (1728–1783)[15] and Jeremiah Dixon (1733–1779).[16] These are, in the first and third parts, the observations of the Transits of Venus in 1761 and 1769 respectively, and in the second part the tracing of the boundary between the provinces of Maryland and Pennsylvania, and the calculation of a degree of latitude in the Delaware peninsula.[17] The first section, "Latitudes and Departures" (chapters 1–25) deals with the expedition to the Cape of Good Hope to observe the Transit of Venus, the first occasion on which Mason and Dixon worked together. Although initially appointed to go to Bencoolen in the Island of Sumatra, the war between the English and French, and the fact that Bencoolen itself was taken by the French meant first a delay and finally a change of plans in their destination. In January 1761, they traveled to the Cape of Good Hope and stayed there until October 1761 when they first met up with the Reverend Nevil Maskelyne at St. Helena. At the end of the first part, Mason and Dixon return to England and sign the contract with the proprietors of Maryland and Pennsylvania that will engage them in drawing the boundary between those two provinces from

1763 to 1768. The second part (chapters 26–73), "America," has as the re-curring theme Mason and Dixon's five-year-long stay in the British North American colonies. During these five years, they become close friends and while carrying out their jobs also get involved in observing and comment-ing on pre-Revolutionary American society. In the third part (chapters 74–78), "Last Transit," back in England Mason and Dixon observe sepa-rately the Transit of Venus from different points. After Dixon's death a decrepit Mason returns with his family to Philadelphia to die there.

Mason & Dixon starts in *media res:* it is Christmas time 1786 and Reverend Wicks Cherrycoke has arrived in Philadelphia in October to attend Charles Mason's funeral, although he was "too late for the Burial, as it prov'd" (6).[18] At his sister's, the reverend has been telling stories in exchange for accommodation, given that "for as long as he can keep the children amus'd, he may remain" (6). The opening scene of the novel focuses on an exchange between the reverend and part of his audience, the twins, Pitt and Pliny, who through these months have already heard "the Escape from Hottentot Land, the Accursèd Ruby of Mogok, the Ship-wrecks in Indies East and West,— an Herodotic Web of Adventures and Curiosities selected, the Rev^d implies, for their moral usefulness, whilst avoiding others not as suitable in the Hearing of the Youth" (7). They now ask for a "Tale about America," "with Indians in it, and Frenchmen" or "French Women" as Pitt comically mutters (7). The sig-nificant exchange, from which the narration stems, requires some unpack-ing. To begin with, there is a humorous suggestion that the young American public in front of Cherrycoke is already craving the ultimate American epic: the frontier tale. Its implied nostalgic reference to the oral traditions of storytelling and the human interaction in the transmission of information characteristic of the past offers an indication of the dialogic nature of the narration to follow. Opinions are exchanged between the storyteller and his audience that account for much of the book's metafic-tional discussions: among other things, they comment on the act of remembering (350, 695). This setting is in turn, related by another narra-tor — the nameless editor of the novel — who will also organize and pre-sent quotations from sources such as Revd Cherrycoke's *Spiritual Journal,* his sermons, and his treatise on *Christ and History.* Such a juxtaposition of materials, the ones used by the heterodiegetic omniscient narrator and those related by the storyteller, provides the novel with the appearance of a collage, out of which the plot and the chronological continuity of the narration emerge.

It is in relation to Cherrycoke's voice that Foucault's questions of "who is speaking?" and "what difference does it make who is speaking?" need to be posed. Cherrycoke, described as Mason's Boswell (718, 744), is *the* witness. He becomes the key character through whom the reader and his audience have access to Mason and Dixon. Both his nostalgic mood and his moral expounding conjure up the history of the two British surveyors as an excuse for his "Tale about America." The storyteller is placed at a privileged viewpoint — 1786, ten years after the Revolution, and twenty after the surveyors' departure from America — from which he can resurvey the past through the many Lines that connect us with history, "into the Mnemonick Deep [. . .] with only their Destination in common" (349). The common destination of time is seen throughout the novel as the principal feature of Enlightenment's new order. Dixon reacts against superstitious warnings before departing for Cape of Good Hope, stating that "'tis the Age of Reason," and that he and Mason are "Men of Science. To huz must all days run alike, the same number of identical Seconds, each proceeding in but one Direction, irreclaimable . . ." (27). This belief in a relentless progress of time is partially contested by Cherrycoke's activity of remembering, but also by those "other times" and "spaces" that constitute themselves as oppositional to "rational time" and "measurable space": the "eleven missing days" of the old English calendar, and Dixon's exploration of the *Terra Concava* (740).

Cherrycoke is a self-styled "untrustworthy Remembrancer" (8) who selects and narrates facts in a consciously "moral" way.[19] His access to some information about the lives of the two British scientists immediately poses questions about the accuracy of the stories, the origin of the materials presented,[20] but also about their moral purpose. The narrator has a contradictory political position from the outset as an exiled member of the Anglican Church who represents, in an American context, dissent and "official" views at once. Cherrycoke's ejection from England characterizes him as an outcast, a "madman." The *Seahorse,* a commercial ship aboard which he travels with Mason and Dixon on their first assignment abroad, is described as an "Engine of Destruction" also used to seclude political dissent. His political activity is identified with madness in a way that recalls the exclusion of social "unreason" in eighteenth-century France denunciated by Foucault in his *Madness and Civilization.* Cherrycoke's political sin, "the Crime they styl'd anonymity," can be read as analogous to Pynchon's artistic standing and his own anonymity, his withdrawal from the public while engaged in a denunciation of technocracy as a conspiratorial entente in which military and economic powers collude. Cherrycoke's "insanity" is reflected in his anonymous activities:

> That is, I left messages posted publicly, but did not sign them. I knew some night-running lads in the district who let me use their Printing-Press,— somehow, what I got into printing up, were Accounts of certain Crimes I had observ'd, committed by the Stronger against the Weaker,— enclosures, evictions, Assize verdicts, Activities

of the Military,— giving the names of as many of the Perpetrators as
I was sure of [. . .]. (9)

All the "Crimes" catalogued here refer to the process of redistribution of
communal properties carried out at the time of the Industrial Revolution
in England, and of which Dixon was an agent as local surveyor in Durham (Robinson, "Dixon" 272). It is Cherrycoke's denunciation of those
Crimes of the "Stronger against the Weaker" that account for his marginal position, for his initial sympathy with margins and excluded people.

For him, America appears to offer an "exceptional" opportunity to
banish the corruption of the Old World, expressed in that continuous oppression of the "Weaker." Cherrycoke explains his wish when he remembers how in 1765: "I was back in America once more, finding, despite all,
that I could not stay away from it, this object of hope that Miracles might
yet occur, that God might yet return to Human affairs, that all the wistful
Fictions necessary to the childhood of a species might yet come true, . . .
a third Testament . . ." (353). America, as the "object of Hope" belongs
to the non-conformist traditions established in the American colonies
since the seventeenth century. Indeed, the religious basis of American nationalism at the time of the Revolution — "the Revolution made prophetic sense" (Stephanson 13) — has been amply demonstrated.
Cherrycoke's "Third Testament" is another version of the coming of the
New Israel, or Berkeley's "Fifth Act" of Westward progress of which
"Time's Noblest Offspring" is the protagonist.[21]

Yet the predestination of the American people and of America's sacred territory is threatened with becoming part of everyday "Despair"
through the enlightened scientists' mapping:

Does Britannia when she sleeps, dream? Is America her dream? — in
which all that cannot pass in the metropolitan Wakefulness is allow'd
Expression away in the restless Slumber of these Provinces, and on
West-ward, wherever 'tis not yet mapp'd, nor written down, nor
ever, by the majority of Mankind, seen,— serving as a very Rubbish-
Tip for subjunctive Hopes, for all that *may yet be true,*— Earthly
Paradise, Fountain of Youth, Realms of Prester John, Christ's Kingdom, ever behind the sunset, safe till the next Territory to the West
be seen and recorded, measur'd and tied in, back into the Net-Work
of Points already known, that slowly triangulates its Way into the
Continent, changing all from subjunctive to declarative, reducing
Possibilities to Simplicities that serve the ends of Governments,—
winning away from the realm of the Sacred, its Borderlands one by
one, and assuming them unto the bare mortal World that is our
home, and our Despair. (345)

Cherrycoke's paradise to come in America is incorporated into the "bare mortal World" at once "home" and "Despair." As the "next Territory to the West" is seen and recorded, and Adorno's "line of destruction and civilization" advances, the "Possibilities" of diversity are encroached, becoming Profane "Simplicities that serve the ends of Governments," homogenized into the "declarative" tense/time of the Westward Empire. Jarvis has pointed out a similar aggression of the colonial forces on the "spaces of myth" in *V.:* "Pynchon's geography of the fall away from what is human hinges upon the expansion of profane places — for as colonial dependencies and supermarkets are built up, so too are all spaces of myth and magic razed to the ground" (58).

The loss of myth and magic that Pynchon had also denounced in "Is it OK to be a Luddite?" is developed even further here, and given a new dimension with the use for the first time in Pynchon's fiction of "real" personages, whose "real" records are reinterpreted through the narrative act. In the novel, Mason and Dixon's slow-growing awareness of the loss of the "subjunctive" is accompanied by an increasing hesitation about the righteousness behind the scientific projects in which they are involved.[22] Mason's non-fictional *Journal* also reveals the "restlessness" (705) that they confess at the end of their trip.[23] However, in the novel their early suspicion about why "they have been hired again" (250) turns into Dixon's conviction that they "shouldn't be running this Line" (478), and Mason finally wonders why he is "doing this" (642). Their growing paranoia is one of the many ways in which the shift from personages into characters takes place in the novel. Unlike other apparently unresolved quests by Pynchon, *Mason & Dixon* finds here a conclusive opinion: the characters finally perceive the Line as "a conduit for Evil" (701).

The point at which author and narrator coincide is precisely in their shared choice of the historical personages, Mason and Dixon, to talk about "Britannia's Dream," to tell through them a "Tale about America." The Rev[d]'s pondering on the future of the "realm of the Sacred" is one of the most explicit examples in the novel of the fictionalization of history in order to politicize it. It is conveniently inserted as a parenthetical digression in the Lancaster episode in which Mason and Dixon visit the site of a massacre committed the previous year against the Conestoga Indians. Pynchon does not need to invent episodes leading to their awareness of racial hatred toward the non-European. They are all taken from historical sources, and their relevance as milestones in the narration is instructive: they are re-narrated and placed at moments of "Enlightenment." In the novel, Mason's visit to Lancaster is conveniently followed by an extract from Cherrycoke's *Christ and History* where he defines history as neither mere "chronologies," which concern lawyers, nor "Remembrance," which belongs to the people. As we were told at the beginning of the novel by that "other narrator," Cherrycoke's histories are "an Herodotic Web of Adventures and Curiosities selected, the Rev^d implies, for their moral usefulness" (7).

Following Cherrycoke's moral theory of history, perhaps the most "morally useful" of the many instances in which Mason the character and the historical Mason coincide is the Lancaster episode. Mason's visit to the scene of the massacre of Conestoga Indians at the hand of the infamous Paxton Boys is recorded in *The Journal* as one of Mason's trips in the winter of '65:

> Left Brandywine and proceeded to Lancaster (distance about 35 miles) a Town in Pennsylvania, distant from Philadelphia 75 Miles, bearing nearly due West. *What brought me here was my curiosity to see the place where was perpetrated last Winter the Horrid and inhuman murder of 26 Indians, Men, Women and Children, leaving none alive to tell.* These poor unhappy creatures had always lived under the protection of the Pennsylvania Government and had Lands alloted [*sic*] for them a few Miles from Lancaster by the late celebrated William Penn, Esquire, Proprietor. They had received notice of the intention of some of the back inhabitants and fled to the Gaol (jail) to save themselves. The keeper made the door fast, but it was broken open; and two men went in and executed the bloody scene; while about 50 of their party sat on Horse Back without; armed with Guns, etc. Strange it was that the Town though as large as most Market Towns in England, never offered to oppose them, though its [*sic*] more than probable they on request might have been assisted by a Company of his Majesties Troops who were then in the Town . . . no honor to them! What was laid to the Indians charge was that they held a private correspondence with the Enemy Indians; but this could never be proved against the men and the women and children (some in their Mothers wombs that never saw light) could not be guilty. (66)[24]

Cherrycoke turns the journal entry into a full episode in which both Mason and Dixon go into the jail, though separately. Dixon puts on Mason's clothes, leaving behind for the first time his "real" red army jacket,[25] both as an external sign of their first ideological identification in the novel, and as a way of including Dixon in a fundamental epiphanic moment of the story. Although there is no documented evidence of whether Dixon accompanied Mason or not on this journey,[26] fiction and fact are mixed with Cherrycoke's assurance: "Dixon told me, that Mason had meant to go alone,— but that at the last moment, mindful of the dangers attending Solitude in a Town notorious for Atrocity, he offer'd to add Muscular Emphasis, tho' Mason seem'd unsure of whether he wanted him there or not" (341). Mason's "real" horrified account is inserted in Cherrycoke's — and Pynchon's — ideological recuperation of history in order to show the way in which the "subjunctive Hopes" may have become "murderous Hopes," and that as the Line progresses, the "indicative" or "declarative" world of the Age of Reason will also advance, wiping out the subjunctive world of the Indians.

Despite Cherrycoke's confessed faith in American exceptionality, in the "subjunctive Hopes" that "may yet be true," Mason and Dixon's comparison between Good Hope and America is constant, even talking about America as just "[a]nother slave-Colony . . ." (248). The Rev^d is also able to recount Mason's realization of the apparent "connection" between the acts of racial violence in both continents:

> Mason did note as peculiar, that the first mortal acts of Savagery in America after their Arrival should have been committed by the Whites against Indians. Dixon mutter'd, "Why, 'tis the d---'d Butter-Bags all over again."
> They saw white Brutality enough, at the Cape of Good Hope. They can no better understand now, than then. Something is eluding them. Whites in both places are become the very Savages of their own worst Dreams, far out of Measure to any Provocation. (306–7)

If "[s]omething is eluding them," it is because they have not yet come to the conclusion that the violent episodes they witness are part of the same project of domination for which they are working. Butter-Bags fill the air every time an act of colonial violence occurs as a metaphysical indication of the outrage, and yet they have not been able to ascertain that "connection." Pynchon's use of Mason and Dixon's African experiences as a preamble for a "Tale about America" becomes clearer: as in *Gravity's Rainbow*, the African element is used in the text as the index of the "original sin" of slavery and domination. In *Mason & Dixon* the comparison between the two colonies re-enacts American utopia just as it was being depleted, turning the "tale about America" into a tale about *the lack of exceptionality of* America.

Mason and Dixon have been made into fictional characters on previous occasions. Susan Lefever, an obscure writer who published an early, bland fictional account of Mason and Dixon's American stay,[27] makes Mason write a letter to Dixon in which he asks: "How did we ever do what we did in that exotic world across the sea?" (326). Mason continues, with a paranoid style familiar to Pynchon's readers, to bluntly confess his close friendship with Dixon:

> And now though I still suffer depression from what we went through and from the ultimate apathy of our superiors I was so sure would honor us, I feel God gave me a greater gift than all the material hon-

ors or promotions that should have been awarded us. He gave me you, Jery. He gave me your friendship, your love, your concern. And never, ever do I wish to lose it. (326)

In Pynchon's infinitely subtler and more complex text, the ideas here condensed in a paragraph are slowly developed. The personages/ characters are yet again conferred what amounts to distrust for their superiors' "ends," a suspicion that is intractable in any of their published scientific articles or in Mason's *Journal*,[28] and which Pynchon elaborates into a full-blown questioning of western values.

A different case is the first recorded instance to my knowledge in which the two surveyors were fictionalized, on this occasion by a Maryland pro-slavery historian, John H. B. Latrobe in his speech, *The History of the Mason and Dixon Line*. In his 1854 address to the Historical Society of Pennsylvania, Latrobe analyzed six years before the outbreak of the American Civil War, the long history of tensions and anxieties on both sides of the Mason-Dixon Line. Latrobe could look back at the moment when the thirteen colonies had declared independence from the British king seventy-eight years earlier and summarize what appeared to him to be a short history of national and intellectual success, the foundation of a Republic "whose rapid development, in all that constituted the true greatness of a people, would be the wonder of the world" (49). Independent American history so far was marked by two geographical events, inscribed on the map of the Mason-Dixon Line East-West and North-South.

The first of these events could be observed in the Line's westward projection, the advance of the country reflected in the replacement of the woodlands' inhabitants, the vanishing Indians, by the "monster and the miracle of modern ingenuity" (37), the train.[29] An achievement which for Latrobe was in marked contrast with the power that the "roving Indians of the wilderness" had had ninety years earlier in cutting thirty-six miles short the assignment of tracing a line between the provinces of Maryland and Pennsylvania.

The other successful event had still to happen and it would consist in the reconciliation of the axis North-South, which the Mason-Dixon Line had come to demarcate: slave holding versus anti-slavery states. In a short history of independence, slavery was to be the major controversy "whose solution, and its consequences, involved the gravest considerations, and had been supposed to threaten the integrity of the Republic" (7). Latrobe's "final" solution to the presence of African slaves is their substitution by cheaper workers: "The slavery question of the United States is a question of interest; and its solution will be found in the increasing white population of the country, the consequent reduction of wages, and the great ultimate result — the production, by free labor, of the chief staples of the country cheaper than they can be produced by slave-labor" (6). Bringing into the country waged white slaves and shipping the Black population to the recently established colony of Liberia are two of his bright antebellum proposals for the forging of a new national consensus. In Pynchon's novel these solutions are parodied when Dixon summarizes the "Elements common" to all their journeys:

> Slaves. Ev'ry day at the Cape, we lived with Slavery in our faces,— more of it at St. Helena,— and now here we are again, in another Colony, this time having drawn a Line between their Slave-Keepers, and their Wage-Payers, as if doom'd to re-encounter thro' the World this public Secret, this shameful Core. . . . Pretending it to be ever somewhere else, with the Turks, the Russians, the Companies, down there, down where it smells like warm Brine and Gunpowder fumes, they're murdering and dispossessing thousands untallied, the innocent of the World, passing daily into the Hands of Slave-owners and Torturers, but oh, never in Holland, nor in England, that Garden of Fools . . .? Christ, Mason. (692–93)

In Dixon's earlier trip to Virginia "though Slaves passed before his sight, he saw none" (398), but at the moment of summing up their journeys, all the encounters with slavery become connected as the "public Secret," "this shameful Core": the prostitutes in St Helena, who were that "slavery within Slavery" (150), and the American slaves, the chattel and the chained, are part of the same technopolitical system based on different forms of slavery. Even northern waged workers can be considered slaves — at least in this point, Latrobe seems to coincide with Pynchon. But in their explicit realization of the destructive results of their collaboration in the Line's — and with it, Enlightenment's — Westward advance, Pynchon's Mason and Dixon appear to have traveled a long way from other characterizations of the two personages.

Latrobe, worried about the coming civil war, argues in apocalyptic tones that if the "blessed people" are finally divided, it may mean the demise of the American dream of "a united and homogenous people." After enumerating the many scientific and political advances which Mason and Dixon would have missed since their deaths, including the foundation of the Republic,[30] he hypothesizes about their reaction to the news by guessing that they would be astonished "[. . .] could they have been told, that the results of this revolution having been power, and might, and majesty, and boundless prosperity, of which every individual in the land was a participant [. . .]" (51). In contrast to Pynchon's, Latrobe's Mason and Dixon are presented as weak, subservient Britons. After all, the surveyors who traced the boundary between Pennsylvania and Maryland until stopped at the "war-path" by the "sylvan monarchs" represent those past times and values banished with the new order to come only with the American Revolution. Latrobe even affirms that "They, probably, were not imaginative men, and it is not likely that they indulged in many reflections as to the future of the world of mountain and forest and boundless plains, on which they thus turned their backs" (48). Quoting Berkeley's famous line about the course of Empire, Latrobe congratulates himself and his audience that now "an observatory [. . .] crown[s] the summit of a hill, looking down on a great city [Cincinnati] near three hundred miles westward of the war-path" (49).[31] Their final reluctance to finish the line into Indian territory was charged to them by Latrobe as a sign of their ignorance of the new Republican imperial values.[32]

In contrast, Pynchon's Mason and Dixon are cast once again as men whose understanding is subject to moral judgment rather than to the colonizing imperatives of the Line: "Having acknowledg'd at the Warpath the Justice of the Indian's Desires, after the two deaths, Mason and Dixon understand as well that the Line is exactly what Capt. Zhang and a number of others have been styling it all along — a conduit for Evil." (701). Mason and Dixon's acknowledgment of the "Justice of the Indian's Desires" in Pynchon's novel credits them with an ability to listen to the Other, and to those other reasons, which is absent from Latrobe's speech. Both Mason and Dixon share their increasingly awed views about the colonial horrors of South African and American slaughter of natives and transported slaves. Their reflection on what they have observed during their journeys leads them to the conclusion that white Europeans are the real savages "out of their own worst Dreams."

Finally, Latrobe puts in the surveyors' mouths "words of prophecy" uttered "for the sake of the unity of [his] discourse" (52) — that is, in order to complete his presentation of the surveyors as weak British "servants" (50); he makes them worry now about the future preservation of the Republic:

> These uses, to which you put the lightning; this erection of cities on river shores, in Indian lands; this tale of battle, and blood-shed and victory; this dethroning of monarchs and uplifting of their subjects, are astounding results that we cannot appreciate, for we see no elements to produce them, and they shock all the prejudices of our education. To time we leave their development. But, that a blessed people beyond all others, in their realization, if realized they *are* to be, and occupying the proudest place among the nations, because of their wondrous unity, under a government that extent of dominion enfeebles not — should willingly permit their Union to be dissolved, we cannot believe; because, here, we are dealing, not with the future of science or politics, but with the principles of humanity common

to all ages; and, depend upon it, whatever the few may wish, the many will be true; and this, our line of survey, will, after all, owe its notoriety to ephemeral oratory, in which it figures as a mere phrase of cant, or to addresses, which will bring to light the few brief records we have left of our transactions. (51–52)

It is at this point that Pynchon's and Latrobe's Mason and Dixon appear as completely diverse personages through their different perceptions of the Line. Latrobe's reconstruction of their voice remains politicized for the sake of his project to save the union, as the "blessed people" need to "be realized." Pynchon's polyphony is equally politicized, but it is engaged in demonstrating Pynchon's obsession with the predestination of the West to spread its "Kingdom of Death" (*GR* 722) throughout the world. His surveyors encounter numerous opinions favoring that view, such as Captain Zhang's: "Nothing will produce Bad History more directly nor brutally, than drawing a Line, in particular a Right Line, the very Shape of Contempt, through the midst of a People,— to create thus a Distinction betwixt 'em,— 'tis the first stroke. — All else will follow as if predestin'd, unto War and Devastation" (615).

Pynchon's final opposition between the two worlds comes to a halt with the surveyors' stop at the Indian Warpath, the "Membrane that divides their Subjunctive World from our number'd and dreamless Indicative" (677). In their discussion, Dixon uses one of Pynchon's syntactic clichés to describe the Line and to speak for the Indians' fear of "this great invisible Thing that comes crawling Straight on over their Lands" (678). Apart from echoing *Gravity's Rainbow*'s opening image of "a screaming [that] comes across the sky" (*GR* 1), the sentence insists on Dixon's earlier conviction that the real "Proprietors" are the Indians (468). For Dixon the Line is therefore an invasion into "its Life's Blood," similar to the V-2 rockets in *Gravity's Rainbow*. A "living creature, 'tis all of us" (678) says Mason to a disconcerted Dixon, whose hesitation is the ultimate paranoid abashment in the novel: "And what of its intentions, beyond killing ev'rything due west of it? do you know? I don't either" (678).

Cherrycoke's reconstruction of history is not so much directed toward claiming truth as toward finding a space for resistance against the dreamless homogenizing drive of the west. His praise of fictional history could stand as a manifesto of the Postmodern Historical Novel:

> Who claims Truth, Truth abandons. History is hir'd, or coerc'd, only in Interests that must ever prove base. She is too innocent, to be left within the reach of anyone in Power,—who need but touch her, and all her Credit is in the instant vanish'd, as if it had never been. She needs rather to be tended lovingly and honorably by fabulists and

counterfeiters, Ballad-Mongers and Cranks of ev'ry Radius, Masters of Disguise to provide her the Costume, Toilette, and Bearing, and Speech nimble enough to keep her beyond the Desires, or even the Curiosity, of Government. (350)

Cherrycoke's faith in America could be read as being parodied through the oppositional elements advanced in Mason and Dixon's discoveries. And yet, Mason and Dixon's story seems to have also transformed the narrator as he has told the story. He explains how his approach to history belongs to the "common Duty of Remembering" of which "our Sentiments" are a part. By "Sentiments," Cherrycoke parenthetically explains, he is referring to "how we dream'd of, and were mistaken in, each other," and those "count for at least as much as our poor cold Chronologies" (695–96). His sentimental history is as much a reconstruction of utopian dreams as a realization of their erring. His America is a thing of the past; it exists in the past subjunctive of the utopia that could have been, but was not. As the novel nostalgically underlines the diversity that was erased through conquest and expansion, readers are asked to confront the history of the birth of the American nation not so much as a historical utopian exception in which liberty and equality were fulfilled, but perhaps as "an instructive history of ethnic cleansing" (Stephanson 24).

The surveyors decide to discontinue the Line, to somehow prevent its movement westward, and Dixon, in a heroic though historically accurate act, threatens to thrash a slave conductor who is being violent towards the slaves (chapter 28).[33] As their actions become oppositional to the world they have helped advance, and they reassert their "thoughts," they also conclude that America *could* have been different, exceptional, but it was not: "No matter where in it we go, shall we find all the World Tyrants and Slaves? America was the only place we should *not* have found them." (693). At this point, instead of the utopian space that was being imagined by the eager founders of the nation, America has become for Pynchon's Dixon a thing of the past, subjunctive.

Notes

To my dear friend Burhan Tufail, whose memory shall endure.

[1] The idea that Native Americans were condemned to either extermination or absorption has been thoroughly studied in McNickle. See also Philip J. Deloria for a study of the appropriation of the Indian in American culture.

[2] See particularly "The Ritual of Consensus," 29–67, and "The Typology of Mission, from Edwards to Independence," 147–67.

[3] In his article on *Mason & Dixon*, David Seed also concludes that "the novel demonstrates a postcolonial alertness to mapping as a culturally inflected exercise,

an exercise in territorial appropriation where the first casualties to be displaced are the native Americans" (99).

[4] Berubé is using here an expression coined by Nina Baym.

[5] In his note to p. 204, Bercovitch explicitly mentions Pynchon as one of the modern practitioners of the American anti-jeremiad.

[6] In Pynchon's case this is true even from a biographical viewpoint; in their well-known monographs Steven Weisenburger and Tony Tanner have commented on Pynchon's puritan ancestry.

[7] As Homi Bhabha has suggested, the question of cultural difference offers a radical challenge to both modernity and the national: "From the margins of modernity, at the insurmountable extremes of storytelling, we encounter the question of cultural difference as the perplexity of living, and writing, the nation" (311).

[8] "Could we ever narrativize without moralizing?" asks Hayden White (25).

[9] Linda Hutcheon's defense of parody in historiographic metafiction as a way of articulating a postmodern political critique clearly resonates in this assertion. In reference to Pynchon, Hutcheon affirms: "Pynchon's intertextually overdetermined, discursively overloaded fictions both parody and *enact* the totalizing tendency of all discourses to create systems and structures" (133).

[10] Similar to those described by Benedict Anderson (55).

[11] Recently described in detail by John Clement Ball, see particularly chapter 1 (9–40). Ball argues that the use of such binaries is a key to understanding the novel's satirical intent (23).

[12] For a study of the novel as a manifesto for Pynchon's Luddite agenda see David Cowart's article.

[13] A "Wahlspruch" or "devise" as Foucault remarks (Foucault, *Lumiéres* 565). For a complete study of the evolution of the motto from Horace through Gassendi and Shaftesbury to Kant, see Franco Venturi (6–9). Venturi asserts the predominant place of the German definition of Enlightenment: "From Kant to Cassirer and beyond, our understanding of the European Enlightenment has been dominated by the philosophical interpretation of the German *Aufklärung*" (1).

[14] Jeff Baker has similarly analyzed the novel's critique of "the revolutionary rhetoric with regard to the hypocritical practices of the colonists" (175).

[15] "We can now be certain that Charles Mason, the astronomer, was born at Wherr in the parish of Bisley in Gloucestershire in the early part of 1728, for he was baptized at Sapperton Church on 1 May 1728" (Robinson, "Mason's" 135).

[16] For a short account of Jeremiah Dixon's life, see Robinson, "Dixon": "Jeremiah Dixon was born at Bishop Auckland on 27 July 1733" (272). See also Hollis.

[17] See Cope, Heidel, and Weld.

[18] For the dates and place of Charles Mason's burial see Cope, "Collecting Source . . ." (114). Also, "He was laid to rest on October 26, 1786, in Christ Church Burying Ground at Fifth and Arch Streets, Philadelphia. The grave is not marked and its exact location is unknown. Benjamin Franklin and his wife Deborah rest nearby" (Cope, "Mountain" 231).

[19] For an interesting contribution on authorship and the role of the narrator see Schaub.

[20] Charles Mason's journal was found at Halifax, Nova Scotia in 1860. George W. Corner, preface, p. vii; A Hughlett Mason, introduction, pp. 1–27, transcribed from the original in the U.S. Archives (Philadelphia: American Philosophical Society, 1969).

[21] It is still unclear who Berkeley refered to when he talked about this offspring: was it European Americans or Native Americans?

[22] The ideological defense of unconquenred territories is carried out through this opposition of "subjunctive" versus "indicative," rather than through that "sharp line between past and present" noticed by E. J. W. Hinds ("Sari" 206). Brian McHale offers a detailed explanation of the uses of the subjunctive in the novel.

[23] The journal is written in the first person by Charles Mason: "Thus ends my restless progress in America" (*Journal* 211).

[24] I have italicized the section of Charles Mason's entry used verbatim by Cherry-coke in the novel.

[25] Another aspect of Pynchon's accurate historical research: "Dixon wore military uniform from 1760 until his death consisting of a long red coat and a cocked hat" (Robinson, "Dixon" 273).

[26] "Whether Dixon accompanied him is not clear" (Cope, "The Stargazers" 206).

[27] Despite efforts to contact this author, I have been unable to this date to trace her current address.

[28] See Mason's articles published in the *Philosophical Transactions of the Royal Society of London*.

[29] Unmentioned albeit clearly suggested, the train is an obvious reference given Latrobe's personal investments in the Virginia/Ohio train company. See Semmes.

[30] Latrobe incurs here one of his many historical inaccuracies because both Mason and Dixon lived to see the first episodes of the American Revolution. Charles Mason died in Philadelphia in 1786.

[31] David Bidney, from a contemporary standpoint, comments: "It is of interest in this connection [contemporary reassessment of attitudes towards Indians] to reflect that the typical rationalization employed by nineteenth-century Americans to validate their claim to expansion on the North American continent and to exclude the Indians from participating in their civilization, was duplicated in the twentieth century by the claims of land-hungry nations of Europe, Germany and Italy, before the Second World War. In their quest for *Lebensraum* similar claims were made as to the rights of powerful civilized peoples at the expense of the so-called less civilized, weaker peoples" (102).

[32] Interestingly, Mason and Dixon charted thirty-six miles fewer than contracted.

[33] "A story is told that one day, whilst in America, Dixon came across a slave driver mercilessly beating a poor black woman. Going up to him he said: 'Thou must not do that!' He received the curt answer: 'You be d. . .d! Mind your own business.' Dixon's reply was: 'If thou doesn't desist I'll thrash thee!' Then righteous wrath overcame his Quaker principles. He was a tall and powerful man, and an

imposing figure, so without more ado he seized the slave-driver's whip and with it gave him the sound thrashing that he richly deserved. Dixon kept the whip as a trophy and took it back with him to Cockfield, where it was long regarded as a family treasure" (Robinson, "Dixon" 273).

5: Postmodernism at Sea: The Quest for Longitude in Thomas Pynchon's *Mason & Dixon* and Umberto Eco's *The Island of the Day Before*

Dennis M. Lensing

> *... all over the World all day long that fifth and sixth of June, in Latin, in Chinese, in Polish, in Silence,— upon Roof-Tops and Mountain Peaks, out of Bed-chamber windows, close to-gether in the naked sunlight whilst the Wife minds the Beats of the Clock,— thro' Gregorians and Newtonians, achromatick and rainbow-smear'd, brand-new Reflectors made for the occasion, and ancient Refractors of preposterous French focal lengths,— Observers lie, they sit, they kneel,— and witness some-thing in the Sky. Among those attending Snouts Earth-wide, the moment of first contact produces a collective brain-pang, as if for something lost and already unclaimable,— after the Years of preparation, the long and at best queasy voyaging, the Station arriv'd at, the Latitude and Longitude well secur'd,— the Week of the Transit,— the Day,— the Hour,— the Minute, —and at last 'tis, "Eh? where am I?"*
>
> *— Mason & Dixon, 97*

THUS DOES PYNCHON'S NARRATOR describe the first great moment of the scientific adventures of Charles Mason and Jeremiah Dixon, and the most significant astronomical event of 1761. For the first time in over 120 years, the planet Venus moved across the face of the sun, providing an unprecedented opportunity for measuring the scale of the solar system. The scientific academies were well prepared for this event, and astrono-mers and their instruments had been dispersed around the world, the better to judge the true magnitude of the Solar Parallax, which would yield an accurate determination of the distance from earth to sun. As David Sellers has noted, Edmund Halley had exhorted the Royal Society forty-five years earlier not to miss this chance, and so, "[i]n 1761, Charles Mason and Jeremiah Dixon observed from South Africa, William Wales from Canada, Jean-Baptise Chappe d'Auteroche from Siberia and

Alexandre-Gui Pingré, from Madagascar. The French astronomer, Guillaume le Gentil set out to observe the transit from India, but unfortunately arrived too late" (par. 4).

The energy of Pynchon's rather telescoped (so to speak) paragraph on the Transit and all that it entailed is certainly well justified. What is striking about this description — and what is especially resonant with one recurrent theme in *Mason & Dixon* — is the passage's culmination. Even as the great moment begins, the sensation felt around the globe is a pang of something "lost and already unclaimable." The bustle of preparation of all the myriad instruments used to capture the moment yields to a focus on what the "at best queasy voyaging" scientists, in all their physicality, had to endure to cross the wide world. And, at last, the countdown to the end of this moment, meant to fix earth's place in regard to the sun, causes utter disorientation: "Eh? where am I?" (97). Such moments of feeling lost, confused, "at sea," are extraordinarily frequent in this tale of two cartographers, who might be expected to have a clearer notion of their location than most. This essay will explore the significance of such disorientation in the context of another, related scientific endeavor of Mason and Dixon's day: the Quest for the Longitude. This quest is a recurrent theme in Pynchon's novel, and is in fact central to Umberto Eco's novel, *The Island of the Day Before* (1994). That two of the more prodigious postmodern authors should concern themselves simultaneously with the Quest for Longitude, two centuries after its resolution, demands comparative consideration, in order to illuminate each work, as well as the development of postmodernism itself, both as literary style and as cultural mode.

The centrality of cartographic problems to both *Mason & Dixon* and *The Island of the Day Before* suggests much about the nature of the postmodern and the situation of these works within the cultural moment of postmodernity. In their novels of the early modern period, Pynchon and Eco deploy a multitude of discursive practices, demonstrating the postmodern insistence on the primacy of multiplicity over any single notion of Truth. Both novels serve as warnings against the excesses to which postmodernism can be prone, excesses in which the untrammeled proliferation of signification leads to the ultimate dissolution of all meaning. By maintaining an insistent commitment to historical awareness, Eco and Pynchon produce a new sort of postmodern novel; their works "not only identify in the past the causes of what came later, but also trace the process through which those causes began slowly to produce their effects" (Eco, *Postscript* 76). And while performing these representations, necessary to any truly historical novel, these two novels draw insistent attention to the difficulties inherent in such identifications and tracings. Pynchon's work takes this process even one step further, illustrating also some possible means of transcending the ideological shortcomings and limitations identified by Fredric Jameson (among others) as weaknesses of the postmodern stance.

The Quest for Longitude

What was the Quest for Longitude? It was the attempt, by countless professional and amateur scientists, to answer the most vexing question of the scientific world in seventeenth- and eighteenth-century Europe: How could one accurately determine one's longitudinal coordinates, especially while at sea? Virtually everyone with any scientific inclinations, from Galileo and Cassini to Newton and Halley, sought an answer to this mystery. And the motivations behind this quest were by no means derived from innocent scientific curiosity; in an age of increasing sea trade and naval warfare, the ability or inability to know one's longitude could literally be a matter of life and death. This reality became brutally clear, at least in the English mind, when, on October 22, 1707, four British warships misjudged their position and ran aground at the Scilly Isles, just southwest of England. Nearly two thousand sailors died as a result. With colonization schemes proliferating, and with the safest sea routes becoming crowded — easy prey for pirates and privateers — every European nation saw the political and military value of this scientific quest. England's Parliament demonstrated its interest dramatically with the Longitude Act of 1714, which promised a reward of £20,000 (the equivalent 12 million dollars today) to the first person who could devise a workable means of determining a ship's longitudinal position within a half degree (Sobel 53).

The longitude project, driven by such practical incentives, led to a wide variety of scientific innovations before any real solution was found. Scientifically, the Quest for Longitude gave rise to the first measurements of the speed of light, the first hard evidence of the earth's motion through space, the calculation of the diameter of Jupiter, and the detection of tiny deviations in the tilt of the earth's axis (Sobel 30, 95). Further, the widespread, though ultimately incorrect, belief that the solution lay in the heavens, as it had for latitude, employed legions of astronomers to chart the movements of the heavens with unprecedented accuracy. Indeed, the effort expended upon this task rendered it perhaps the first scientific investigation ever to enter so thoroughly the public mind; in the years between the Longitude Act and the eventual discovery of a solution, "the concept of 'discovering the longitude' became a synonym for attempting the impossible" (Sobel 156).

The resolution of the problem of the longitude was produced by a clockmaker, John Harrison, who spent decades developing a clock that would keep accurate time even at sea. By comparing the clock's time, which would be the time of day in London, with the time of day at the ship's location, one could easily calculate the longitude. Harrison's Watch, his fourth model, passed the test for accuracy on a trip from England to Jamaica in 1762. However, the members of the Royal Society, especially astronomer Nevil Maskelyne, were so wed to the idea that the solution lay in the stars, that they denied Harrison's claim to victory for many more years, until King George III was finally induced to intervene in 1773.

In light of the general consciousness of the mystery of longitude throughout the seventeenth and eighteenth centuries, one can hardly feel surprise that this scientific project should be mentioned in the literature of the decades leading up to Harrison's eventual success. As Dava Sobel points out, longitude appears not only in Jonathan Swift's *Gulliver's Travels,* but also in the poetic works of John Donne and John Milton, separated by many years. The study of the heavens, associated with the ability to determine longitude even in the early seventeenth century, inspires Donne's religious musings in *An Anatomie of the World.* Donne writes of the stars:

> But yet their various and perplexed course,
> Observed in divers ages, doth enforce
> Man to find out so many Eccentrique parts,
> Such divers downe-right lines, such overthwarts,
> As disproportion that pure form . . . (258–62)

Later, Donne criticizes the analytic drive of astronomers further:

> For of Meridians, and Parallels,
> Man hath weav'd out a net, and this net throwne
> Upon the Heavens, and now they are his owne. (283–85)

Even in Donne's time, the cartographic projects associated with astronomy are connected with appropriation and ownership. Men's hubris taints the heavens and ensnares the earth, debasing God and exalting humanity beyond its true worth.

However, the religious impulse evident in Donne's poetry, as in Milton's, need not lead inevitably to such a Tower-of-Babel interpretation of scientific enterprise. John Milton was well versed in the astronomical knowledge of his day, and uses it to great effect in *Paradise Lost.* In Book Ten, he imagines a complete prelapsarian astronomy, asserting that the tilt of the earth's axis is a direct result of God's displeasure at human disobedience. Because of the original sin, God bids "his angels turn askance/The poles of earth twice ten degrees and more/From the sun's axle" (668–70). Thus, eternal equinox, and eternal spring, are ended, and

Eden is lost. Milton goes on to mention the "noxious" astrological effects of this alteration, revealing just how intertwined were what we consider the separate categories of science and superstition, a commingling seen clearly in the later life and thought of Isaac Newton himself.[1]

While the appearance of such astronomical concerns in the literature of the era is interesting in its own right, it is no more surprising, given the ubiquitous presence of the longitude problem in the popular consciousness, than the appearance of nuclear physics in post–Second World War literature. And, considering the scholarly thoroughness demonstrated by both Pynchon and Eco in their earlier masterworks, *Gravity's Rainbow* and *The Name of the Rose*, the longitude problem would virtually *have* to appear in their two newer novels, at least in passing. What is noteworthy is that the cartographic problems involved in the Quest for Longitude are *central* to both *Mason & Dixon* and *The Island of the Day Before*. This renewed fascination with one of the greatest scientific quests of the modern age, and the manner in which Pynchon and Eco use it, suggest as much about the nature of the postmodern cultural mode as they reveal about the historical facts of the quest itself.

While Pynchon's book ranges far and wide among the scientific and political projects of the eighteenth century, simultaneously enacting — and gesturing beyond — the postmodern moment of the late twentieth century, Eco's work is far more focused and rigorous with regard to the Quest for Longitude as it played out in the seventeenth century. *The Island of the Day Before* also commits, perhaps even limits itself, to the task of warning against postmodern discursive excess. In this sense, this novel serves as a reprise and extension of some of Eco's concerns elaborated in *Foucault's Pendulum*. The death of Roberto, resulting from his belief in the truth of his own fanciful imaginings, recalls Diotellevi's claim in the earlier novel: "I am dying because we were imaginative beyond bounds" (468). And the obsession of *The Island of the Day Before*, the *Punto Fijo*, resonates with the reflection of the narrator of *Foucault's Pendulum* near the tale's end, on Belbo's death, resulting from his own quest for "the Mystic Pole . . . the only Fixed Point in the universe" (524). Eco remains stern in his insistence that we allow ourselves to get carried away (in Roberto's case, literally) at our own risk and inevitable expense.

The Elusive *Punto Fijo*

Eco's *The Island of the Day Before* takes place in 1643 during the early stages of the quest for longitude. At this time, only the most preliminary steps were being made toward a viable solution; Dutch scientist Christiaan Huygens would not even invent the pendulum clock, the first innovation on the long road to the Harrison Watch, for another fourteen years

(Klarreich par. 3). Therefore, the problem of longitude is inevitably unresolvable within this text, a fact which permits Eco to explore the issues connected with the quest in an open-ended manner, consistent with the lack of closure and resolution commonly associated with postmodernism. Indeed, the futile quest for the *Punto Fijo*, or fixed point of longitude, drives the entire narrative; many characters are in search of the meridian which lies precisely opposite the prime meridian, the latter variously situated running through Jerusalem, Paris, and London. The protagonist, Roberto della Griva, is forced by the Machiavellian Cardinal Mazarin to serve as a spy aboard the *Amaryllis;* another passenger on board that vessel, Dr. Byrd, is suspected by the Cardinal to be developing a solution to the mystery of longitude. Ironically, the *Amaryllis* sinks in a storm, and only Roberto escapes, managing to climb aboard the *Daphne,* which is anchored near an island believed to lie directly on the anti-meridian. Roberto, unable to swim, cannot reach the island, and thus spends the majority of the narrative shipwrecked aboard a ship, within sight, but just out of reach, of his goal.

In the course of Roberto's ill-fated journey, he interacts with a variety of characters, each of whom permits Eco to explore the various scientific and political oddities associated with the search for longitude, and by extension with scientific pursuits in general. As Peter Bondanella has pointed out, the myriad schemes proposed by scientists and illustrated by Eco serve a "double purpose" within the novel. First, they are "intrinsically amusing"; second, and more importantly, they demonstrate "Eco's belief that there is no 'system' in scientific method that can explain the sum totality of the universe" (179). Further, Eco undertakes in the fictional mode the very sort of discursive practice advocated by Michel Foucault in *The Order of Things.* Foucault insists that "the historical analysis of scientific discourse should, in the last resort, be subject, not to a theory of the knowing subject, but rather to a theory of discursive practice" (xiv). Eco's treatment of seventeenth-century science in *The Island of the Day Before,* accomplished via the variety of characters seeking the longitude, serves in the end to deprivilege the discourse of science, which has come to serve the twentieth century as a master narrative and thus to offer a superior means of accessing Truth. Put another way, Eco's novel acts as a site at which scientific discourse may be dialogized in the Bakhtinian sense; science comes to be seen as but one language among many, an achievement beyond the scope of conventional histories of science, such as Dava Sobel's *Longitude,* published in 1995. Thus, the reader is led to an "incredulity towards metanarratives," the very definition of "postmodern" according to Jean-François Lyotard (xxiv).

Of the characters encountered by Roberto, three in particular function to accomplish Eco's goals: the Knight of Malta, Doctor Byrd, and

Father Caspar. Each espouses a different solution to the mystery of longitude, and each works from different motives. That the Knight, admittedly a minor character, has been all but completely overlooked by critics analyzing the novel reveals to just how great an extent the twentieth-century mind separates the spheres of science and religion, even more so than those of science and superstition. The Knight's motivations are purely religious, as are his methods. He has reasoned on the basis of a passage in the Bible, stating that visitors from the edge of the earth brought gifts to King Solomon. Having heard of the existence of the Solomon Islands, he has deduced that these islands must be the origin of these visitors, and therefore must in fact lie on the 180th meridian, exactly opposite Jerusalem. And in the mind of the Knight, his goal has deep spiritual significance, equivalent to salvation and escape from, in Roberto's words, "all the assassins of this merciless world" (226). Lest the point Eco is making here by means of the mystic Knight of Malta be missed by the reader, Eco elaborates upon this intermingling of discourses in the more sophisticated character of Father Caspar, a Jesuit priest and, of course, a scientist.

Before examining the complexities of Father Caspar's character and role in the novel, I will turn to the eccentric Dr. Byrd, fellow traveler of Roberto and the Knight aboard the *Amaryllis*. Here, the object of Eco's ironic attentions is not religion, but pseudo-science and science themselves; when reading of Dr. Byrd, one cannot but recognize that it is often difficult to distinguish the former from the latter. Only from a distant, privileged vantage point can these terms be applied at all, and that vantage point is always denied us when we consider our own era. Dr. Byrd is convinced that he has solved the problem of longitude, but his "solution" seems utterly ridiculous today.

Dr. Byrd has a wounded dog hidden in one of the ship's holds, its wound carefully prevented from healing. Every day, precisely at noon, in London, the Powder of Sympathy, or *unguentum armarium*, is applied to the weapon that inflicted the wound. In the seventeenth century, this substance was widely believed to aid in the healing of a wound, at any distance, when brought into contact with the weapon, although not without some discomfort experienced by the injured party. Thus, when the wounded dog should whimper precisely at midnight, Dr. Byrd would stand assured that he was upon the 180th meridian, measured from London. This magical solution to the problem of knowing the time of day in faraway places, in order to determine one's own longitudinal position, seems so ludicrous to us today that Dava Sobel felt it necessary to write "The Longitude Problem," a brief essay about Eco's novel. In this essay, Sobel iterates that this scheme is not a creation of Eco's fancy, but was in reality advanced as a legitimate possible solution. Eco's point is not merely that ideas advanced as science can be absurd, but that the result of these ideas is often appalling cruelty. Roberto himself reflects upon this, after Byrd has revealed the dog to him, thinking, "And was not he, Roberto, involved in this adventure in order one day to tell Mazarin and young Colbert how to populate the ships of France with tortured dogs?" (226).[2]

While Eco's presentation of Fr. Caspar does not continue to address the inhumane consequences which may result (and in the twentieth and twenty-first centuries most certainly have resulted) from unfettered scientific curiosity, the words and actions of the Jesuit certainly serve to call master narratives, such as religion and science, into serious question. Caspar, whom Roberto encounters while stranded upon the *Daphne*, is the most sophisticated religious thinker and the most advanced scientist Roberto has met. Although he also espouses the reasoning developed by the Knight of Malta, deducing longitudinal position from Biblical authority, he seeks to confirm these beliefs by means of scientific instrumentation. Throughout his education of Roberto, these two discourses constantly flow into one another. When Roberto, having been made to work assembling Caspar's instruments, protests that it is Sunday, Caspar replies that Roberto is not working. Rather, the strenuous labor is "an exercise of art, the noblest of all arts," and, since the work would lead to "an increase of knowledge of the great Book of Nature," it was "the same as meditating on the Sacred Scriptures, with which the Book of Nature is closely associated" (326).

The intermingling of discourses in Caspar's mind appears clearly from the moment he and Roberto meet; soon after their first encounter, Caspar confirms his belief in the Knight's theories, saying: "You guess now why the Islands of Solomon are so named? Solomon dixit: Cut baby in two. Solomon dixit: Cut Earth in two" (253). In fact, Caspar's primary reason for seeking the *Punto Fijo* is essentially religious, involving an elaborate consideration of the Great Flood, the metaphysical possibility and historical reality of which Caspar longs to prove. If he can find the 180th meridian, the line separating one day from another, he will have solved the question paramount in his mind: Where did God get all the water? His tortuous answer: God moved water from the "yesterday" side of the line to the "today" side, therefore not having to create or destroy matter, which actions would transgress His nature. Eco reinforces Caspar's ridiculousness by means of Caspar's own instruments. A slapstick, futile attempt to use his "Instrumentum Arcetricum," a device similar to Galileo's "celatone" (Sobel 26), to determine the *Daphne*'s longitude, results in Caspar soaked in oil, looking "like a piglet ready for the oven," and his spyglass broken (296). Caspar then resolves to reach the island, upon which is his "Speculum Melitensis," a device he believes will enable him to determine his position once and for all. Thus, he descends into the ocean in his aquatic bell, planning to walk to the island; he never reappears and pre-sumably drowns (339).

The cumulative effect of all these men, each so thoroughly convinced of the merits of his solution, each obsessed with longitude for his own peculiar reasons, is one of grim amusement. The reader is situated very much in line with the young Roberto — skeptical, but always willing to attempt to understand the men with whom he interacts. As each method is attempted, and fails, Roberto and the reader move toward a thorough-going doubt with respect to all these grand schemes, designed to organize and explain the world once and for all. Thus, Eco's novel effectively produces a postmodern sensibility in the reader, a sensibility which Eco associates strongly with the baroque aesthetic; he defines this aesthetic, returning in postmodernism, as "dynamic," an aesthetic which "induces the spectator [or, in this case, the reader] to shift his position continu-ously" (*Open* 7).[3]

Mason & Dixon on Land

Eco's masterful use of palimpsest and pastiche, as he layers and juxtaposes myriad discourses within his text to inspire a postmodern stance in the reader, is the most visible stylistic similarity linking Eco's novel with Pynchon's *Mason & Dixon*. Indeed, Pynchon's use of these techniques leads virtually every critic and commentator to make mention of it, as Charles Clerc has enumerated in his overview of the novel and its recep-tion, *Mason & Dixon & Pynchon*.[4] Pynchon's novel, more than Eco's, is a loose and baggy monster (to borrow the Jamesian phrase), filled with as many various discourses as Pynchon (and his sometime narrator, Cherry-coke) can plausibly — and not so plausibly — work into the text. Among the ceaselessly multiplying asides and digressions, the need to determine one's longitude recurs compulsively, as do specific references to the Lon-gitude Act and the men who sought to claim its prize. Rather than serv-ing as the central, controlling trope, as in Eco, questions of longitude here consistently feed into a variety of other issues, adding to the pleni-tude of *Mason & Dixon*.

For a novel dealing with eighteenth-century events taking place in such far-flung locales as Cape Town, St. Helena, England, Ireland, and North America, *Mason & Dixon* spends very little time describing the par-ticulars of ocean travel. As Clerc notes, "The narrator is highly selective in relating events. For example, all details of sea voyages between America and England, east or west, are entirely excluded. As readers, we are sud-denly just there, at one place or another" (88). Significant description of seagoing is offered only in the context of Mason and Dixon's abortive at-tempt to sail to Bencoolen to view the Transit. Aboard the *Seahorse*, they sail down the English Channel, past, as a sailor informs them, "the Tail of the Bolt . . . where the *Ramillies* went down but this year February, losing seven hundred Souls. They were in south-west Weather, the sailing-master could not see,— he gambl'd as to which Headland it was, mistaking the Bolt for Rame Head, and lost all" (34). This, the very first sentence describing Mason and Dixon at sea, immediately invokes a maritime disaster caused by a miscalculation of longitude — one very similar, in fact, to the Scilly Isle disaster of 1707, which is itself mentioned later in the novel (323). The master of the *Seahorse*, Capt. Smith, avoids this fate, "bending late and dutifully over the lunar-distance forms," which were the best but far from perfect means of guessing one's position available in 1761 (35). Unfortunately, Mason and Dixon's ship is set upon by the French, and their journey is thwarted.

Interestingly, although actual descriptions of sailing the world's oceans are scarce, nautical metaphors abound in passages of narrative dealing with Mason and Dixon's adventures and difficulties on land. When they reach Africa, having been redirected from Bencoolen to Cape Town, that continent is described as "the unreadable Map-scape of Africa" (58). They are barely ashore before encountering Bonk, an agent of the Dutch East India Company, who instructs them:

> From Guests of our community, our Hope is for no disruptions of any kind. As upon a ship at sea, we do things here in our own way,— we, the officers, and you, the passengers. What seems a solid Continent, stretching away Northward for thousands of miles, is in fact an Element with as little mercy as the Sea to our Backs, in which, to be immers'd is just as surely, and swiftly, to be lost, without hope of Salvation. (59)

Thus, the unknown (to them) lands into which Mason and Dixon must venture in the name of science and order are figured as at least as hazardous as the uncharted seas.[5] This is but the most overt of such nautical allusions; lesser references are common, such as when Benjamin Franklin's friend Dolly mocks Dixon with his magnetic compass as a "Sailor among the Iron Isles,— Circumferentor Swab," and warns him to "Beware" (301).

By novel's end, however, the likening of land to treacherous and deceiving seas, on which longitude cannot be known, has been turned on its head. First, in the interpolated captivity narrative of Eliza, the massive and intricate Jesuit Telegraph is described as having "an extensive Rigging, even more mysteriously complex than that of a Naval Ship," because "the whole Apparatus [of balloons and kites] must stand absolutely still in the Sky" (516). Those who are made to operate the machine are extensively trained, to be "sailors upon dry land" (516). Here, the image of a ship is invoked to demonstrate that the seas can be conquered through advanced technology; again, this obliquely recalls Harrison's Watch, which works as though perfectly still, even on the stormiest of seas.[6]

The reversal of the trope "land-as-sea" is complete by the time Mason and Dixon finally return east from drawing their Line in America. Asked by an old acquaintance what they plan to do next, Dixon replies, "Devise a way . . . to inscribe a Visto upon the Atlantick Sea" (712). Mason plays along, producing a plan for an

> "Arrangement of Anchors and Buoys, Lenses and Lanthorns, form-ing a perfect Line across the Ocean, all the way from the Delaware Bay to the Spanish Extremadura," — with the Solution to the Question of the Longitude thrown in as a sort of Bonus,— as, ex-actly at ev'ry Degree, might the Sea-Line, as upon a Fiduciary Scale for Navigators, be prominently mark'd, by a taller Beacon, or differ-ently color'd Lamp. (712)

Waxing poetic, they imagine a continuing broadening of the "Sea-Road of a thousand Leagues," until a trans-Atlantic city evolves, and the "Land-Speculation Industry" finally and inevitably moves in (712). Unknown lands, likened to uncharted seas, have given way to seas charted so thor-oughly that they might just as well be land. That the establishments named by Mason and Dixon here are entirely places of trade ("Wharves, Chandleries, Inns, Tobacco-Shops, Greengrocers' Stalls, Printers of News, Dens of Vice, Chapels for Repentance, Shops full of Souvenirs and Sweets" [712]) is hardly accidental. This vision of the completion of the cartographic project is overtly tied to notions of absolute expansion of capital. All local differences, even down to the very difference between land and sea, are emptied out, as every locale finally can be expressed in degrees, hours, minutes, seconds of longitude and latitude, just as capital renders all labor and all products ultimately expressible solely in terms of exchange value, in terms not of "different qualities, but . . . merely differ-ent quantities" (Marx 305).

What makes this grand and horrifying vision even more striking in the context of this essay is that the notion of deploying a string of vessels across the Atlantic actually *was* proffered as one possible solution to the problem of the longitude. In 1714, mathematician Humphrey Ditton suggested that a chain of stationary ships be deployed across the Atlantic, each of which would, at an agreed time, fire its cannon a mile into the air, providing a landmark for all vessels nearby. Of course, this plan was en-tirely unfeasible. Even if the ships could be held in place on the high seas, and even if the expense of manning such a fleet could be managed, a ship whose location was known would be utterly vulnerable to pirates or en-emy fleets. These obvious flaws notwithstanding, Ditton's was among the more realistic solutions offered to the Royal Society. As noted above, certain of these solutions play central roles in *The Island of the Day Before*. Pynchon's novel is not as obsessed with the issue; the only other appearance of the multitude of "solutions" generated in the hopes of fame and wealth in *Mason & Dixon* comes in an early flashback to the days when Mason was assistant to Astronomer Royal James Bradley, when one of his chores was to review the hundreds of letters that poured in. The Quest for the Longitude was, for many, "at least a chance to Rattle at length to a World that was ignoring them," leading them to write "Suggestions, Schemes, Rants, Sermons, full-length Books," which betrayed "unhealthy naivete," "an inner certainty that the Scheme would never work anyway," and occasionally "Insanity" (141).

Generally speaking, though, the specifics of the Quest for the Longitude do not interest Pynchon to the extent that they do Eco. Rather, the longitude is deployed in *Mason & Dixon* largely to reveal the Royal Society as being less a disinterested scientific body than an institution wielding political and financial power. That Pynchon's depiction has substantial basis in fact is made clear by the realities of Harrison's struggle to gain the reward that was his due, for years after he had perfected his watch. The Royal Society in Pynchon's novel, as in history, was dominated by "Lunarian Stalwarts" such as Waddington and Maskelyne, who could not conceive that the solution would lie anywhere other than in the stars (74). Mason, whose own ambitions lead him to resent the well-connected Maskelyne, specifically complains to Dixon of the new Astronomer Royal's "usage of poor Mr. Harrison, and his Chronometer, how contemptible. Few are his ideas, Lunarian is his one Faith, to plod is his entire Project" (437). In the end, of course, the Harrison Watch proves to be triumphant, much to Maskelyne's chagrin. Toward the end of the novel, the narrator relates: "Once more the Harrison Watch, like an Hungarian Vampire, despite the best efforts of good Lunarians upon the Board of Longitude to impale it, has risen upon brazen wings, in soft rhythmic percussion, to obsess [Maskelyne's] Position, his dwindling circle of Time remaining upon Earth, his very Reason" (728). Harrison, in *Mason & Dixon*, certainly seems to be the exception to the rule, in his ability finally to wrest victory from the recalcitrant Society. Throughout the novel, the Royal Society acts as an obscure and powerful force, willing to direct Mason and Dixon into combat with the French at the start of the novel, and able to deny Mason's claim to prize money for his refinements of Mayer's Lunar Tables at the end of his life (730, 762). Mason's widow, in the end, is in "utter dependence upon the Board of Longitude," and it is quite clear that this is an unfortunate state of affairs (761).

However, to claim that Pynchon's treatment of the Royal Society or of its Board of Longitude rises to the level of conspiracy theory, as seen in his earlier works, would be an overstatement. Concerning this aspect of *Mason & Dixon*, critical reaction is extremely varied. Charles Clerc, for example, insists that "there's no more than moderate concern with paranoia, a previously ubiquitous subject in Pynchon, and only a few conspiracy theories manage to sneak in" (91). On the other hand, Elizabeth Jane Wall Hinds argues that "Pynchon's trademark paranoia, the search for patterns in time and space evidenced in *The Crying of Lot 49*'s 1960s California and *Gravity's Rainbow*'s European 1940s runs as deep in *Mason & Dixon*'s culture of the Web, wherein the primary players, unsure of their place and agency, enact a late-twentieth-sensibility" (205). Without becoming involved too deeply in this argument, I would simply say that, although hints at deeper machinations abound in Pynchon's latest novel, usually in pub or coffee-house conversations, the sheer variety of possibilities offered regarding the nature of any supposed conspiracy renders this trope less central, less controlling than in his past work. The sheer proliferation of characters and subplots exceeds any one conspiracy. The question, then, becomes: What is the role of conspiracy here, and what, if not conspiracy, might be said to be the dominant logic of the narrative? With this question, we have navigated our way back to the central topic of this essay: the reasons for the return of the Quest for the Longitude, and the lessons about the nature of postmodernism we can derive from this return.

Conclusions: Postmodernism at Sea

In 1995, Dava Sobel published her eminently readable scientific history of John Harrison and the Longitude Problem, a short book which was made into a movie by the Arts and Entertainment network five years later. Within this brief period, Umberto Eco and Thomas Pynchon published monumental novels, treating this same era, and these same concerns, serving to contextualize the Quest for Longitude, to reveal science in all its historical messiness, alongside all the competing and conflicting discourses struggling for validation. As noted before, the cumulative effect of the extensive discursive pastiche at work in these novels is the deprivileging of scientific discourse; science is not the handmaiden of any objective Truth, but merely one voice among the panoply of voices produced by humanity, today just as centuries ago. Given all this, the question yet remains: Why does the centuries-old search for a reliable longitude so deeply fascinate two of the preeminent postmodern novelists writing today?

One very simple answer is suggested by Fredric Jameson's definition of postmodernism: postmodernism is the cultural logic of late — that is, global — capitalism. At present, capital is penetrating the farthest corners of the world, rearranging every society and culture with which it comes into contact. Therefore, the Quest for Longitude, crucial to the visualization of earth as a whole, suggests itself readily as a topic of concern in the postmodern moment. The charting of the earth's spaces in accordance with rational thought was never an innocent project, as both Pynchon and Eco demonstrate. Eco's protagonist, Roberto, embarks upon his quest not out of detached scientific curiosity, but as a result of the workings of political power, embodied in Cardinal Mazarin. Pynchon addresses this point even more overtly, generally through the voice of Jeremiah Dixon; Dixon, always the more uneasy of the pair, describes the company of men formed to mark the Line as "a single great Machine,— human muscle and stamina become but adjunct to the deeper realities of Steel that never needs Sharpening, never rusts" (443). As the Line progresses, extending toward the heart of the continent, Dixon becomes even more nervous, and more blunt, remarking to Mason, "We are Fools . . . We shouldn't be runnin' this Line" (478).

Related to this uneasy concern with the process of the re-creation of the world as a globe by reason and capital is another motivation, again suggested by Jameson's notions of the postmodern. According to Jameson, another common characteristic of postmodernism is nostalgia (*PM* xvii), that is, a fascination with "pastness" (*PM* 19). To Jameson, developing his ideas from the architectural notion of "historicism," postmodernism is thus characterized by "the random cannibalization of all the styles of the past," a situation which serves to preclude any real or effectual historical awareness on the part of the postmodern subject (*PM* 18). Therefore, it is less than surprising that Pynchon's, or Eco's — or anyone's — postmodern text is drawn to past events as its topic. Of course, what renders these texts remarkable is the extent to which they transcend the limitations diagnosed by Jameson. In a sense, Pynchon and Eco choose to *enact* nostalgia in order to parody its emptiness, or rather, in order to satirize its ineffectuality. Thus, they transcend the merely nostalgic in order to perform precisely the historical — and this, in a form supposedly most resistant to historical awareness: the postmodern narrative.

Closely related to the unprecedented atemporality of postmodern nostalgia is a new sort of space to which the postmodern body is constantly subject, one involving "the suppression of distance [. . .] and the relentless saturation of any remaining voids and empty places" (Jameson, "Cognitive" 351). The combination of these two aspects of the postmodern can thus be seen to lead to concerns such as those explored by Eco and Pynchon. In the early days of global commerce, the map still had blank spaces; information was not yet such a relentless, ubiquitous force. In fact, Pynchon alludes directly to this situation, describing a diabolical plot on the part of the sinister Jesuits (a favorite secret society of both Eco and Pynchon) to construct a telegraph and thus "enjoy their d----'d Marvel of instant Communication" (287). In a postmodern novel concerned with the time before today's "perceptual barrage of immediacy" ("Cognitive" 351), any such plan will inevitably appear ominous. Eco and Pynchon, rather than producing Luddite railings against such eventualities, however, explore the origins of the postmodern "crisis of space" in order to "invent a new space" (Jameson, "Regarding" 60).

This new space constructed within the saturated space of postmodernism by Eco's and Pynchon's texts specifically works to resolve another postmodern crisis identified by Jameson: the failure of cognitive mapping. Jameson develops his concept of cognitive mapping from Kevin Lynch's *The Image of the City,* in which Lynch asserts that "the alienated city is above all a space in which people are unable to map (in their minds) either their own positions or the urban totality in which they find themselves" (*PM* 51). Jameson suggests that the concept becomes even more useful when projected outward and applied to the global spaces which constitute the multinational capitalist system. Combined with Althusser's definition of ideology as "the representation of the subject's Imaginary relationship to his or her Real conditions of existence" (162), the cartographic problems identified by Lynch can be applied "in terms of social space" (*PM* 52). Jameson argues that present global realities are "inaccessible to any individual subjectivity or consciousness," and that the "incapacity to map spatially is . . . crippling to political experience" ("Cognitive" 353). Thus, the Quest for Longitude resonates strongly with the postmodern subject; the project of mapping terra incognita in the eighteenth century serves almost as an allegory for the twentieth-century desire to map "societas incognitas."

If this analysis is accurate, then the idea of cognitive mapping as an impossible task for the postmodern subject at the present moment explains more than just the fascination with longitude seen in Pynchon's and Eco's two most recent novels; further examination reveals cognitive mapping as a means of comprehending the authors' obsession with conspiracy, seen clearly in earlier works such as *The Crying of Lot 49* and *Foucault's Pendulum.* As a result of the postmodern inability accurately to situate oneself in relation to a society and an economy which have taken on global dimensions, attempts to comprehend the world generally result in conspiracy theories, "the poor person's cognitive mapping in the postmodern age" ("Cognitive" 356). Interestingly, in the novels concerned with longitude, the interest of both authors in conspiracies, though still readily visible, seems to be on the wane. As Michael Wood writes of *Mason & Dixon,* "No overarching conspiracy, or even the steady suspicion of one, unites the unravelled strands of this book" (128); rather, as noted above, Mason and Dixon's fears of hidden powers directing the events of their lives are generally expressed only during anxious, inebriated barroom chats. Eco, too, moves away from conspiratorial concerns; the only evil genius present throughout the book is Ferrante, Roberto's twin, who thwarts him at every turn, in Roberto's mind, but who does not actually exist.

Thus, these two works, so postmodern in so many respects, cannot simply be pigeon-holed as "postmodern" in any simple or negative sense. On the contrary, both works seem to be moving toward something beyond postmodernism, something at present only glimpsed amid the shifting narrative pastiche. While it is true, as Wood asserts, that *Mason & Dixon* (and the same may be said of *The Island of the Day Before*) can accurately be described as "unravelled" in one sense, in another sense both novels gesture towards some — not unity — but coherence of a sort not yet seen in postmodernist fiction. In these two works, Eco and Pynchon are performing the work advocated by Jameson in a 1986 interview with Anders Stephenson: Jameson encouraged a critique that would seek

> [t]o undo postmodernism homeopathically by the methods of postmodernism: to work at dissolving the pastiche by using all the instruments of pastiche itself, to reconquer some genuine historical sense by using the instruments of what I have called substitutes for history. (59)

Each novel achieves this new coherence and this new critique in its own particular way, Eco's negatively, as a warning against postmodern excesses, and Pynchon's positively, indicating new possibilities for making sense of the world. An examination of the latter parts of each novel illustrates these gestures.

Roberto's tale ends badly. Unlike his literary predecessor, Robinson Crusoe, in that Roberto is never rescued, Eco's protagonist gradually loses his grasp of reality, especially in the wake of Fr. Caspar's death. Instead of rejoicing at Roberto's salvation, the reader is "marooned in mirages of damnation, loss, futility, grief" (Kelly 3). Isolated, Roberto indulges more and more in the weaving of improbable tales of his evil twin Ferrante and his paramour, Lilia, both of whom have haunted him throughout his ordeal. But just as did his previous anxieties regarding the imaginary Ferrante, so too do these narratives get the best of him. Finally, in desperation, Roberto tells himself that Lilia has escaped Ferrante's deceptive clutches and been set miraculously adrift on the sea. Her helpless travels bring her, of course, to the "eastern shore of the Island of Solomon, that is to say, the side opposite the one of which the *Daphne* rode at anchor" (492). Though this tale is of Roberto's own making, constructed from fragments of Romances he has heard since he was a boy, Roberto permits himself to be seduced by it. Finally, his tale becomes so real to him that he acts on it. Though he knows he is not able to swim well enough to reach the island, he resolves to make the attempt anyway. There, the story discovered years later by Eco's narrator comes to an end. Thus, Eco's novel culminates in a warning against the seductions of an absolute abandonment of oneself to the postmodern condition, in which Truth is so utterly lost that one may as well act on the instigation of any one narrative as on that of any other, however improbable and dangerous. Turning his back completely on any good that the nascent Enlightenment may offer (his last act before abandoning the *Daphne* is to throw overboard all the clocks brought along by Caspar), Roberto recklessly retreats into self-indulgence, striking out for an absurd, unreachable, and nonexistent goal. In doing so, Roberto succumbs to the "universal abandon" identified as central to postmodernism by Andrew Ross, in his book of that name, and serves as a warning against such postmodern excess.

Pynchon's novel ends with a similar postmodern uncertainty, spending its last pages offering unsubstantiated hypotheses regarding the activities of Mason and Dixon in their later years, just as Eco refuses to confirm Roberto's death absolutely. One of the final confirmed events of *Mason & Dixon*, however, illustrates the positive project of Pynchon's novel. Dixon, having been appalled by the omnipresence of slavery throughout his travels, finally acts upon his unpopular convictions, seizing a slaveowner's whip and releasing the slaves he has been abusing (698–99). Slavery is one of the few constants in this novel, appearing wherever Mason and Dixon roam. In South Africa, "coiled behind all gazes the great Worm of Slavery" (248). In America, Dixon is appalled to find once again "this public Secret, this shameful Core," even though "America is the one place we should *not* have found [slaves]" (692–93). In the end, Dixon rebels against this ubiquitous injustice, striking out at an abusive slavedriver, and then fleeing the angry mob that quickly gathers.

This event functions as the overt culmination of a central project in *Mason & Dixon:* the recuperation of voices lost to the postmodern historical consciousness. Rather than merely offering a warning against the dangers of postmodern excess, Pynchon reminds the reader that our present condition was never, and is not now, inevitable. If we examine the origins of contemporary society carefully, we find a polyphony of discourses, among which we may pick those which most forcefully oppose today's brutalizing hegemony. Thus, we can see that Pynchon's "jokes and anachronisms are not incidental" (Wood 126). Rather, his allusions to such things as pizza, *feng shui,* and surf music (235, 229, 264) are reminders that our world has emerged from that inhabited by Mason and Dixon. As Hinds has asserted, "The pun and other wordplay bubble up out of the past [. . .] to challenge the falsely intellectual mapping urge strangling Mason and Dixon's compeers" (206). In fact, such humorous, superficially postmodern maneuvers also function to situate *Mason & Dixon* as a new sort of historical novel, overcoming postmodern nostalgia "without affect" (Jameson, *PM* xvii). Thus, Pynchon not only warns against postmodernism, but points toward a way to recuperate an historical awareness; he satisfies in a new way Lukács's insistence that true historical novelists must "see the specific qualities of their own age historically" (20). Pynchon's *Mason & Dixon* simultaneously enacts postmodern techniques, warns against the failings of postmodernism, and gestures toward possibilities beyond the limits of postmodernism.

The tremendous scientific undertaking in the seventeenth and eighteenth centuries to devise a technique for determining longitude accurately returns to us in the late twentieth century as a fictional tool for getting our own bearings, in the midst of postmodernity. These two novels, led to the topic of longitude due to its strong resonance with the postmodern sense of being adrift, without bearings, treat the quest in such a way as to point beyond the failings and confusions of postmodernism. Looking back hundreds of years, Eco and Pynchon unearth the multitude of voices which actually existed, revealing that our present world arose from a multiplicity of origins; there is no one narrative teleology which renders this world inevitable. And in revealing the complexity of the past, these authors derive the possibility of a future beyond the postmodern, offering, if not an absolute *Punto Fijo*, at least a few tentative meridians by which we might begin to orient ourselves.

Notes

[1] Pynchon plays this relationship between the two ways of studying the stars for bawdy laughs in *Mason & Dixon*, when Nevil Maskelyne points out to Mason that "Kepler said that Astrology is Astronomy's wanton little sister, who goes out and sells herself that Astronomy may keep her Virtue" (136). He goes on to wonder, "how many Steps may she [Astronomy] herself indeed already have taken into Compromise?" (136).

[2] Interestingly, Roberto discerns that "the dog suffered or experienced relief as the waves alternately jarred or lulled him" (225). The prevention of accurate timekeeping due to the sea's motion was, in fact, the very problem that Harrison's Watch had to overcome; thus, another connection is implied between the scientific and the mystical.

[3] It should be noted that Eco's own hermeneutic theories of literature shy away from the thoroughgoing relativism toward which postmodernism often tends. As Guy Raffa has noted, Eco's notion of the "model reader" deployed by the text serves to privilege some interpretations over others, to the extent that "Eco's hermeneutics have no place for the uncooperative or resisting reader" (168).

[4] Clerc himself, it should be noted, believes that, in *Mason & Dixon,* Pynchon's "technique is to go beyond pastiche" (109). I agree with this assessment, insofar as "pastiche" is defined, in the manner of Fredric Jameson, as a dead end, or "blank parody," as will be shown later in the essay (17).

[5] The reasons behind their excursion are also comically presented by Pynchon is his scene depicting the conversation of the British and the Cape clocks; the imposition of Western racination is shown as an undercutting of Western mastery, as the clocks converse, one even going so far as to declare that "Maskelyne is insane" (123).

[6] Further, this apparatus, controlled by the Jesuits and operated largely by "Telegraph Squads, elite teams of converted Chinese, drill'd, through Loyolan methods, to perform with split-second timing" could even be taken as symbolic of the technological and economic structure of our present "information age," the infrastructure of which is largely controlled by the West, but the construction and maintenance of which are heavily reliant upon the labor of the Third World, including in particular that of Asia (287).

Enlightenment Microhistories

6: Haunting and Hunting: Bodily Resurrection and the Occupation of History in Thomas Pynchon's *Mason & Dixon*

Justin M. Scott Coe

> *For if the dead rise not, then is not Christ raised:*
> *And if Christ be not raised, your faith is vain; ye are yet in your sins.*
> *Then they also which are fallen asleep in Christ are perished.*
> *If in this life only we have hope in Christ, we are of all men most*
> *miserable.*   — I Corinthians 15:16–19 (KJV)
>
> *These times are unfriendly toward Worlds alternative to this one.*
>   — Revd Cherrycoke, in *Mason & Dixon* (359)
>
> *What?*   — John Calvin, *Institutes*

JUST BEFORE PUBLICATION OF *Mason & Dixon*, Thomas Pynchon wrote a review of Gabriel Garcia Marquez's *Love in the Time of Cholera*, in which he says that "to assert the resurrection of the body [is] today as throughout history an unavoidably revolutionary idea" ("Heart's Eternal Vow").[1] In other essays, such as "Is it OK to be a Luddite?," Pynchon almost defensively asserts that he is not being "Insufficiently Serious" in his ecomiums to "violations of the laws of nature," especially "the big one, mortality itself." Again, in "The Deadly Sins/Sloth," he risks accusations of naïve historical nostalgia by recalling for us "the long-ago age of faith and miracle, when daily life really was the Holy Ghost visibly at work and time was a story, with a beginning, middle and end. Belief was intense, engagement deep and fatal." In "Luddite," Pynchon traces this age to just before the eighteenth century, the religious and historical setting for his 1997 novel *Mason & Dixon*, when there was a

> deep religious yearning for that earlier mythical time which had come to be known as the Age of Miracles. In ways more or less literal, folks in the 18th century believed that once upon a time all kinds of things had been possible which were no longer so. Giants, dragons, spells. The laws of nature had not been so strictly formu-

lated back then. What had once been true working magic had, by the Age of Reason, degenerated into mere machinery. As religion was being more and more secularized into Deism and nonbelief, the abiding human hunger for evidence of God and afterlife, for salvation — bodily resurrection, if possible — remained.[2]

This statement, though flippant on the surface, collapses the distinction between nostalgia and hard-core history by introducing the "deep religious yearning" that creates nostalgia for historical times and places, including a need to believe in future times and places that extend beyond the present life.[3] In other words, the influence of religion on history is not so much nostalgic as it is futuristic, much like the mystical influence of stars on one's life; history creates a desire for a future that makes the present worth living. In *Mason & Dixon*, Pynchon takes up this eighteenth century yearning and hunger for both history and "futurity," science and miracles — "bodily resurrection" in particular, the revolutionary desire to overcome ultimate history, or death — and demonstrates how they, in a religious nation, necessarily haunt and hunt each other.

Mason and Dixon are the two famous and very historical men who surveyed their Line straight into the American wilderness, using astronomical observation to navigate their way inland in order to settle a property dispute between the Penns and the Byrds. The formerly "divine" stars and spheres are used by Mason and Dixon, both men of science — an astronomer and a surveyor, respectively — as quantifiable points of reference that can be counted on to cross the zenith of the sky at an exact time when seen from a corresponding point on the globe, thus making it possible to locate one's coordinates, or position, on it. The Line's position in the story-line corresponds not just with a physical and latitudinal boundary but also with a metaphysical force which, combined with the similar lines of longitude, creates a rationally based but spiritually constrictive, all-encompassing grid of right-angled linearity. Zhang, a Chinese feng shui master who accompanies the surveyors, warns that such a project(ion) has serious spiritual implications, both dangerous and diabolical: "To mark a right Line upon the Earth is to inflict upon the Dragon's very Flesh, a sword-slash, a long, perfect scar [. . .] How can it pass unanswer'd? [. . .] Tho' Degrees of Longitude and Latitude in Name, yet in Earthly reality are they Channels mark'd for the transport of some unseen Influence . . ." (542, 547). The plot of the novel, therefore, paradoxically revolves around what the Line delineates, inclusively and exclusively, in the history of its own creation, incorporating the sources of its origination and recreating boundaries between the spiritual and physical realms that were just then being conceived at the time of its creation.

Though referring to *Gravity's Rainbow*, Molly Hite is equally correct in reference to *Mason & Dixon* when she states that "any comprehensive system for putting everything together is ultimately a variant on the Judeo-Christian myth because it appeals from a time-bound order to a transcendent perspective" (105). This appeal to transcendence in the eighteenth-century Age of Reason, however, did nothing to simplify the Christian belief in Jesus rising from the dead, which became an increasingly difficult proposition to put together with new scientific discoveries. Mason and Dixon, eighteenth-century "Men of Science," are, as Richard Poirier describes their twentieth-century counterparts in *Gravity's Rainbow*, "haunted, visited, obsessed and parano[id]" (160), caught unawares in the intellectual paradox of personal tensions between their faiths (Anglican and Quaker, respectively — the gamut of Anglo-American Calvinism) and their scientific longings, findings, measurements, and doubts. Calvin, in the book of the *Institutes* on the Lord's Supper, himself expresses this paradox in referring to the doubt of "hyperbolical doctors" who try to substantiate the transubstantiation of Christ's body in the Eucharist, and thus "transfigure Christ, after divesting him of his flesh, into a phantom" (7),[4] pulling his divinity down to our earthly level:

> [I]t is impossible for the mind of man to disentangle itself from the immensity of space, and ascend to Christ even above the heavens. What nature denied them, they attempted to gain by a noxious remedy. Remaining on the earth, they felt no need of a celestial proximity to Christ. Such was the necessity which impelled them to transfigure the body of Christ. (15)

Rev[d] Cherrycoke clearly takes up Calvin and goes even further to express this dilemma in another form of what he elsewhere calls his religion of "planet-wide Syncretism" (356), meshing these paradoxical impeti in a riff on the heretical necessity of an "Ascent to Christ" through doubt itself:

> The Ascent to Christ is a struggle thro' one heresy after another, River-wise up-country into a proliferation of Sects and Sects branching from Sects [. . .] into an Interior unmapp'd, a Realm of Doubt [. . .] the America of the Soul.
> Doubt is of the essence of Christ [. . .] The final pure Christ is pure uncertainty. He is become the central subjunctive fact of a Faith, that risks ev'rything upon one bodily Resurrection. . . . Wouldn't something less doubtable have done? a prophetic dream, a communication with a dead person? Some few tatters of evidence to wrap our poor naked spirits against the coldness of a World where Mortality and its Agents may bully their way, wherever they wish to go. . . . (511)

The Rev[d]'s "Ascent" into doubt, recasting the heretical "noxious remedy" of Calvin's scientific doctors, is continuously demonstrated in Mason and Dixon's act of surveying their various lines. They become less and less sure about their readings the further they progress south to South Africa, west into America's "Interior unmapp'd," north to Scotland and the Pole, and finally East to home and their own pasts. Their doubts range from wondering who they're working for, manipulated by agents of mortal power — the Royal Society, the East India Company, the Jesuits, Benjamin Franklin's business cronies — to their own desires in making the Line, variously described as a "Vector of Desire," a "Coaching-Road of Desire," or by its "Dimensions of Desire." The relationship of their desires with those of other interests acts, as Stefan Mattessich observes, "to fold desire and the object, the time that desire actualizes and the space that the object defines, into one textual . . . surface." The message of this space/time text is an "implication in a totality, an envelopment of the subject in a pre-personal 'depth' that, beneath or coterminous with geometric space, commits that subject to an existential immediacy irreducible to acts of comprehension" (par. 8–9). Thus, the Line that Mason and Dixon draw onto (and into) the continent's space in turn draws their desires, and especially Mason's desire for an afterlife, closer to the pre-personal depth of the age of faith, in which miracles such as bodily resurrection and the transfiguration of flesh into spirit are possibilities rather than mere theological necessities. The Line which the novel presents and represents is a communal desire bridging the corporeal and the spiritual in Western culture, housing within it, as we find at the end of the novel, a stellar message, or "text," that envelopes its subjects.[5]

Pynchon's message is a survey of history itself, and in particular our ability to survey time and space with the instrument of Christ's resurrection, aiming at an exposition of "the Despair at the Core of History,— and the Hope" that this promise offers. Rev[d] Cherrycoke explains to his listeners:

> As Savages commemorate their great Hunts with Dancing, so History is the Dance of our Hunt for Christ, and how we have far'd. If it is undeniably so that he rose from the Dead, then the Event is taken into History, and History is redeem'd from the service of Darkness,— with all the secular Consequences [sic], flowing from that one Event, design'd and will'd to occur. (75–76)

If this is compared to the passage from I Corinthians 15 cited at the beginning of this essay, we find that the Rev[d] follows the latter part of Paul's logic, in which history is based upon Christ rising from the dead, thus supporting the historical — even "secular" — necessity that the dead also must rise again. Mason, however, when reading further into this same chapter of Corinthians (after, appropriately, being thrown from his horse), discovers that Paul's "case for Resurrection" doesn't connect with Mason's eighteenth-century reading:

> Recovering from his Fall, Mason in fact spends his waking time reading I Corinthians, in particular Chapter 15, in which Paul's case for Resurrection proceeds from Human bodies to Animal Bodies, and thence to Bodies Celestial and Terrestrial, and the Glories proper to Each, to Verse 42,— "So also is the Resurrection of the Dead."
> "Excuse me?" Mason aloud. "'So also'? I don't see the Connection. I never did." (409)

Mason, in attempting to prove what Paul stipulates at the outset, that "the dead rise," stumbles on Paul's seemingly simple analogy between the human and the divine. At this point, ironically, when Mason's Enlightenment rationality cannot connect with the "Glories" proper to humanity, a voice from "Beyond" tells him he's thinking too much, a voice that is not "exactly" his deceased wife Rebekah's, but close enough for him to save it, along with "Lesser Revelations" that he has "gathered" throughout the novel, "in a small pile inside the Casket of his Hopes, against an unknown Sum, intended to purchase his Salvation" (409) — in other words, the bodily reunion with his beloved. Yet without the assured salvation of Christ's resurrection and return — if the miracle did not/will not take place, "in time" as it were — then history can no longer be the "Connection" between "Bodies Celestial and Terrestrial," nor the progression ("how we have far'd") to our cumulative, destined salvation; it merely serves as a record at "the service of Darkness,— with all the secular Consequences" thrown in. The hunt for Christ then becomes the "unknown Sum" of all Western hopes, not just for an afterlife, but for a history that is not in the service of darkness. Without that assurance, as Paul says, "we are of all men most miserable."

Mason, the ultimate representative of this misery (Revd Cherrycoke stipulates in the end that he may have died from "Melancholy"), spends most of the novel simultaneously seeking out and doubting a series of visitations from Rebekah. Her existence in the world to come, however, becomes increasingly questionable as the novel progresses — even though her visitations do not cease. Joel Black says, concerning the experience of the characters in *Gravity's Rainbow,* that "[a]s the evidence of Order in the world becomes increasingly rare . . . such Order nevertheless appears to them in increasing abundance" (244). This is explained, apropos of the eighteenth-century setting of *Mason & Dixon,* by Leo Braudy: "As the order of God loses explanatory force, there arises a longing for other orders . . . Before the Renaissance, God was the only Creator. With the eighteenth century he became one of many" (622). By setting his later novel within this time period, Pynchon calls attention to the shift from a God-oriented to what Kenneth Burke would call a multi-"god-termed" universe (106 passim), where any signifier of power and primacy can re-place — and therefore replicate — the significance of God and His pow-ers. The result is that Mason is left attempting to find, in whatever order it might exist, any assurance about the possibility of life-after-death. His investigation begins early in the novel with his question to the seemingly miraculous anthropomorphic Learned English Dog, or "L.E.D.," who sings and dances and also carries on extensive philosophical conversations. Mason hesitantly asks it, "Have you a soul,— that is, are you a human Spirit, re-incarnate as a Dog?" The L.E.D. replies by comparing Mason's question to certain oriental "*religious Puzzles* known as *Koan*," for which it is "necessary for the Seeker to meditate upon the *Koan* until driven to a state of holy Insanity" when the answer comes up "Mu!" (a la "moot"). The L.E.D. then redirects Mason's search onto a more reasonable path: "But please do not come to the Learned English Dog if it's religious Comfort you're after. I may be preaeternatural, but I am not supernatu-ral. 'Tis the Age of Reason, rrrf?" Instead, Mason is directed to rely on "Provisions for Survival in a World less fantastick" (22, his emphases).

The L.E.D.'s off-putting message can be read through the "raffish Gleam in its eye" (18),[6] and his rendition of his and his kind's evolution is *thoroughly* fantastic, employing the Scheherazade survival motif by "nightly delaying the Blades of our Masters by telling back to them tales of their humanity" (22). Significantly, this format had already been intro-duced earlier as a condition for Cherrycoke's own storytelling, that "as long as he can keep the children amus'd, he may remain,— too much evidence of Juvenile Rampage at the wrong moment, however, and Boppo! 'twill be Out the Door with him, where waits the Winter's Block and Blade" (6–7). The opening setting of both science and storytelling is a mode of survival "in a World less fantastick," a world, ironically, that requires fantasy for that very survival, or at least for one's sanity. Followed logically, myth and science must therefore occupy this same plane of sur-vival, for which the messages from the L.E.D. (both on power line and on paw) and from Rev[d] Cherrycoke, on whom the novel's tale relies for its own survival, are both "but an extreme Expression of this Process" (22).

Building upon this early exchange, Pynchon sets up a controlling dia-lectic within the novel between the different worlds of scientific reality and mythical fantasy, another version of the troubled Christian dichotomy between body and spirit. Dialectic may not be the correct term here, however, because, in proper Pynchonian fashion, the worlds are increas-ingly commingled to the extent that it is hard in most passages to tell the difference between the real historical experience of Mason and Dixon and the various fantastic worlds that swirl at their side. In Hite's terms, Pynchon is again "undermining the stability of that apparently rigid entity, the past" (139). Pynchon employs a variety of methods to destabilize a chronological, linear rendering of history so that a space is opened for events and people which exist within the outmoded or forgotten structures, both religious and historical, of past times. There is, in a sense, an occupation of the space of history in the novel by those left out of a chronological, secular history which does not include the "Event" of Christ's resurrection (via bread and/or flesh). Elizabeth Jane Wall Hinds has explored already one such method, anachronism, which works to destabilize the text and erase lines.[7] But as she sees slippage between the eighteenth and twentieth centuries as primary, I suggest that even more so is the extreme tangle of corporal and spiritual "Lines," as is explained in the prefatory passage to chapter 35 from the Rev^d's fictitious book, entitled *Christ and History:* "History is not Chronology," but rather "a great disorderly Tangle of Lines, long and short, weak and strong, vanishing into the Mnemonick Deep, with only their Destination in common" (349). This tangle of lines cuts across not only chronology but also the boundary that was supposed to exist between sacred and secular history.

The destabilization begins by what may be called a transubstantiation of historical moments and personal destinies. While discussing the possible plots in the Royal Society involving the East India Company, Mason and Dixon allude to a haunting feeling they've had since their disastrous encounter on the Seahorse with the French Frigate Defiant which made them turn back from their first outing to South Africa. This horrific moment of irrational violence causes them to doubt not only their scientific but also their personal and religious eschatologies. Mason floats two possible, and equally fantastic, explanations: one, that they mistakenly acquired "a piece of someone else's History," or, two, that there may be "no single Destiny" but an "unredeemable" teleological culmination in the choices one makes, which is "reduc'd" to one's destiny as light through a lens reduces a "vast Field of View [. . .] to a single Point" (44–45). Revd Cherrycoke describes this experience as "patently a warning to the Astronomers, from Beyond. Tho' men of Science, both now confess'd to older and more Earthly Certainties" (47), namely the immediacy and irrationality of their original plan, and a need for contingencies in order to placate the "Beyond" that seemed to be out to get them. But this Beyond is exactly (if vaguely) what the Rev^d describes as the "Destination" of history's tangled lines, and the moment seems an inverse replication of Paul's encounter on the Road to Damascus, as well as his assertion in the same chapter of Corinthians that "we shall all be changed, In a moment, in the twinkling of an eye" (vs. 51–52). The event of Christ's resurrection can be replaced by other events, and subsequent events flowing from them may be less salvational and more horrific "secular Consquences [. . .] design'd and will'd to occur."

Mason and Dixon are thus forced by such a momentous warning from Beyond to confess to *less* earthly certainties concerning these disparate plots they seem to be experiencing simultaneous to their own:

> "Yes, yes, upon the face of it, quite straightforward, isn't it? [Mason says] . . . And yet, d'ye not feel sometimes that ev'rything since the Fight at sea has been,— not a Dream, yet. . ."
>
> "Aye. As if we're Lodgers inside someone else's Fate, whilst belonging quite someplace else . . .?"
>
> "Nothing's as immediate as it was. . . . We might have died then, after all, and gone on as Ghosts. Haunting this place, waiting to materialize,— perhaps just at the moment of the Transit, the moment the Planet herself becomes Solid. . . ." (75)

This moment, we find out near the end of the book through Dixon's trip to the Earth's hollow center, is when the volume of the planet will be known (thanks to their own Parallax of Venus measurements taken before and after drawing the Line) and the creatures and space below will disappear as a result of scientific measurement. Mason and Dixon's disastrous moment behind them prefigures the one before, and they at present haunt their own history, both in the past and future, neither of which is fully theirs. History thus doubles as the haunting possibility of both a literal (i.e. scientific) future as well as a mythical (i.e. storied) past, with the former hunting the latter into nonexistence. And both are archetypically prefigured in the haunting of (and "Hunt for") Christ, who died but rose again, and therefore will, one hopes, reappear at the appropriate salvatory and/or apocalyptic moment in history, incorporating all destinies. It seems that Pynchon, in surveying the intrusion of Western history into the American continent in the form of the Line, is assessing in terms of this doctrine the definite secular consequences of the eighteenth century's loss of faith as a loss of any salvational destiny whatsoever.

One secular consequence of the conjunction between belief and doubt is that the callings or beckonings from the Beyond that Mason is continually experiencing are matched with revelations that there is not only no Beyond but also a profound lack where it should be. This revealing absence is illustrated in Mason's visit on St. Helena to Jenkin's Ear Museum,[8] which begins with him looking at a miniature of a ship named *Rebecca* about to be boarded. The scene forms a miniature of his transformation at the moment of his own "metaphysickal escape" at sea, as if "the Event [was] not yet 'reduc'd to certainty.'" This moment he terms a "Dispensation," but an ironic one which throws him out of his certainty (for a reunion, or boarding, of the real Rebekah), away from "his last morning of Immortality" into the profound New World of doubt — "the America of the Soul." He is forced to face the realization that his own line, incorporating his life, his lineage, his science, and his faith, will never intercept Rebekah, that she is irredeemably lost, at least to his well-worn eschatology of other-worldly existence. The Ear itself redoubles this ironic play on this now existential Dispensation,[9] signifying "the Void" as "the very anti-Oracle," devouring "human speech" with a "great Hunger, that never abates." Mason, caught up in "the Metaphysicks of the Moment," faces the real possibility that all his longings for an after-life, for the Christian promise of history as a redemptive enterprise with a teleological and reunifying resolution on the other side, is merely a *"Calling into a Void"* (emphasis in original) of a divine ear well-practiced at "revealing nothing, as it absorbs ev'rything. One kneels and begs, one is humiliated, one crawls on" (177–79).

This less-than-hopeful "miracle" is among many Mason and Dixon witness in South Africa and on St. Helena which, combined, represent a condensed eighteenth-century version of *Gravity's Rainbow*'s European "death culture" (Hume 89) and its communication, through colonial forays, into "other worlds." The town of St. Helena symbolizes the madness and darkness of the island's past:

> A very small town clings to the edge of an interior that must be reckoned part of the Other World. No change here is gradual,— events arrive suddenly. All distances are vast. The Wind brutal and pure, is there for its own reasons, and human life, any life, counts for close to nought. (107)

The island is described as a lost Paradise, beholden to the Serpent, the "great Worm of Slavery" (147) that "Rules the Island, whose ancient Curse and secret Name, is Disobedience" (135). The island, a "conscious Creature" in its own right, we later find is exclusively the creation of the East India Company, down to the very thoughts and dreams therein, which offer "the only Choices within one's Control, those between Persistence and Surrender. Within their first week upon the Island, all visitors have this Dream" (108). It is "the visible and torn Remnant of a Sub-History unwitness'd" (162), as described by its European occupant (and Mason's erstwhile friend) Maskelyne, an astronomer who is doing observations there when Mason arrives. Maskelyne's ravings create the impression of a land blighted by divine retribution: "Aahckk! Mason, can y' not feel it? This place! This great Ruin,— haunted . . . an Obstinate Spectre,— an ancient Crime,— none here will ever escape it." Yet Maskelyne's awareness of St. Helena's diabolical and contrived past is itself cast into doubt by his own ambiguous semi-diabolical "place" on this fallen topos, not only as the soon-to-be Royal Astronomer (which, but for his low social status, would have been Mason's post) but also as "the pure type of one who would transcend the Earth,— making him, for Mason, a walking cautionary Tale" (128–34). We are left uncertain with the impure knowledge of whether this European-contrived nether-kingdom is an embodiment or a fantasy of moral corruption, due to the unreliability of its translation into Christian archetypes by its seemingly demented Adamlike occupant.

Later, when Dixon visits the East India Company Lodge in South Africa, he witnesses yet another "fallen" topos in a classic Pynchonian scene of European debauchery. The Dutch sado-masochism, represented first by the Vroom women's attempts at seducing Mason (through multiple bodice-rippings and invitations to spank) for the purpose of reproducing slaves, is further accentuated in a similarly contrived orgy — described as a ritualistic opportunity to transcend societal norms and delineations — where "Lust is schedul'd, splashing outside the Church-drawn boundaries of marriage, as across racial lines." The slave women serve as a "dangerously beautiful Extrusion of everything these white brothers, seeking Communion, cannot afford to contain" (151). The search for transcendence in Western history is transmogrified into a diabolical Christian Eucharistic "service." There is even a Beyond, a horrific "one Room further" in which any bounds of decency or sympathy are broken in the dark, morally and topographically ambiguous space of miraculous ecstasy and persecution, ever attempting to connect the "Bodies Celestial and Terrestrial" of which Paul spoke through pain:

> The Penetralia of the lodge are thus, even to those employed there, a region without a map. Anything may be there. Perhaps miracles are still possible,— both evil miracles, such as occur when excesses of Ill Treatment are transform'd to Joy,— quite common in this Era,— and the reverse, when excesses of Well-being at length bring on Anguish no less painful for being metaphysickal,— Good Miracles. (151)

This miraculous dichotomy with reversed attributes is again represented in the crucificial reproduction of the Black Hole of Calcutta, which Pynchon calls "some Zero-Point of history" — some colonial mythic touch-stone for the resultant sado-masochistic fantasy which we call modern history — literally, a "Horror," which, as the Rev[d] explains, "If one did not wish to suffer [it] directly [. . .] one might either transcend it spiritually, or eroticize it carnally" (152–53).

The first section of the novel sets up not just the moral but the mortal, carnal scene on which the West's search for transcendence ends up playing its dirty games. Transcendence is but one option in relation to the horror of sexual and racial slavery, the other following a debauched Eros into carnality on a mass scale, something Pynchon doesn't dismiss out of hand but lifts up to equal status with spiritual transcendence. Mixed together in the metaphoric Hole, one has an analogue to the Anubis orgy in *Gravity's Rainbow*, a communal apocalyptic orgasm, "some single slow warm Explosion," yet with heightened overtones of the terminal suffocation. The "Moral" of the Hole (which is all the Rev[d] Cherrycoke recounts to his listeners) is "a small Metaphor of this continental Coercion [. . .] practis'd in Reverse" (153), a recreational representation of victimhood writ large, communicating the necessity of employing "evil miracles" such as the Black Hole of Calcutta to "Reverse" the implication of slavery on those who inflict it. The denial of a transcendent end is not so much a barrier but instead a Zone in and of itself through which Mason enters personally the sexualized miasma of Western culture's love affair with death. In South Africa and on St. Helena, just like in the German-controlled Sudwest Africa of *V*.'s "Mondaugen's Story," Pynchon "creates a space in which Pynchon can stage 'orgies of the signifier,' which, in analogy, 'take the place' of meaning, creating fetish countries of increasing complexity." In like manner, here as in his earlier work, "Pynchon follows the sexually dead body into its equally dead culture," thus representing "psychic and cultural colonization" (Berressem 72). Mason's encounters with Rebekah on St. Helena, "if sexual, were profoundly like nothing he knew," permeated as they were by the West's colonization of his sex life, a colonization that doesn't quite take the place of meaning but instead takes place within the very meaning of the miraculous. Thus, colonization itself is permeated by miraculous interventions of both the evil and good kinds. Mason's experience, though thoroughly mediated by the "many-Lens'd Rebekah," is also mediated by other "mediating instruments" which turn out to be mutations of Christian liturgical practice — namely by commerce, slavery, and the contrived morality of the gallows (195).

The defining frame of the South African scene, concentrically replicating Mason and Dixon's first meeting at a London hanging and defining the attributes of all their other loci, is the gallows and slavery, which in turn frame Pynchon's overarching concern with international human commerce, "for Commerce without Slavery is unthinkable, whilst Slavery must ever include, as an essential Term, the Gallows,— Slavery without the Gallows being as hollow and Waste a Proceeding, as a Crusade without a Cross" (108). The Christian reference, though on the surface only a simile (like Paul's), is remarkably apt when the imagery of crucifixion as a rallying cry of international military action is superimposed upon the institution of slave commerce. Death as but another form of Christian commerce — Calvin's "diabolical" exchange of flesh for spirit and vice versa — works as a potent symbol, and part of its potency is the reassurance that it is a redemptive death one seeks to buy, one which guarantees to crusader and trader alike the gift of eternal life. Instead of redemption, what is created is, as Mason finds when reflecting on South Africa's slavery, a "Collective Ghost" incorporating all the "Wrongs" inflicted on the Slaves and, "propitiated, Day to Day, via the Company's merciless Priesthoods," which eventually "brings all but the hardiest souls sooner or later to consider the Primary Questions more or less undiluted," leading to as high a suicide rate among Whites as Blacks (68–69).

The divine carnality that these southern regions represent is consistently replicated in Pynchon's use of the Eucharist miracle to embody the fear of earthly violence entering, or even originating from, the other side. The intelligences that exist in the realm of "death transfigured" in *Gravity's Rainbow* are given liturgical agency through the most sacred and prophetic (for Western history) of Christian rites — the literal transfiguration of bread into flesh. Mason's disgust with sheep in South Africa is likened to the Eucharist, which in turn connects with his relationship to his father, a baker. This communal element is shared by the novel's main characters, including Revd Cherrycoke (driven out of England by his father), who writes empathetically in his journal: "Lamb of God, Eucharist of bread,— what Mr. Mason could not bear, were the very odors of Blood-Sacrifice and Transsubstantiation, the constant element in all being the Oven, the Altar wherebefore his Father presided" (86).[10] As Calvin preached, God, by serving up Christ as a "spiritual feast," "performs the office of provident parent" (1) — that is, for everyone except the son being sacrificed. The connecting symbols of son-sacrifice and the oven are not only symbolic of Europe's genocidal bent, but also suggests personal as well as religious sources for the desires which lead to death-commerce. The Rev^d is later more explicit about the dubious efficacy of the Lord's Supper as a "good Miracle," fearing that it might symbolize instead "some ultimate Carnality":

> The question I cannot resolve is whether real Flesh and real Blood are themselves, in turn, further symbolick,— either of some mystickal Body of Christ, in which participants in the Lord's Supper all somehow,— mystickally, to be sure,— become One,— or of a terrible Opposite . . . some ultimate Carnality, some way of finally belonging to the doom'd World that cannot be undone,— a condition, I now confess, I once roam'd the Earth believing myself to be seeking, all but asphyxiated in a darkling innocence which later Generations may no longer fully imagine. (386)

The reason later generations might miss this is because, as many critics suggest in reference to *Gravity's Rainbow*, the "Christian structure of crucifixion" has given way to "something more frighteningly inclusive," a terrible Opposite melding Synthesis and Control into a "dangerous resurrection," one that leads not to an afterlife, but to "death transfigured" (Hume 91–92; Poirier 157). This is what Calvin feared would happen to Christ if the mind attempted to rise above the heavens and entangle Christ's divinity in the earth-bound immensity of space. The Rev^d, here, visiting this question of trans- or consubstantiation as pertaining to a more-than-academic situation, sees in the blood-rite of Christ a threatening transcendent carnality of Europe, a mutation of Western cultural archetypes and its instruments, including ovens and altars and scientists, into divine accoutrements, all performing very real "Blood-Sacrifice."

The transformation of bread to flesh is intertwined with the equally miraculous transubstantiation of matter to measurement, and from starlight to message. Venus's Transit is a symbol of the Enlightenment reversal or inversion of a corporeal and mythic "body," when "all shall suddenly reverse" as the "Goddess descended from light to Matter" (92). What actually occurs is a double transformation from light to matter to the measurement of the Parallax's Arc, as Dixon later explains to the already thoroughly corrupted Vroom sisters: "One day, someone sitting in a room will succeed in reducing all the Observations, from all 'round the World, to a simple number of Seconds, and tenths of a Second, of Arc,— and that will be the Parallax" (93). This transformation into what Pynchon calls "Mathesis" is what functions as the ultimate hope of transcendence as expressed by Maskelyne, all the stars making up "some single gigantick Equation [. . .] to us unreadable, incalculable" (134). DePugh, the Rev^d's academic listener who "has shown an early aptitude for figures," earlier describes such encoding as the Parallax's "Vector of Desire," whereby, as the Rev^d attempts to describe, "the Telescope, in mysterious Wise, were transporting us safely thro' all the dangers of the awesome Gulf of Sky, out to the Object we wish to examine" (96). Such a transport, Dixon later explains to Mason, is exactly the same as the Quaker quietist doctrine requiring one "to sit quietly" for the "Working of the Spirit," which then abates, and so "another such Visit soon becomes necessary": "'tis all Desire,— and Desire, but Embodiment, in the World, of what Quakers have understood as Grace" (101). Though Mason immediately and comically makes failed attempts at this direct experience of Christ ("he keeps jumping up, to turn and interrupt Dixon, who is trying to do the same, with news of his Progress"), Mason later in the book cannot help but suffer from this doubled stellar and spiritual phenomenon, feeling himself constantly projected into the stars until he can no longer stand to look up at them.[11] The calculations made by the astronomers and those sitting in a room are to transform, both scientifically and religiously, with the help of the stars, the nature of earth-knowledge, but it does nothing to change the actual message of the stars, which remains until the end unreadable. If the mantras of Pynchon's previous novels were any help — V.'s "Stay cool, but care" and *Gravity's Rainbow*'s "proverbs for paranoids" — Mason and Dixon's repeated claim that "as above, so below" both establishes and destabilizes the grasp their numbers have on the earth. Thus begins the reconfiguration of myth, through the filling in of the earth with matter, to the architectonics of information, which again become light in the form of electrical grids of L.E.D. and fiber-optics, and (as Hinds and others point out) the Internet.

Luckily for the surveyors, and especially for Mason, they never are quite able to attain this ultimate and destructive knowledge. Mason's personal desire to eventually earn his place in the Royal Society's "purer region, where Mathesis should rule" is foiled by his father's lineage (one "line" failing another), and he is packed off once again, this time to Scotland to observe the second Transit of Venus, forced to continue his tedious exposure to "Stars and Mud" (724). On the way back from Scotland, he experiences the dangerous mixture of these motifs in a ship's hold where the fat of dripping and sliding sheep carcasses creates a frictionless floor, "Mason instantly recognizing the same proximity to pure Equations of Motion as he felt observing Stars and Planets in empty Space" (736). The proximity of this farcical situation to the blood sacrament of the Eucharist is not lost on the reader, nor is the realm of the Beyond to which such rites give access. The sacrificial sheep themselves occupy "a category beyond Dead, in its pointless Humiliation, its superfluous Defeat," all performing a very different but comparable "Dance of our Hunt for Christ" in their zombie-like "Ball of the Dead." The lambs also have their afterlife, a further "Abasement" (they are later thrown in the sea during a food riot) whose symbolic destiny, beyond usefulness or liturgical value is, like Mason's, unclear (735–37). This image can be compared with an earlier reference to the Eucharist by Armand, the Line-drawing expedition's chef, in which he describes Mason and Dixon's time in America as, literally and symbolically, sandwiched between the two Transits of Venus: "Disks of secular Bread, enclosing whilst concealing slices of real Flesh, yet a-sop with Blood, under the earthly guise of British Beef, all,— but for the Species of course,— Consubstantiate, thus . . . the Sandwich, Eucharist of this our Age" (367).

Finally, Mason's vision of the occupation of the eleven days by a band of pygmies and then by himself is another reversed religious metaphor, a possible redemptive inversion of the sadomasochistic Black Hole. The metaphor does not offer the possibility of freedom or liberation or retribution, but instead illustrates the metaphysical implications released once Time is *"denied its freedom to elapse"* (194, emphasis in original), becoming occupied by the chronological colonization of calendar reform. In

Mason and Dixon's field journals (ominously printed by "an ingenious Jesuit device") Revd Cherrycoke finds that cycles of eleven day intervals occur repeatedly, "suggesting," as he says, "a hidden Root common to all [. . .] the famous Eleven Missing Days of the Calendar Reform of '52" (554). Mason earlier in a frontier bar drunkenly refers to this usurpation of time, offering to the revelers a fantastic story about these outlawed days which were taken over by a band of Pygmies who have since set up plantations of their own in Time, "eleven days to the Tick behind us." The "more curious" Pygmies are "ever pursuing us, as might Historians of Times not yet come," and Mr. Hailstone's reported sighting of one Mason interprets as a mutual experience: "You haunted each other" (196–97). We are to these dwarfed historians, he stipulates, "a mystery Nation [. . .] a vast Hive of Ghosts not quite vanish'd into Futurity" (196). The inhabitants of both worlds are temporalized only in the relationship between being faithful and being followed, which coalesce in the sense of being haunted and hunted, chased by strange beings across the border of a doubly occupied time.

Mason later gives Dixon a dubious account of how he himself entered the vortex of the missing eleven days in 1752, transforming their fictive space in the novel from a drunken, "fantastick" fable (with dwarves, et al.) to a temporal anomaly which attaches itself to the present moment, both narrated in the story of the Line and more abstractly considered: "a slowly rotating Loop, or if you like, Vortex, of eleven days, tangent to the Linear Path of what we imagine as Ordinary Time, but excluded from it, and repeating itself,— without end" (555). This vortex of unanswered insult visits the "Ordinary Time" of the novel repeatedly as a periodic occupation of the present by the forgotten, cut-off past. Eliminated by the scientific elites, this time/space/place thus comes to haunt, by its very non-linearity, the further scientific act of line-making. What's more, within this vortex Mason finds "wild Creatures" who subsided into the missing days of magic possibility because, like the L.E.D., they were "ownerless" and thus "disconnected as well from calendars" (557). In contrast, Mason does not find Bradley, the deceased Royal Society chief and his mentor, probably because the "unexpected depth of his complicity in an Enterprise so passionately fear'd and hated by most of the People" — namely the Calendar Reform — places him firmly in the scientific elite (or, to use religious terminology, the Elect), who seem not privy to the Time they exorcised and thus are not among those who are able to haunt (and hunt others in) the alternate history of the eleven days. These days are further claimed for the passed-over by "the sensible Residue of Sin that haunted the place,— of a Gravity, withal, unconfronted, unaton'd for," harkening back to the centrifugal significance of gravity in *Gravity's Rainbow*.[12]

In this propitious, in-between-life state, Mason seeks ancient wisdom on the Bodleian Library's "Secret Shelves, where [normally] none but the Elect may penetrate." He is haunted there, too, by "something I never saw," rummaging with him in the "ancient Leaves" and seemingly trying to communicate, saved from this fearful yet hoped for encounter by the most lowly, yet sacramental, desire of all — hunger (think Jenkin's Ear). He rushes into streets endlessly moonlit, filled with "all that Reason would deny," a veritable "Carnival of Fear" with which he "thrill'd" in a fantasy of flight and moral anarchy, to the point that he wishes to join in and make "a Druidical Bonfire of the Bodleian." But, falling short of "Human Prey," his "Evil Appetite" falls away to melancholy, and he finds when returning to the Bodleian that he is "Exil'd from the Knowledge" by a "Barrier invisible," a silent suggestion of "Spiritual Unease":

> I receiv'd, tho' did not altogether hear, from somewhere, a distinct Message that the Keys and Seals of Gnosis within were too danger-ous for me. That I must hold out for the Promises of Holy Scripture, and forget about the Texts I imagin'd I'd seen. (560)

Put together, Mason's fantastic adventure exercises the cohabitation of corporeal hunger and spiritual faith in the Eucharist, a need for certainty that both cannot and cannot help but cross the Line into the realm of secret knowledge, through cannibalistic consumption as represented by the West's colonial conquests of meaning, yet must ever reside in a mel-ancholic hope for a promised salvation, even without "the Keys and Seals of Gnosis" to connect him to anything beyond. As a result, after hearing this message, Mason himself becomes the literal embodiment of the carnal/transcendent conjunction, briefly "Meditating upon bodily Resur-rection," and then resurrecting his paunch in a "Bacchic interlude" (which was too good to recount), thus renouncing the gnostic gleam of knowledge for the L.E.D.'s "raffish gleam," the naïve scriptural promise of the integrity and the necessity of the flesh.[13] The disconnected and dispossessed, like Mason, are left to take care of their bodies and not expect any consumption beyond simple nourishment and promises. The typically Christian moral to Mason's travels that he tells Dixon is that his life, like the eleven days, will end and he (paunch and all) "will be to-gether again" with Rebekah (560–61).

Simplistic as the end of this tale is, the stipulated vortex offers a glimpse of how the lines of the past and the future, and the corporeal and the spiritual, can intertwine. Reflecting on this lost chance at Gnosis, which Mason describes as lying in the center of the vortex, he felt "ob-lig'd" to aim across it "a bit upstream, or toward the Past" — Pynchon's Age of Miracles. Instead he becomes aware at that moment that the ghostly presences he'd been sensing at the corners of his vision were "haunting me not from the past but from the Future," that is, from the day ahead of the Eleven Days to which the rest of humanity had already jumped. Whether Mason learned his lesson, or whether he missed his chance, his exploration of the vortex outside of ordinary time sharpens his and Dixon's ambivalent existence in the present, whose only function serves, as with the Eucharistic sandwich, to define an unknown, unsubstantiated knowledge at the center of their tale's spinning: "None of this may be about either you or me. Our story may lie rather behind and ahead, and only with the Transits of Venus, never here in the Present, upon the Line, whose true Drama belongs to others" — namely we Americans. Mason fears that he has "merely dream'd it, even this very moment, Dixon, which I know is real. . . ." (610). His fear is palpable in that his experience in the eleven days, from which he drew his scriptural moral of redemption and reunion, itself might be a dream (as Dixon suspects), and thus, like the biblical myths, devoid of true flesh-like experience and therefore suspect, its promises vain. For Mason's troubled religious sensibility, if miraculous events are not allowed to occur, then reality becomes ever more tenuous. Zhang calls this dilemma the "failure of perfect Return, that haunts all for whom Time elapses" (629).[14]

The pygmies later reappear in Dixon's equally dubious account of his travels to the Inner Earth, and identify themselves in response to Dixon's questioning eerily reminiscent of *Gravity's Rainbow* — "They are We." But this Zone of seeming equivalency never reached in *Gravity's Rainbow* is exceedingly tenuous, and "will vanish" when the earth is "calculated inescapably at last," forcing them "to seek another Space," perhaps "thy own Surface." They ask Dixon if he truly wishes to "bet ev'rything upon the Body? — this Body?," a question he leaves "in abeyance" (741–42). Outside of these opportunities of transcendence and resurrection, we are left with the ambiguity of the novel's tale-telling, mediated by Mason and Dixon's "Boswell," the Revd Cherrycoke, who, like the real Boswell Mason meets in Scotland, is "a sort of Shadow ever in the Room who has haunted you, preserving your ev'ry spoken remark" (747). Yet beyond this is Revd Cherrycoke's own Boswell, or Boswells, the legion of those dispossessed by Time and other desacralizing measurements, who haunt the "Room" of his storytelling, caught in the "Hook of Night" during which he tells his story — significantly, a night near the Advent:

> When the Hook of Night is well set [. . .] slowly into the Room begin to walk the Black servants, the Indian poor, the Irish runaways, the Chinese Sailors, the overflow'd from the mad Hospital, all unchosen Philadelphia [. . .]. They bring their Scars, their Pox-pitted Cheeks, their Burdens and Losses, their feverish Eyes, their proud

fellowship in a Mobility that is to be, whose shape none inside this
House may know. (759)

The procession of Mobility, of the dispossessed, in which Mason can
grudgingly claim fellowship, come to haunt the room once reserved
for Mathesis and European sadomasochistic rites, telling by their very
presence "tales of their own humanity," inspiring the Rev^d's sacralized
"host" (by now only his brother-in-law, who is an arms dealer) to repeal
the Scheherazade threat with an expression of a humanity "less fantastick," namely aid for Mason's sons who are left in America.

Throughout, the validity of these stories, of or by Mason and Dixon
and the Rev^d, is constantly in doubt, but they nevertheless offer a very real
alternative to "poor cold Chronologies," reverting rather to the develop-
mental and evolutionary value of the preternatural tale, as opposed to supernatural history. In defending his rendition of the all-too-familiar story
in which Dixon frees slaves from a seller, the Rev^d stipulates that such tales
must be "perfected in the hellish Forge of Domestick Recension, generation 'pon generation, till what survives is the pure truth" (695). Plugged
into his theory of history (and in turn plugged into the role of Christ's
resurrection within Western history), Dixon's Mosaic tale becomes part of
a quasi-biblical "common Duty of Remembering" which requires fantastic events to inhabit the communal memory of humanity —"how we
dream'd of, and were mistaken in, each other." Thus, the purpose of
these miraculous tales, saved from their European pre-occupation in
Europe and its death-kingdoms of the South, is resurrected here by
Pynchon as a controlling motif through which quotidian dreamscapes
can, if not occupy, be at least radically summoned into real earth-bound,
enclosed, and circumscribed human experience. The Native Americans
and other southern races, undreamed of by us, through the extravagance
of our violent and sexualized "occupations" (marveling that we sell them
guns to shoot us with), end up in turn occupying our dreams, our
repeated "Fears" (697), our occluded times and places, including within
them the Christian dream of reunion with loved ones in the bodily resurrection. More immediately, Mason's Line is replaced by the tangle of lines
which he himself casts — his sons, the final "cast" of the novel (they've
gone fishing) — who are, like himself, the progenitors of and participants
in "a Mobility that is to be." One could call this Pynchon's Dispensation, incorporating all that came before into this future Mobility, even as
we try to repress — forget — these other histories of oppression, death,
and ideology by having them occupy a non-linear vortex of ever-present
storytelling tangential to our own violent past and ominous future.[15]

Christ's death and resurrection are written large over the history of
the West, particularly as it is written over the histories of spaces consid-

ered blank, such as the American wilderness. The historical texts, however, do not mesh with the grid-lines and networks of points simultaneously plotted on the land with enlightened rationality, creating what Zhang calls "Bad Energy" (542), a series of mutations on the Christian theme of redemption and the new Dispensation embodied in Christ's resurrection and its prefiguration in the Lord's Supper. As the eighteenth-century Deistic God withdraws from the corporeal Earth, the possibility of the miraculous in general and bodily resurrection in particular takes on forms of horror, such as human commerce and genocide, which emphasize the carnal rather than the spiritual manifestation of Christ's (and our) transformation between flesh and spirit on this continent, as on others. Thus, in conquering and mapping the earth through rationalized methods of science, the West has infected the weighed and measured globe with a religious sensibility gone horribly wrong.

We should remember, though, that what drove Mason and Dixon to measure the Parallax, as described by the Rev^d, is not "the Heavenly Event by itself, but rather that unshining Assembly of Human Needs, of which Venus, at the instant of going dark, is the Prime Object,— including certainly the Royal Society's need for the Solar Parallax, but what of the Astronomers' own Desires, which may have been less philosophical?" (102). We might see in Pynchon's own practice, as he saw in Garcia Marquez's, a world "haunted less by individual dead than by a history which has brought so appallingly many down, without ever having spoken, or having spoken gone unheard, or having been heard, left unrecorded" ("Heart's Eternal Vow"). Pynchon's record itself exists in the interstices of Paul's situating of the promise of redemption in the raising of the dead, offering that promise in a new, transubstantiated form which holds all hope in abeyance but invests it with such power that it cannot be ignored. The occupation of history by the dispossessed, while threatening Mason and Dixon's Enlightenment sensibilities, lives on in their haunting presence on the American geopolitical landscape and, more importantly, in the dreams of Mason's children. In a temporally reflexive move at the novel's conclusion, Mason's sons haunt his dreams with their dreams of going fishing with their father, as he did with his. This mutual dreaming can also be read as a radical restructuring of Christ's purpose in making his disciples, characters in another story, another kind of hunter — namely, fishers of men. What they, disciples and sons alike, end up fishing for is a history made of flesh and blood, caught in their tangled communion of lines "with only their Destination in common."

Notes

This essay was first published in *Reconstruction: Studies in Contemporary Culture* 2.1 (Winter 2002). www.reconstruction.ws.

[1] That this revolutionary idea is essentially a *religious* one is a fact that many Pynchon critics attempt to placate by identifying in his works a secularization of religious themes. Robert Hipkiss identifies, in place of religion, "a search for an operative spiritual force" in Pynchon's previous novels, which he assures us is "not to say that Pynchon finds no validity in religion," but that this "natural emanation of man's desire for transcendence, an extension of the life force" no less, is merely a setting for "ideals of conduct" (19, 21). Charles Hohmann's observation of *Gravity's Rainbow* applies equally (and as disturbingly) to *Mason & Dixon:* "Either the values the novel seems to promote are unfounded or at least far-fetched, or the humanist conventions it flouts are judged inadequate. I believe the latter explanation applies." This is based not on any religious values, but upon the "anti-rationalism lying at the heart of the novel" (89). John Krafft asserts that Pynchon's religious "concepts . . . are almost exclusively secular [even "grossly secular" later on], retaining only the resonances of their formerly sacred significance," and leaving us only with "a desire of transcendence no longer quite believed in" (56, 63, 72). In Kathryn Hume's mythography of Pynchon, she finds that, though he "certainly leaves open the possibility of an afterlife," Pynchon faults religions for "try[ing] to make death palatable" (129). And Molly Hite suggests that "*Gravity's Rainbow* confronts its readers with the spectacle of a *post-religious* society" (157, emphasis added), a spectacle that, as we can see, is replicated in Pynchon scholarship. Though easily considered part of the spectacle, Joseph Slade in a way explains it: "Among the many ironies of Protestant rationalization is that an impulse originally religious has led to the secularization of the world" (66). Harvey Cox makes the most forceful argument for secularization as the logical and ultimate culmination of Protestantism in his groundbreaking work on postmodern theology, *The Secular City* (1965).

[2] David Cowart, in "The Luddite Vision: *Mason & Dixon,*" makes this same connection between Pynchon's earlier essays and his newest novel (344 passim). He, too, cites "the mounting evidence of Pynchon's spiritual and metaphysical (even religious [!]) seriousness" (361) and establishes a helpful, if by now conventional and slightly reductive, postmodern Americanist alignment of Pynchon's work against technological hegemony and historical metanarratives.

[3] "Like their earlier counterparts, 20th-century Luddites looked back yearningly to another age — curiously, the same Age of Reason which had forced the first Luddites into nostalgia for the Age of Miracles" ("Luddite?").

[4] All references to Calvin are to the section numbers in chapter 17 of volume IV of the *Institutes.*

[5] A psychoanalytic reading of these repeated uses of "Desire" to describe the Line's peculiar energy, often likened to a great "Engine" and even a "Weapon," is

eminently, well, desired, and one could find much in Freud and Lacan (and Derrida for that matter) to inform on this pathway of desire. Also apropos would be the anti-psychological "desiring-machine" of Deleuze and Guattari (cited in Baringer 45), which can be compared to the "Phantom Shape" that Mason reads in the stars at the end of the novel, seeing "a great single Engine, the size of a Continent" (772). Especially relevant, and deserving its own comparison to *Mason & Dixon*, is Deleuze's postulated rhizomatic "lines of flight" in *A Thousand Plateaus* (1987), which offer a possible postmodern recuperation of organized resistance to desire as a totalizing mechanism.

[6] "L.E.D." is, of course, also the ubiquitous Light-Emitting Diodes we rely on at sporting events and on bank marquees. A technical Internet manual gives an interesting description that may be relevant to the dog's preternatural role: "In electronics terms, a diode is a semiconductor device through which *current can go in only one direction*. As a side effect, light-emitting diodes produce visible light. LEDs require very little power and are often used as *indicator lights,* including (most likely) the drive access lights on your computer" ("Game Monitor Scoreboards," my emphases).

[7] According to Hinds, *Mason & Dixon* is "a most anxious exploration of temporal possibility. Recorded time in *Mason & Dixon* keeps slipping away, though it be so much an object of finer and fine recalibrations; this kind of time does not perform consecutively, will not stay within prescribed lines" (197). Later she states that the novel, "infused with anachronism, warps the map of history to an extent that eighteenth- and twentieth-century culture, action, and language are virtually inseparable" (205). One wonders if, in addition to culture, action, and language, she sees the same anachronistic cross-over between eighteenth- and twentieth-century religious belief.

[8] Pynchon invents this museum to house the ear Robert Jenkin reportedly lost to Spanish torturers, a claim that started "The War of Jenkin's Ear" in 1739. Jenkin in fact served as the governor of St. Helena for the East India Company, leading Pynchon to imply a "quid pro quo" (175) for his services to his "country."

[9] The OED's theological definition of "Dispensation" is "A religious order or system, conceived as divinely instituted, or as a stage in a progressive revelation, expressly adapted to the needs of a particular nation or period of time, as the patriarchal, Mosaic (or Jewish) dispensation, the Christian dispensation; also, the age or period during which such system has prevailed." The first example is from The Westminster Confession of Faith (1877), an earlier version of which would have been Mason's Anglican catechism: "There are not therefore two covenants of grace, differing in substance, but one and the same under various dispensations." A few lines below: "The Christian dispensation is the dispensation of grace, a favour;" a still later writer clarifies: "Christianity is the last dispensation." It seems that Mason's Dispensation is one past the last.

[10] According to Hohmann, "there is only one genuine form of 'transformation' in *Gravity's Rainbow* and that is the one enacted in 'the bitter intestinal oven' . . . , the artificial oven man has created which appears as a 'Rocket' and for which Weissman has 'fattened' Gottfried" (86). Mason's oven, though with more paternal connotations, carries with it the odors of *Gravity's Rainbow.*

[11] What he sees is the dark side of History's occupation by the dispossessed: "Mason has seen in the Glass, unexpectedly, something beyond simple reflection,— outside of the world,— a procession of luminous Phantoms, carrying bowls, bones, incense, drums, their Attention directed to nothing he may imagine, belonging to unknown purposes [. . .] a conscious Denial of all that Reason holds true. Something that knows, unarguably as it knows Flesh is sooner or later Meat, that there are Beings who are not wise, or spiritually advanced, or indeed capable of Human kindness, but ever and implacably cruel, hiding, haunting, waiting,— known only to the blood-scented deserts of the Night,— and any who see them out of Disguise are instantly pursued,— [. . .] Spheres of Darkness, Darkness impure,— [. . .] of Spirits who dwell a little over the Line between the Day and its annihilation, between the number'd and the unimagin'd,— between common safety and Ruin ever solitary . . ." (769).

[12] Black: "Gravity represents the compacting and densitizing force that constitutes the brute substance of History" (239). In a more recent recuperative gesture, Alessia Ricciardi contrasts Pynchon's stylistic "values" from those of Italo Calvino, and finds Pynchon's to be more "grounded": "Rather than lightness, quickness, exactitude, or visibility, more appropriate signifiers for Pynchon's writing might be 'gravity' or, perhaps, 'rupture'" (1071).

[13] Harold Bloom's famous formula, based on "The Story of Byron the Bulb" in *Gravity's Rainbow,* that "Pynchon's is a Gnosis without transcendence" (3) is here reversed, as Mason is made to transcend (at least momentarily) without gnosis, and seems none the worse for wear. Mason's alternate form of transcendence is suggested by Thomas Moore's reading of Byron's story as a "parable of preterition," seeing Byron's "election for subversive, redemptive purposes is set against the debased neo-Puritan sense of 'election' to serve entrenched power" (146). Hohmann also sees a Gnostic root in the Deistic "hidden God" of the story, thus leaving the earth ruled instead by "archons" whose "Creation they administer is programmed to destroy itself" in a "deliberate resurrection," a "staged and controlled holocaust." In Byron's tale, Phoebus "sees to it that violent destruction and controlled reincarnation is maintained" (182–83, qts. *GR* 415). However, Hohmann's helpful gloss on the relationship between Gnostic and Christian salvation seems in keeping with most of Mason and Dixon's experiences: "Redemption [in Gnosticism] is found in gnosis, a kind of mystical knowledge or grace which opens the Gnostic's eyes to his true destiny . . . [This] awakening causes some to be tempted to liken Gnostic salvation to Christian resurrection. However, the association would be fallacious. While Christian redemption is founded on a teleological view of history, Gnosticism conceives of it in terms of *a sudden violent irruption into human time and history.* For the Gnostic true time proceeds 'by quantum jumps' and revelation is always subjective, discontinuous and anarchic" (177–78, last emphasis added).

[14] For more complete treatments of Pynchon's use (and abuse) of Time in *Mason & Dixon,* see Cowart (349 passim), Pagano (Chapter 2), and Hinds.

[15] Ricciardi makes a similar point: "Pynchon's method of rescuing the postmodern for himself and for readers of conscience is to reframe the story of Mason and Dixon's explorations from the epistemological standpoint of a postcolonial con-

sciousness, making clear . . . the perils and the limits of ethnocentrism. . . . In *Mason & Dixon* it seems possible to recognize a minimalist form of political commitment that may not lead to a call for action, exactly, so much as a call for attention to human suffering, that most haunting and irreducible link between past and present" (1072–74).

7: "Our Madmen, our Paranoid": Enlightened Communities and the Mental State in *Mason & Dixon*[1]

Ian D. Copestake

MADNESS AS BOTH A BLANKET DESCRIPTION for a host of abnormal mental states and the way in which these states are perceived by the sane, has been a recurrent presence in Pynchon's work throughout his career. His fiction of the 1960s and 70s established a particularly powerful and enduring association with paranoia, while Pynchon's novel, *Vineland* (1990), saw Zoyd Wheeler struggling to assume a post-radical state of socialized normalcy in the Reagan era through receipt of a "mental disability check." The novel opens with Zoyd contemplating the fact that "unless he did something publicly crazy before a date now less than a week away, he would no longer qualify for benefits" (3). Abnormal mental states, sometimes even madness, become identified with the sea in Pynchon's novels beginning with *The Crying of Lot 49* and reaching a novel-length thematic in *Mason & Dixon*. The symbolic identification of madness and the sea that Pynchon plays upon is in part informed by romanticism and concepts of the sublime, in which the spectacle of nature offers man a means of affirming the interconnection between selfhood and Godhead. But more influential is a longer and specifically American tradition that Pynchon is well aware of and subsequently brings to the fore in *Mason & Dixon*, a tradition linking madness, divine election, and national selfhood.

Pynchon's concern with the sea prior to *Mason & Dixon* has been peripheral, but *The Crying of Lot 49* serves as an interesting corollary to the later work through the role of sea-consciousness and in particular Oedipa Maas's projection on to the sea of her own idealism.[2] At times of confusion in the face of the unraveling of Oedipa's sense of normality she turns to the sea and becomes aware of its presence. The novel can be seen to chart the progress of her relationship to the idealism the sea embodies for her as she struggles to find a release from the perplexities, confusions, and paranoia that increasingly grip her.

Paranoia quickly becomes a way of life for Oedipa in the wake of revelations about Pierce Inverarity's business dealings she discovers in executing his will. From this starting point Oedipa's quest for meaning begins to suggest answers to more personal questions, including her suspicion that she has been enclosed in a tower throughout her life and that exposure to potential revelation suggests a way of regaining contact with some more significant and revelatory meaning. Such a summary of Oedipa's motivations and expectations as she begins to soak up references to Pierce's businesses throughout the city of San Narciso, only really does justice to the ambiguity of what it is she hopes to find, and what her sense of enclosure really signifies.

Her quest sees her begin to doubt all she had held to be true, to attempt to turn back from this path of revelation, and return to her world of comfortable isolation. This means she must deny the existence of desires she has already identified. If she attempts to do this, these desires must be seen as fictions. As figments of her own imagination they must be dismissed, ignored, or painted over by her conviction that they do not exist and that she is happy to "fall back on superstition, or take up a useful hobby like embroidery, or go mad or marry a disc-jockey" (13). It is not possible for her to backtrack without taking advantage of the most powerful of these options, namely by embracing a delusion, by going mad. Thus paranoia itself begins to be seen as an indicator of the world of questions without answer she has entered, and not something that should be rejected as delusory. To deny the truth with which paranoia connects her would not constitute a return to reality but rather return her to the madness of a deluded existence.

Her desire for meaning is at least, via the Tristero, given a name. This postal system represents the desires of a community of people who, like herself, want to keep open a channel of communication with their own desires for something different and more hopeful than the set of ideals and values realized within their disenchantment of the conventional society of America. Proving the existence of the Tristero seems to restore the possibility and viability of hope itself in the face of hidden and controlling forces. However, confirmation of its existence would also confirm the frightening reality of the powers which necessitate its existence, a stark reality reflected in the bleak options facing Oedipa at the end of the novel. At the auction awaiting the revelatory crying of lot 49, she confronts the need to recognize her irrevocable state of insanity:

> Either Oedipa in the orbiting ecstasy of a true paranoia, or a real Tristero. For there either was some Tristero beyond the appearance of the legacy America, or there was just America and if there was just America then it seemed the only way she could continue, and man-

age to be at all relevant to it, was an alien, unfurrowed, assumed full circle into some paranoia. (126)

Frank Palmeri rightly argues that there is in Pynchon's work a progression "away from the representation of extreme paranoia, toward a vision of local ethico-political possibilities" (par. 5). The key to this point is the cultivation within each individual of an awareness of his or her relationship to the determining factors and powers which seem to render individual action insignificant. In *The Crying of Lot 49* Oedipa's awareness of her relationship to the world around her undergoes a sea-change, and it is this which must come before any subsequent action can be taken to improve that relationship. The possibility of action is explored in *Mason & Dixon*, while the earlier novel charts Oedipa's first steps to an emergent realization of the need to confront her own responsibility for understanding the life around her:

> The position of Mason and Dixon more nearly resembles that of Oedipa Maas, who comes to see more than she saw at first, to whom revelations happen which may or may not add up to evidence of a wide-ranging conspiracy, but which are nevertheless historically significant and demand an ethical response. (par. 31)

An alternative to the madness at the end of every avenue of possibility open to Oedipa had potentially been envisaged by the role of sea-consciousness within the book. Early in her quest Oedipa senses the presence of the Pacific, and the narrator describes the comfort she derived from the significance she gave to it when in the past she viewed the Pacific as an "inviolate" embodiment of "some more general truth," (37) a hope that life in Southern California could become less ugly than it appeared to be on the surface.[3] The narrator also, however, immediately undermines the integrity of Oedipa's vague sense of hope by stating that though she "had believed in some principle of the sea as redemption for Southern California," it excluded "her own section of the state, which seemed to need none" (37). Re-instated here is the prevalent self-absorption and insulation from reality which Oedipa is only now beginning to challenge. The change of tense here, the fact that she "had believed" in the sea as an embodiment of redemptive hope, suggests not only that her idealism belongs to a time before her quest began, but it also allows the narrator to suggest the very different nature of the enlightenment both she and the reader should expect to confront at the quest's end: "Perhaps it was only that notion, its arid hope, she sensed as this afternoon they made their sea-ward thrust, which would stop short of any sea" (37).

The sea's role in the novel changes and becomes a means of assessing the degree to which Oedipa is willing to accept the changed status of meaning in her world. For her to achieve a true sense of reality and her relationship to it necessitates resisting any desire to retreat to her former state of insulation. Her willingness to continue will be reflected in her attitude to the sea which, the narrator implies, should no longer indicate to her the comforting possibility of redemptive meaning, but reveal to her the presence of its absence. Oedipa's quest inevitably leads her to a choice between her nostalgia for the comforts of her past idealism, and hence to a delusion, or to a new world of deconstructed truths and textual meanings in which she must try to make herself at home.

Throughout the novel we are given reminders of the sea's peripheral presence via the role the various lakes play in revealing the identity of the Tristero. Oedipa's prior sense of the sea as an incorruptible model of a spiritual life that she wanted affirmed on the land finds another representative in the person of the aptly named Driblette. As director of a Jacobean play that gives Oedipa her first clue to the existence of the Tristero system, Driblette is frustrated at Oedipa's seemingly obsessive textually grounded search for meaning at the expense of "the invisible field surrounding the play, its spirit" (105). He soon rejoins the appropriate symbolic realm of his own vision of meaning when he commits suicide by walking into the Pacific.

The suggested division between the land and the sea, between the possibly fruitless pursuit of texts and some more spiritual perception of truth, is also made to stand out when Oedipa reaches the lowest ebb of her quest. With the disappearance of a voice on a phone, seemingly her last possible contact with vital information about the Tristero, she faces the prospect of never finding out whether it was all a joke, whether such a system really existed, or whether it was a nightmare of her own concoction. At this moment the narrator describes Oedipa's sense of loss in terms which confirm her irrevocable distance from the sea and her past idealism:

> She stood between the public booth and the rented car, in the night, her isolation complete, and tried to face towards the sea. But she had lost her bearings. She turned pivoting on one stacked heel, could find no mountains either. As if there could be no barriers between herself and the land. (122)

Oedipa's absorption by the land seems complete, and this unsettling but revelatory experience of isolation and disorientation informs her encounter with the novel's final representative of the sea, the sailor suffering from delirium tremens. The genuine emotion and sense of loss conveyed in the scene is reflective of Oedipa's recognition of the need to abandon not the sailor, but the nostalgia which preserved the sea for her as a realm symbolic of a vaguely defined and flawed sense of hope.[4] Through a literally touching act of recognition, Oedipa's desire to comfort the sailor demonstrates the distance she has now come from her prior state of insulation from the world around her:

> She was overcome all at once by a need to touch him, as if she could not believe in him, or would not remember him, without it. Exhausted, hardly knowing what she was doing, she came the last three steps and sat, took the man in her arms, actually held him, gazing out of her smudged eyes down the stairs, back into the morning. (87)

While she can give physical comfort to this damaged and washed-up representative of the sea's symbolic realm she can no longer offer him the same hope which that realm had formerly signified to her:

> She felt wetness against her breast and saw that he was crying again. He hardly breathed but tears came as if being pumped. "I can't help," she whispered, rocking him, "I can't help." (87)

Pynchon is aware of the confusions inherent in America's historical relationship to forms of idealism and delusion that its Puritan heritage continues to influence. For Sacvan Bervovitch the "sacred drama of American nationhood" (132) is constituted by the confluence of sacred and secular history, in which The Great Migration and the War of Independence are linked by evolved perceptions of Providence in the wake of the growth, power, and influence of scientific rationalism. While the Divine Order remained reflected in the laws of nature which science brought to light, this revised cultural framework facilitated the emergence of an American national self-identity that outgrew its origins in the outmoded typology of Providence, and yet preserved in adapted form a cultural authority which endorsed the myth of America's Manifest Destiny. What is so often at stake for American writers and their fictional characters when they confront the sea or water, what draws Thoreau to Walden Pond, or gives significance to the final sight of the sea at the close of *The Great Gatsby*, is the repeated need to find an answer to the question of whether a conception of America is necessary for it to exist, or whether a society is possible outside the delusions or ideals which historically have determined its identity.

Oedipa Maas confronts this question at the end of her personal quest for answers and finds avenues toward different forms of insanity awaiting her. In *Mason & Dixon* Pynchon moves back into history to expose the larger delusions at the heart of America's quest for national identity. At the heart of *Mason & Dixon* is Pynchon's concern to chart the movement man can hope to make away from the prison-house of paranoia to a home within the changed world such paranoia indicates.

The supposedly enlightened age which *Mason & Dixon* illuminates is one in which madness abounds. Mason suffers from hyperthrenia, or excess in mourning, brought about by the death of his wife, Rebekah, casting him under the shadow of a deep melancholia. The Rev[d] Cherrycoke is keen to point out his acquaintance with mania, having avoided imprisonment for his crimes by allowing himself to be declared insane. Among the many realms both ghostly and geographic visited in the book is the island of St. Helena from which, due to the incessant beating of the sea against its mountainous sides, all are said eventually to go mad. The southeast winds of Cape Town are another element responsible for legendary examples of insane behavior. We can add to this list of conventional insanities the more fabulous examples never more than a page away throughout the novel — characters, realms, rituals, and inventions the absurdity of which break through any prolonged pretense at historical realism. From the mechanical duck and talking dog to the Lambton worm, Pynchon celebrates through them the colorful diversity of imagination's realms, and sets them against the cold line drawing and divisiveness which bring Mason and Dixon into history.

The dividing line between sanity and madness in the age of reason is rendered less clear by the reactions of "Sunny, bustling and order'd" Cape Town to the bouts of madness it experiences among minds seemingly "in the rosiest fullness of Sanity" (151–52). When deemed too dangerous the mad "are kept as a responsibility of the Company, confin'd in padded rooms in the Slave Lodge" (151). The dehumanization of the mad goes hand in hand with the heritage of slavery on which "order'd" Cape Town was built. The interrelatedness of reason and its supposed opposite is given an ironic twist by the image of democracy among the confined mad of the Slave Lodge, who are "of every race, condition, and degree of Affliction, from the amiably delusionary to the remorselessly homicidal" (152). The confinement allows for sadistic pleasure to be taken by Cape Town's hierarchy who revel in their sense of difference from the mad through displays of power which only confirm their inhumanity:

> Sometimes for their amusement the Herren will escort a particularly disobedient employee to a Madman's cell, push her inside, and lock the door. Next to each cell is a Viewing Room where the gentlemen may then observe, through a wall of Glass disguis'd as a great Mirror, the often quite unviewable *Rencontre*. (152)

The sea is again perceived as the metaphoric realm of the mad, a fact that underlines the definition of them as other from the order desired on the land:

Some of them hate women, some desire them, some know hate and desire as but minor aspects of a greater, Oceanick Impulse, in which, report those who survive, it is unquestionably better not to be included. Again, some do not survive. When the Herren cannot return their Remains to their villages, they dispose of them by sea, that the Jackals may not have them. (152)

Pynchon, like Foucault, is aware of the historical changes in the perception of the mad.[5] In *Mason & Dixon* he utilizes a wide variety of perceptions of the insane which serve both to foreground their provisionality and underline the intimate relationship between the human need for definition and the imposition of inhumane division which this can foster. The fate of the mad in Cape Town reflects stoic conceptions of the sea as a realm of fearful chaos and uncontrollable power. By being returned there the dead confirm that in return for hegemony over the fate of the mad, the enlightened authorities have thrown their own humanity into the sea, and conform to Lillian Feder's definition of insanity as:

A state in which unconscious processes predominate over conscious ones to the extent that they control them and determine perceptions of and responses to experience that, judged by prevailing standards of logical thought and relevant emotion, are confused and inappropriate. (5)

The madness of the Age of Reason is, as Pynchon figures it in Cape Town, confirmed by its failure to distinguish between the symbolic product of unconscious processes which turn the sea into a symbol, and its own conscious authoritative acts.

There are parallels here with the manner in which Pynchon's *Mason & Dixon* comes to be related by its narrator, the banished Rev[d] Wicks Cherrycoke. The tale is made possible by Cherrycoke's escape from imprisonment in England, which he avoids by claiming to be insane and so taking advantage of the authorities' endorsement of the belief that "Sea voyages in those days being the standard Treatment for Insanity, my Exile should commence for the best of Medical reasons" (10). Cherrycoke's liberty is made possible by medical Reason's perception of the sea as a restorative to mental health. Mason is also aware of the sea's regenerative influence. His desire to alleviate his hyperthrenia makes him "eager to be aboard a ship, bound somewhere impossible,— long voyages by sea being thought to help his condition" (25). Such views have gained currency in the world of the novel. Outside it this power to misconceive myth as reality, fiction as medical fact, mirrors Thomas Szasz's condemnation of the practices of twentieth-century psychiatry in the wake of Sigmund Freud's impact upon it.

Szasz argues that Freud's work dramatically influenced perceptions of the insane, which gave credence to forms of treatment that were not only ineffective but inhumane. In relation to Pynchon's novel, Szasz's theories offer a historical model for the "literalization" of the treatment of mental illness which the Enlightened authorities fall back on in their efforts to assert control over a seemingly unknowable condition. Szasz claims that

> when the early (nineteenth century) psychiatrists spoke of mental diseases or diseases of the mind, they understood, and often explicitly stated, that these expressions were figures of speech or metaphors. (140)

For Szasz, a change occurred with Freud's success in jettisoning "the linkage between insanity and somatic illness and [his substitution of] an analogy or putative identity between insanity and a normal, everyday feature of inner (mental) experience, namely, dreaming" (141). A consequence was the "literalization of the metaphor of mental illness," which for Szasz was

> exemplified by Freud's cryptochemical theories of *actual neurosis* (and other mental illness) and by the neurochemical fantasies of contemporary psychopharmacologists [. . .]. After the Freudian revolution got under way [. . .] psychiatrists began to insist — as they now typically do — that mental illness, far from being a metaphor, is literally an illness *like* any *other illness* (that it is always and without doubt a disease of the brain). (141)

In Szasz's view the status of medical treatment also changed, for "if the conditions psychiatrists seek to cure are not literal diseases, then the procedures they use cannot be literal treatments" (163). By viewing insanity as related to the brain rather than the body highly invasive medical practices from lobotomy to electrotherapy gained credibility.[6] For Szasz the nature of such treatments reflected the spurious fantasies which the Freudian revolution had given credence to and made legitimate.

Pynchon's depiction of Cherrycoke's "insanity" brings to the fore further recent models used in the definition of mental illness that differ from those of Feder and Szasz. For R. D. Laing, "true sanity [. . .] entails in one way or another the dissolution of the normal ego, that false self competently adjusted to our alienated social reality" (*The Politics of Experience* 144–45). As Feder explains,

> A central idea in Laing's *The Politics of Experience* is that human beings having lost their "selves," have "developed the illusion that we are autonomous egos." He contrasts the "transcendental experiences" which are "the original well-spring of all religions" with what he calls the "egoic" approach to reality of most people; the experi-

ence of "the world and themselves in terms of a consistent identity, a me-here over against a you-there, within a framework of certain ground structures of space and time shared with other members of their society." To Laing, "egoic" experience [. . .], is essentially a form of "socially accepted madness," on the other hand, a state of "ego-loss" generally regarded as psychotic, may be for the person involved "veritable manna from heaven." (Feder 281–82)

Aspects of Laing's contentious but influential views inform Cherrycoke's explanation of the circumstances leading to his exile at sea. The narrator of *Mason & Dixon* relates that he had committed "one of the least tolerable Offences in that era, the worst of Dick Turpin seeming but the Carelessness of youth beside it,— the Crime they styl'd 'Anonymity'" (9). He goes on to declare that

> I left messages posted publicly, but did not sign them. I knew some night-running lads in the district who let me use their Printing-Press,— somehow, what I got into printing up, were Accounts of certain Crimes I had observ'd, committed by the Stronger against the Weaker,— enclosures, evictions, Assize verdicts, Activities of the Military,— giving the Names of as many of the Perpetrators as I was sure of, yet keeping back what I foolishly imagin'd my own, till the Night I was tipp'd and brought in to London, in Chains, and clapp'd in the Tower. (9)

Cherrycoke is seen to have lost the self he felt he had, and in its place is confronted by the fact that what he had considered his own (his name, his freedom), was nothing next to the power the Enlightened authorities of his age had over all these elements. The challenge he offered these authorities, through the moral act of his exposés, was to withhold his own name and so attempt to assert a form of selfhood unsanctioned by them. The realization that the autonomy of his own self was a myth in the face of the repressive and all-pervasive power of Reason's authority, is brought home to Cherrycoke in an ironic vision of transcendence:

> It took me till I was lying among the Rats and Vermin, upon the freezing edge of a Future invisible, to understand that my name had never been my own,— rather belonging, all this time, to the Authorities, who forbade me to change it, or withhold it, as 'twere a Ring upon the Collar of a Beast, ever waiting for the Lead to be fasten'd on . . . One of those moments Hindoos and Chinamen are ever said to be having, entire loss of Self, perfect union with All, sort of thing. (10)

Here Cherrycoke's experience of, to use Laing's term, "ego-loss," confirms that his own former belief in the autonomy of his ego was a form of "socially accepted madness." From the moment in Cherrycoke's account that this bleak realization is reached the tone of his narration changes, as with growing relish he begins to recount the manner of his escape from this plight:

> Strange Lights, Fires, Voices indecipherable,— indeed, Children, this is the part of the Tale where your old Uncle gets to go insane,— or so, then, each in his Interest, did it please ev'ryone to style me. (10)

Realizing he has no autonomous selfhood that is not the property of Reason Inc., he embraces the epithet "insane" and the non-identity it confers, and in doing so enters a state in which the self is truly lost. For Cherrycoke it is a state which perfectly reflects his new realization that in the world of the sane he was never free.

Insanity, as is it did for Zoyd Wheeler in *Vineland,* offers a means of escape from hegemonic forces and social control, and provides the narrator of *Mason & Dixon* with a passport to a new form of selfhood. What Pynchon recognizes in *Mason & Dixon* is the need to acknowledge the validity of the delusions of others, to recognize the legitimacy of values and beliefs which by their very existence contradict conventional assumptions and beliefs. The fact that Zoyd Wheeler's social conformity is outwardly confirmed through an act of irrationality highlights the prevalence of an order of values that can only be defined by its perceived distance from such acts. Figured here is Pynchon's recognition that the opposed states of rationality and irrationality are intimate bedfellows, as the existence of one depends on the existence of the other. Wheeler's recognition of this fact turns his act from one of mere conformity to a deliberate and positive compromise, allowing him to maintain his freedom through his role as madman.

To fail to make such compromises is to insist on oppositions and a drawing of boundaries which define out of existence all that is on the other side. In *Mason & Dixon*'s Cape Town the imposition of a privileged selfhood by the town's authorities dehumanizes them at the same time as it deconstructs the opposition between sane and insane. The claim for the exclusive legitimacy of its own power is based on the annihilation of that which it perceives to be other. Cherrycoke's new identity is, however, one that sees him make a home in the contentious spaces which boundaries create, while attaching himself to no side but his own. Liberty is again associated with madness, but both Wheeler and Cherrycoke consciously embrace it as a role allowing them to highlight and transcend the divisions within their respective societies while retaining their freedom.

Cherrycoke's sea-bound exile, if we compare it with the Laing model of insanity, sees him embrace a status consistent with Laing's "inner" or "true" self. This state, which exists in opposition to the "egoic self," is seen by Laing to be "occupied in maintaining its identity and freedom by being transcendent, unembodied, and thus never grasped, pinpointed, trapped, possessed" (94–95). Cherrycoke's new identity is appropriately shifting and changeable. As the "nomadic Parson" and "Family outcast" (10) his seaborne life makes him both exotic and mysterious, providing him with license to fulfill his role as storyteller, while his fabulous histories leave his audience continually aware that the territory he patrols is the boundary between truth and falsehood.

Mason & Dixon is Cherrycoke's tale and it continues to embody the characteristics of the exposés for which he was condemned by taking the form of an account of the perverse ethics inherent in the Age of Reason which underlay the divisive product of Mason and Dixon's partnership. His status as a wanderer by sea and land, and a teller of fantastical tales, his melancholy following the passing of Mason (8), and his role as the timekeeper of the novel, make him a true child of Saturn. Such associations are bolstered by the acronym of the book's title, M. A. D, the use of the ampersand in the written title helping to underline the different resonances given to the title when it is spoken. In such ways Pynchon emphasizes the importance of the history of insanity to his memorialization of man's need for division and definitions which nevertheless give credence to the inhumanity of conflicts such as the Mason-Dixon Line.

To recognize complicity is, in *Mason & Dixon,* a vital sign of the awareness that Pynchon looks to promote as offering hope of the possibility of ethical action and resistance amid a world of division and conflict. The role of the sea in the novel brings to the fore Mason and Dixon's own recognition of their responsibility as the novel concludes with an acknowledgment that the sea is also the means by which the spread of reason's authority is assured, and with it the evil being perpetuated in its name all over the globe. At the end of the novel Dixon asks of his cohort:

> "Ev'rywhere they've sent us,— the Cape, St. Helena, America,— What's the Element common to all?"
> "Long Voyages by Sea" replies Mason, blinking in Exhaustion by now Chronick. "Was there anything Else?"
> "Slaves. Ev'ry day at the Cape, we lived with Slavery in our faces,— more of it at St. Helena,— and now here we are again, in another Colony, this time having drawn a Line between their Slave-Keepers, and their Wage-Payers, as if doom'd to re-encounter thro' the World this public Secret, this shameful Core. . . . Pretending it to be ever somewhere else, with the Turks, the Russians, the Companies, down there, down where it smells like warm Brine and Gunpowder fumes, they're murdering and dispossessing thousands untallied, the innocent of the World passing daily into the Hands of

Slave-owners and Torturers, but oh, never in Holland, nor in England, that Garden of Fools? Christ, Mason." (692–93)

The sea which Oedipa longed for but never came near to, and the hope
embodied within it, is also, prior to Mason and Dixon's last transit, the
subject of their projected hopes and dreams for the future:

> "[. . .] what'll yese do now?"
> "Devise a way," Dixon replies, "to inscribe a Visto upon the
> Atlantik Sea."
> "Archie, Lad, Look ye here," Mason producing a Sheaf of Pa-
> pers, flapping thro' them,— "A thoughtful Arrangement of Anchors
> and Buoys, Lenses and Lanthorns, forming a perfect Line across the
> Ocean, all the way from the Delaware bay to the Spanish Extre-
> madura," — with the Solution to the Question of the Longitude
> thrown in as a sort of Bonus,— as, exactly at ev'ry Degree, might the
> Sea-Line, as upon a Fiduciary Scale for Navigators, be prominently
> mark'd by a taller Beacon, or a differently color'd Lamp. In time,
> most Ships preferring to sail within sight of these Beacons, the Line
> shall have widen'd to a Sea-Road of a thousand Leagues, as up and
> down its Longitude blossomed Wharves, Chandleries, Inns, To-
> bacco-shops, Greengrocers' Stalls, Printers of News, Dens of Vice,
> Chapels for Repentance, Shops full of Souvenirs and Sweets,— all a
> Sailor could wish,— indeed, many such will decide to settle here,
> "Along the Beacons," for good, as a way of coming to rest while
> remaining out at Sea. (712)

This imagined utopia at sea is soured in the instant that it is dreamed, for
the narrator's extended contemplation on this vision of Mason and
Dixon's retirement finds the outstretched hand of Reason Inc. acquiring
the rights to the oceans:

> Too soon, word will reach the Land-Speculation Industry, and its
> Bureaus seek Purchase, like some horrible Seaweed, the length of the
> Beacon Line. Some are estopp'd legally, some are fended directly
> into the Sea, yet Time being ever upon their Side, they persist, and
> one Day, in sinister yet pleasing Coral-dy'd cubikal Efflorescensce,
> appears "St. Brendan's Isle," a combination Pleasure-Grounds and
> Pensioners' Home, with ev'rything an Itinerant come to Rest might
> ask, Taverns, Music-Halls, Gaming-Rooms, and a Population ever
> changing of Practitioners of Comfort [. . .]. 'Tis here Mason &
> Dixon will retire, being after all Plank-Holders of the very Scheme,
> having written a number of foresighted Stipulations into their Con-
> tract with the Line's Proprietor, the transnoctially charter'd "Atlantic
> Company." Betwixt themselves, neither feels British enough any-
> more, nor quite American, for either Side of the Ocean. They are

content to reside like Ferrymen or Bridge-keepers, ever in a Ubiquity of Flow, before a ceaseless Spectacle of Transition. (712–13)

Such a projected retirement at sea suggests Mason and Dixon's complicity in the appropriation of the many realms they have encountered. As a result, their own identity is left to merge with the ceaselessly flowing element that has facilitated the world's transition into sameness.

With madness taking over the land and insane reason seemingly also setting its sights on the sea, there is a need for a new refuge that can hold out the possibility of resistance to the divisive and inhumane values taking root fast throughout history. In *Mason & Dixon* the motif promoted in the light of the threat both to insanity and the sea as embodiments of escape or redress is the value of fiction-making itself. As in *The Crying of Lot 49*, the act of metaphor is still very much "a thrust at truth and a lie" (89), reflecting as it does in *Mason & Dixon* the capacity for the authorities of the Enlightenment to believe in the fictions they inherit, and so impose their beliefs through the etching of dividing lines across the globe. A part of *Mason & Dixon*'s own thrust at truth is carried by the novel's celebration of the absurd, the puncturing of its historical realism with flights of fantasy, in which the human imagination is allowed free reign. Palmeri states that Pynchon's earlier novels, including *The Crying of Lot 49*, resist suggesting a way forward from the paranoia which grips these novels' characters:

> [Pynchon] implies instead that it is necessary if almost impossible somehow to combine the urge to order and meaning with a skepticism that recognizes the fruitfulness of disorder and unpredictability. (par. 24)[7]

A way forward from this point is through the promotion of an awareness which recognizes the delusory nature of all ideals and so sees us follow Cherrycoke to the liminal states and boundary lines enabling us to see more clearly our own relationship to the contending positions of power which dominate society. By not rejecting the form and order which beliefs and ideals give to a society we are all responsible for the injustices which result, but by recognizing that fact and the provisionality of the ideals and values which define and legitimize them, independent ethical action remains possible. To recognize and accept the inevitability of delusion is the key, and it is this that turns Pynchon's celebration of the imagination in his novel into a stance of ethical resistance as he populates his novel with creations of the human imagination that do not insist on being seen as anything other than unreal and fantastical.

Notes

[1] A version of this article appeared in *American Postmodernity: Essays on the Recent Fiction of Thomas Pynchon,* edited by Ian D. Copestake (Oxford: Peter Lang, 2003), under the title "'Off the Deep End Again': Sea-Consciousness and Insanity in *The Crying of Lot 49* and *Mason & Dixon.*"

[2] See Kiely 215–37; Guzlowski 48–60.

[3] I am grateful here to John Krafft for his suggestions concerning the ambiguities inherent in Oedipa's view of the sea.

[4] Guzlowski suggests that Oedipa in fact desires "to further the estrangement" that exists between herself and the physical sea in the novel, and which cuts her off from the "inner sea of emotions" it is seen to represent (51). Using this meeting to support his claim that Oedipa does not desire contact with the redemption that the sea represents, Guzlowski sees her as failing to respond to the cries of the sailor by abandoning him "and the inner emotional seas he might have guided her to" (52).

[5] See Foucault 9–10. Palmeri notes extended patterns of similarity between Pynchon and Foucault's work, while both Palmeri (par. 38) and Collado Rodríguez (500) note explicit references to Foucault's work in *Mason & Dixon.*

[6] See also Valenstein.

[7] Reflected here are Pynchon's continued efforts to locate the modern self between extreme polarities of order and chaos which Tony Tanner identified as a vital characteristic of American fiction from the 1950s to the 1970s. See Tanner 153–73; O'Donnell 10–11.

8: General Wolfe and the Weavers: Re-envisioning History in Pynchon's *Mason & Dixon*

Frank Palmeri

Throughout his novels, Thomas Pynchon combines strict fidelity to previously forgotten historical records with conjectural or fantastic narratives which nevertheless contribute to making a moral or political argument. In *Mason & Dixon,* he employs this characteristic strategy with events at the intersection between two kinds of narrative in eighteenth-century history. The first concerns labor history, and in particular the wages for weavers, who were among the first workers to experience the effects of an early industrializing economy. This narrative interest figures in *Mason & Dixon* because of the efforts of weavers in the southwest of England in late 1756 and early 1757 to obtain an increase or at least to avoid a decline in wages through group action such as strikes, public assemblies, and machine breaking. The second, intersecting strand at work in Pynchon's novel is military and imperial history, specifically the presence of Colonel (later General) James Wolfe in Stroud and surrounding areas of Gloucestershire to keep the peace in late 1756. Pynchon's account of the events that brought together the weavers and General Wolfe is striking and illuminating for the accuracy of many of its elements, for the way it re-animates this important episode in English history, and for its substantial inaccuracies and fictionalizing. Through this combination of scholarly accuracy and imaginative fabrication, Pynchon shows Mason and Dixon's ability to move outside their expected ideological positions, but he misses the opportunity to recognize Wolfe making the same step.

In *Mason & Dixon,* Pynchon's protagonists condemn the enslavement of Africans and the violent dispossession of Native Americans. When Mason and Dixon resist these patterns of oppression, they give evidence of their ability to sympathize and identify with groups outside their own presumed subject positions as white male English professionals. Political theorists Ernesto Laclau and Chantal Mouffe make an argument that correlates closely with Pynchon's way of thinking about political action in his narrative. For Laclau and Mouffe, it is crucial that people are not confined — as they are in the theories of ideology of Marx and Althusser — to a single subject position defined by their class, race, religion, or education. The ability to assume the subject position of others in groups to which one may not belong by birth, and to identify not upward but across or down the social scale enables the establishment of connections between groups that may have equivalent interests in eliminating their unjust treatment by the dominant social group (Laclau and Mouffe, 127–34, 176–93).

Mason and Dixon show themselves capable of drawing such equivalences when they recognize and protest against the mistreatment of African slaves and dispossessed Native Americans. Through Mason's account of the weavers' strike of 1756, Pynchon extends the equivalence between slaves and Native Americans to include British workers, as all three groups are unjustly deprived of liberty, property, or the means of life by dominant groups in English society. However, in the course of re-animating this history and demystifying General Wolfe as a hero of empire, Pynchon's account denies Wolfe's own ability to see outside his subject position as a military officer.

* * * * *

The specifics of the weavers' agitation in 1756–57 emerge through two dialogues in the novel: the first between Mason and a truculent American colonist; the second, somewhat later and longer, between Mason and Dixon. The American argues that Englishmen without property, such as Mason, are no more free than African slaves, but are owned by whoever employs them. Although Mason protests against the equating of wage-earning with chattel slavery, which he has observed both in South Africa and North America, he is put on the defensive when the American learns he is from Stroud (in fact, from Oakridge Lynch, a few miles from Stroud).[1] The colonist maintains that the clothiers depend for the enforcement of their will on rifles wielded by soldiers just as the slavemasters depend on whips wielded by overseers. Although the weavers receive wages, he says, "I think you know how weavers are paid — tho' Wolfe preferr'd to settle the Pay-list with lead and steel, keeping his hand in between Glorious Victories, thinking he'd use weavers for target practice, nasty little man . . ." (407). Mason does not continue the interchange but instead falls into a recollection of "that autumn of '56, when the celebrated future Martyr of Quebec, with six companies of Infantry, occupied that unhappy Town after wages were all cut in half . . . and a weaver was lucky to earn tuppence for eight hours work . . . [S]oldiers were beating civilians and slaughtering sheep for their pleasure, fouling and making sick Streams once holy" (407). As these events were occurring, Mason remembers, he was just about to leave his "Golden Valley" to take up a position as assistant to James Bradley, the Astronomer Royal. Mason thus loses his Edenic garden twice here — not only must he leave it behind to pursue his chosen field of knowledge, but also this is a "doom'd Paradise" because of its desecration by Wolfe and his troops.

The second conversation and set of memories concerning the weavers has a number of continuities with the first, but it is cast in a more sublime and heroic rather than an elegiac mode. Again, Wolfe's soldiers behave brutally; stopping occasionally at his orders to use as target practice any animal that strikes their fancy, they leave behind them "a path scarlet with hundreds of small innocent lives wild and domestic" (501). This time Mason, rather than the American colonist, sees a parallel between the weavers and a dispossessed group: "Wolfe," he speculates, "may have felt the same contempt for British Weavers as did Braddock for American Indians,— treacherous Natives, disrespectful, rebellious . . . " (501). Pynchon suggests here that Africans, Native Americans, and English workers are all treated unjustly by the British Empire and its army.

But in this conversation, Mason also explains the details of the weavers' grievances, and their actions, which on at least one occasion provided a memorable example — one might say a revelation of group solidarity in the pursuit of justice. During the depression of 1755–56, Mason recalls in indirect discourse, the local Justices of the Peace "reduced by half the Wages set by law" for weavers (501). After telling Dixon that his wife's family were weavers, Mason remembers the "wondrous night" in October, 1756, when the streets were filled with all the weavers from in and around Stroud — altogether "thousands of angry Men," including Rebekah's family and Mason himself: "torches everywhere, Looms dress'd in Mourning, . . . and the Murmur,— ever, unceasingly, the great, crisp, serene Roar,— of a Mobility focus'd upon a just purpose" (502). Dixon offers that he too demonstrated in the streets, in support of keelmen in Newcastle. However, after providing this support of other working men by Dixon, the rest of the passage undercuts the idea of the heroic or sublime solidarity of the weavers. In a somewhat deflating detail, Dixon reports that the sound of a mob reflected by bricks in the north must be different and less sonorous than in the southwest. From there, the conversation quickly descends into a squabble about whether weavers or keelmen make better drinking companions. At the end of the exchange, in what seems to be a farcical invention, we learn that on one of those October nights in Stroud, several clothiers were besieged by a mob at an inn and were compelled to jump from a second-story window to escape.

Thus, in Pynchon's representation of the depression and related events in Gloucestershire in autumn, 1756, the weavers, faced with a reduction in their already subsistence-level wages, take collective action, which includes striking, protesting in the streets, and even rioting. However, six companies of infantry are brought in under then-Colonel Wolfe, and the workers' demonstrations are violently suppressed by English soldiers beating and shooting at English workers. The historical record shows that in what concerns the weavers, Pynchon's narrative is extremely accurate, even when it might seem most imaginative. However, in what concerns Wolfe and the soldiers, Pynchon's account is almost entirely inaccurate — in some ways misleading, in others fabricated and counterfactual.

* * * * *

In *The Crying of Lot 49* and *Gravity's Rainbow*, Pynchon represents a fabricated historical entity — Tristero in the former, the Counterforce in the latter — that metaphorically represents the dispossessed who have been ignored by history. His portrayal of the weavers in *Mason & Dixon* departs from his previous practice by providing not a metaphorical, but more forcefully, a literal basis for the equivalences suggested in the novel. In the depression of the mid-1750s, weavers had to struggle against attempts to lower wages by employers, who also faced pressure to lower prices themselves. At this time, the majority of weavers were earning four pence for approximately sixteen hours of work. They almost all worked at home on their own looms, and were paid by the piece, not by the hour (Moir, "Gentleman Clothiers," 252).[2] At first, the weavers agitated for wages to be set in accord with an act of 1727 for regulating their wages and resolving disputes between the workers and the clothiers. But a parliamentary committee that investigated the situation in the fifties found that the clothiers had never paid these wages because they had "entered into an Association not to pay" the rates set by local Justices of the Peace in 1728 in accordance with this act.[3] As a result, a new act was passed in 1754 (27 Geo. II, c.33), again empowering justices to fix wages. The weavers petitioned for them to do so in 1755, arguing that they could barely survive on the wages then being paid; but the clothiers counterpetitioned, stating that wages needed to be kept low or their businesses would not survive. Declaring in this case that no equitable rate could be determined, the court in effect decided with the clothiers, and did not set wages.

In early October 1756, the frustrated weavers went on a strike that was to last for six weeks and cause a loss to the county of £15,000 to £20,000 (comparable in contemporary purchasing power to at least several million dollars). There were loom-wreckings and mass demonstrations. At one meeting, held at Stroud on October 11, several thousand weavers from around the county presented their proposals for wage rates to some clothiers who had come together to discuss the situation. Pent up by the mob in a room at the inn, the masters agreed to the weavers' demands, and, as the crowd surged in from outside, several clothiers had to jump from a second floor window. After this incident, soldiers were called in to protect the peace. Still, when the next quarter session of the court sat in Gloucester on November 6, the justices accepted the rate which the weavers had demanded and which the clothiers had agreed to under pressure. The strike came to an end, and soon afterward the soldiers were removed from the county.

The success of the weavers, however, was short-lived. In February, 1757, the clothiers petitioned Parliament, and, after carefully selected testimony favoring the masters had been heard, the clause of the previous act allowing justices to set wage rates was repealed (30 Geo. II, c.12). Some "poor and distressed" weavers from Stroud presented a petition against this repeal at the beginning of March, followed a week later by a petition against the repeal from several gentlemen and landlords from Gloucestershire (Moir, 257). However, the repeal took effect, and the newly won wage rates were overturned (it is not clear they were ever paid); this victory by the masters can be seen as establishing in the clothing industry the principle of laissez faire that would not become official national policy for another fifty years.[4]

The account just given of the events surrounding the Gloucestershire weavers' strike of 1756 bears out the arguments made by E. P. Thompson about the moral economy of the crowd and by E. J. Hobsbawm about machine-breaking in the eighteenth century. In his now-classic study, Thompson argues that riots and acts of property destruction by crowds of workers in the early modern period were not pointless, purely destructive expressions of collective anger. Rather, riotous destruction usually followed a rational calculus and served the purpose of recalling employers and local authorities to their traditional responsibility of caring for the people, at least not letting them starve ("Moral Economy"). Thus, a moral impetus and a conservative presumption underlay and helped shape the actions of rioters such as weavers in the southwest or keelmen and colliers in the northeast. Numerous reports from the autumn and winter of 1756–57 speak of workers and country people forming crowds and rioting, often appropriating foodstuffs at less than sellers' prices and sometimes plundering goods outright. In November, in Shropshire, a mob of colliers and common people, "for many days before having had nothing but grains and salt to subsist upon," at last broke into the houses of grocers, bakers, and farmers, and plundered them of provisions; at Broseley and other market towns, similar crowds forced farmers to reduce the price of wheat from 8 to 5 shillings a bushel, then went on to take grain for nothing (*Gentleman's Magazine*, v. 26, 544). At an inquest in

Gloucestershire in late January into recent seizures and plundering of grain from barges, the defendants claimed that such grain was forfeited to them by law (*Gentleman's Magazine*, v. 27, 43). Although they were convicted and fined heavily, their defense provides a contemporary articulation by the rioters of the moral argument that Thompson sees as underlying and helping to explain riots and destruction throughout the long eighteenth century.

Hobsbawm similarly contends that during the same period, the destruction of machinery often did not arise from a suspicious antagonism to new machines, but instead constituted part of a strategy to put pressure on employers to raise wages, or, more often, not to lower them. Thus, workers burned masters' barns, broke into storehouses and destroyed supplies as well as machines ("Machine Breakers"). In 1726–27, in Gloucestershire and other counties in the southwest, weavers broke into the houses of masters and blacklegs (scabs), destroying wool, looms, and utensils of the trade. The result of these actions was the law of 1727, which authorized justices to establish minimum wages for the weavers. Citing this example as well as others, Hobsbawm writes that "wrecking was simply a technique of trade unionism in the period before, and during the early phase of, the Industrial Revolution," and he singles it out as having been particularly effective for weavers, coal-miners, and seamen (59, 66).

We can now assess how accurately Pynchon represents the weavers' actions in the strike of 1756. Mason's representation of the average wage for a broadcloth weaver at the time is precise: "tuppence for eight hours' work" (409). Even though he makes the questionable assertion that the Justices of the Peace in 1756 cut the weavers' wages in half (501), he correctly shows the weavers struggling against reductions in wages more often than gaining increases. Moreover, his description of Stroud and the large public meeting of the weavers conveys a sense of the workers' indignation, anger, and solidarity at their unfair treatment. Since the population of Stroud in 1756 was only a little over two thousand, the fact that several thousand people attended this meeting means that most or almost all of the populace of Stroud and the valley must have been present.[5] Pynchon captures the significance of the event, in accord with Thompson's claim, in the sound made by the crowd in the town's small and usually empty streets — "the great, crisp, serene Roar,— of a Mobility focus'd upon a just purpose" (502). Even the somewhat farcical and seemingly imaginary picture of the clothiers forced to jump from the second floor of what was probably the George's Inn (where Wolfe would stay a week later) is, as we have seen, attested to in earlier historical accounts (Moir, 257). Pynchon's addition of the cartoonish detail of the masters not having had time to take their lit pipes out of their mouths or to put down their punch cups as the crowd surges in — the kind of supporting detail that is usually allowed to the historical novelist — displaces the masters' having agreed to a higher wage rate before they had to jump. Still, Pynchon's historical imagination is operating on a high level in this depiction of the sights and sounds as well as the important moral and political purpose of the striking weavers' public meeting and riot on what must have been October 11, 1756.

But Pynchon goes even further in extending the implications of this scene when he has Mason remark by way of introducing what he experienced among the mob of striking workers: "I have look'd on Worlds far distant, their Beauty how pitiless" (502). This cryptic assertion carries strong intertextual relations with two significant twentieth-century works. In the first of these, "Easter 1916," William Butler Yeats asserts that as a result of the violence and the deaths caused by the Easter uprising against British rule in Ireland, "All is changed, changed utterly. / A terrible beauty is born" (87). Pynchon, then, associates the "pitiless" beauty of the striking weavers — their ethical determination — with the political violence of the Irish who were determined to throw off British rule: in both cases, harshness and violence are linked with efforts to seek political justice.

Through Mason's statement, Pynchon also alludes to Ridley Scott's *Blade Runner* (1982), where, just before he dies, the android Roy Batty tells the detective who has been pursuing him, "I've seen things you people wouldn't believe true . . . Attack ships on fire off the shoulder of Orion." The close parallels between the lines of Batty and Mason may help explain some of the peculiarities in the latter's account. Perhaps Mason has "look'd on Worlds far distant" in the sense that they are far different from the everyday world of his time. His expression implies that his experience of participating in a large crowd of striking workers focused on their just purpose constituted an epiphany for him, a sublime utopian moment that opened up the possibility of another world within the familiar one, like the awful but beautiful vision Batty has had of an exploding warship in another solar system.

The echo of *Blade Runner* also establishes a relation between the late eighteenth-century past and the late twentieth-century future. This equivalence between historical periods functions like the equivalences already discussed between diverse groups in a single historical period. The parallel in this case links an historical human and a fictional android. However, the fact that Batty was brought into the world only to be exploited, that he has been denied selfhood and human rights, that he has rebelled against and returned from the off-world work colonies — these elements tie his story together with the stories of the other dispossessed groups in *Mason & Dixon:* slaves, Native Americans, and workers. Batty is both a machine and yet also more human than the other characters in the film: he has seen and experienced more; like the workers, he has felt and rebelled against his exploitation. He can also exercise compassion rather than making a living by killing. His status as both machine and human renders him comparable to the ethical mechanical characters in *Mason & Dixon*, including Vaucanson's Duck and the conversing chronometers. Finally, the anachronistic echo of a twenty-first-century science fiction character by an earlier historical figure paradoxically has the effect not of undermining, but of providing a retroactive authorization to the earlier fiction. Thus, rather than historical elements such as documents, events, or well-known figures providing a sense of reality to fictional characters — as is common in historical novels — in this case, the entirely fictional character underwrites the historical figure.

There is also a striking omission in Pynchon's treatment of the weavers. Although his attitude toward machines has been compared to that of the Luddites — not least because of his 1984 essay, "Is It O.K. to Be a Luddite?" — in *Mason & Dixon*, Pynchon makes no mention of the loom-breaking that accompanied the 1756 strike. One can imagine that in earlier works, Pynchon might have dwelt on the possible threat posed by new technologies or the conflict between workers and machines. However, the looms destroyed in 1756 and throughout the eighteenth century were not new machines, and as Hobsbawm points out, an antagonism to machinery as such was foreign to the attitudes of English workers, apart from the years of the Luddites proper, 1811–13. In fact, Pynchon's omission here indicates an accomplishment: by not attributing to the workers a hostility to machinery as such, Pynchon avoids an anachronism and maintains the accuracy of his narrative.[6]

However, a certain fluidity also characterizes the historical situation that is not registered in Pynchon's account. For example, Pynchon has Mason say that the Justices of the Peace, "upon easily imagin'd arrangements with the Clothiers, reduced by half the [weavers'] Wages set by law" (501). It is true that the Justices of the Peace declined at this time to establish a higher wage rate, although they were authorized to do so by the act of 1754; however, there is no evidence that local J.P's cut weavers' wages in 1756. In fact, it was not the case that the local justices would always side against the weavers or other workers throughout the eighteenth century. It has already been noted that the 1728 wages for weavers, which the clothiers considered too high and would not observe, were established by the local justices. Indeed, there is evidence that during much of the century, clothiers considered some or many J.P.s not as allies but as antagonists. A pamphlet published in 1739 which is harshly critical of the workers, complains that the 1727 act was biased against the clothiers, and sees most of the magistrates as "exceedingly" partial to the laborers

(Philalethes). The general attitude of the justices may have changed in the second half of the century.[7] However, as late as January, 1757, a meeting of Justices of the Peace, clergymen, and others took place in Durham to form a society to relieve distressed workers by selling them grain at a moderate price (*Gentleman's Magazine*, v. 27, 43). And, in the southwest, maltsters in the same month agreed not to buy any barley at the market because of its "exorbitant" price; they also encouraged purchasers of grain in other market towns to follow their example, "for the benefit of all in general and of the poor in particular" (*Gentleman's Magazine*, v. 27, 43). These are only two indicators from the winter of the Stroud strike of the concern of the Justices of the Peace and other country gentlemen with the effects of high grain prices on the working poor.

* * * * *

According to the fullest and most widely available collection of his letters, Colonel Wolfe received orders on October 19, 1756, to march six companies of foot soldiers into Gloucester "to assist the civil authority," in Wolfe's words, "in suppressing riots, etc." (Willson 304). By October 24, Wolfe was in the neighborhood of Stroud, but he gives no evidence in his letters of contempt for the weavers or of a desire to suppress them brutally. He writes that "the Gloucester weavers and I are not yet come to blows nor do I believe we shall" (304). In fact, he calls the expedition a "harmless piece of business," and anticipates it might be a means of recruitment because the people are "so oppressed, so poor, and so wretched" that they may prefer taking their chances in the army to their life in Stroud (304–5). In November 1756, he writes in striking support of the workers' position and their grievances against the clothiers: "the poor half-starved weavers . . . beg about the country for food, because, they say, the masters have beat down their wages too low to live upon, *and I believe it is a just complaint.* Those who are most oppressed have seized the tools and broke the looms of others that would work if they could" (306; italics added). He concludes by expressing concern that they will commit "some extravagancies" that would "force the magistrates to use our weapons against them" (306). Far from revealing a bloody-minded contempt for the workers, Wolfe in his letters agrees that they are not receiving a living wage, and he considers their grievances well-founded. Even the loom-breakers who destroy property and deprive others of the chance to work do not arouse his anger or indignation; the weavers would have to resort to more extreme measures before he could justify ordering his troops into action against them.

The picture presented by other contemporary accounts of the activities of Wolfe's troops in Gloucestershire is consistent with the attitude expressed in these letters. In a time of severe economic distress, with many people near starvation, Wolfe's troops do not appear to have been operating under the orders of a brutal and eager oppressor of the workers or poor. For example, the "Historical Chronicle" in the *Gentlemen's Magazine* reported that in December 1756, when Wolfe and his soldiers were about the leave the county, a river barge with two thousand bushels of wheat for a Worcester distillery was stopped by a mob of colliers a few miles below Gloucester. The colliers and some country people were about to carry off the grain when a party of Wolfe's soldiers appeared, dispersed the rioters, and rescued about six hundred bushels of grain (*Gentleman's Magazine*, v. 26, 591). Neither this report, nor other descriptions of encounters between Wolfe's troops and the striking workers of Gloucestershire in autumn, 1756, mentions Wolfe's men firing on, killing, beating, or severely wounding the workers. One might suggest that killings occurred but went unreported, because the lives of the poor were considered beneath notice. However, Wolfe's own letters indicate that the killing of Englishmen by English soldiers would have caused angry protests; and the killing of a small number of workers sixty years later at Peterloo (St. Peter's Fields outside Manchester) did cause widespread and lasting outrage.

The question arises, then, why Pynchon has chosen to represent Wolfe and his soldiers as brutal enforcers of an internal oppression. Such a portrait serves two main purposes, one of which I have already touched on. Wolfe's presence in Mason's hometown less than ten years before the drawing of the Line provided historical grounds for equivalences between British workingmen — weavers from the southwest, colliers and keelmen from the northeast — and slaves and natives in the American colonies.[8] All are deprived of what is rightly theirs by the empire whose will is enforced by an army of redcoats under officers such as Wolfe.[9] But, in addition, Pynchon's narrative is very interested in debunking conventional and strongly entrenched heroes, including the idea of General Wolfe as the Martyr of Quebec who, by sacrificing his life in the battle on the Plains of Abraham, obtained the victory of the English over the French in North America and established the greatest extent of the first British empire.[10]

In Pynchon's earlier works, even if the historical conspiracy with which the plot is concerned cannot be established as historical fact, it can nevertheless be understood metaphorically, as pointing to inconvenient or unacknowledged historical truths, especially the condition of being lost or left behind, which is shared by many in Pynchon's fictions.[11] In *Mason & Dixon,* the condition of the weavers is not a metaphor for the oppression of workers, and it carries greater weight because it is historically accurate. The portrait of Wolfe may be intended as a metaphor or synecdoche of the brutal imperial enforcer, but the James Wolfe who figures in *Mason &*

Dixon is a counterfactual fiction.[12] Pynchon is not merely extrapolating from suggestive facts, filling in parts of a picture for which the evidence has not come down to us. We have evidence — indeed all the relevant evidence points in the same direction — and it contradicts the portrait Pynchon draws of Wolfe among the weavers.[13] On the other hand, apart from the representation of Wolfe, *Mason & Dixon* marks a significant advance over the historical imagination at work in the earlier narratives in that the historical existence not only of the weavers, but of the most powerful and sinister forces in the narrative — the Jesuits and the East India Company, one dominant in the economic sphere, the other in the religious — is well established. Such a firm anchoring in history contrasts these institutions with V., Tristero, or Them, which are Pynchon's fictions not based on historical characters or documents.

* * * * *

Although Pynchon's acts of historical imagination and reconstruction in *Mason & Dixon* are impressive in many ways, he has also flattened out some complications in the historical situation that he depicts. He is correct that the local J.P.s did not help the weavers in 1756, and an "arrangement" between magistrates and clothiers is, in Mason's words, "easily imagin'd" (501), but such an imagined conspiracy turns all J.P.s into villainous agents of the manufacturing interest. The alignment of magistrates with manufacturers would become characteristic in the 1790s and throughout the nineteenth century. However, in the mid-eighteenth century, J.P.s were not homogeneously antagonistic to workers, and in their thinking and actions some, perhaps many in certain places, inclined to favor the workingmen over the innovating manufacturers, even though such a position may seem to contradict their subject position, based on nineteenth- or twentieth-century class alliances. Unfortunately, projecting later attitudes back onto the eighteenth-century magistrates parallels the more serious counterfactual portrayal of Wolfe as a brutal oppressor of English workers. In these instances, Pynchon does not take sufficiently into account that individuals, even in charged historical circumstances, may make judgments and pursue actions that are not entirely consistent with their expected or official subject positions. Such contradictions or departures from a presumed monolithic subject position by a James Wolfe or anonymous country magistrates set them apart from the stereotypical villainous oppressor.

In the depiction of Mason and Dixon themselves, Pynchon represents the possibility of identifying outside one's own biographical, economic, or professional subject position. He offers an instance of such an identification in the passage before us when he has Mason express his solidarity with the weavers: "They're people, Dixon, whom I saw daily, they work'd, they ate when they came off shift, good for a Cob or a Batch-Loaf a Day. Or a Mason's Bap,— that was my Dad's own speciality" (501). However, along with farmers and the manufacturers themselves, bakers were one of the groups most likely to have their goods plundered during food shortages, times of high prices, and labor disputes. Mason thus identifies apart from his economic subject position as the son of a baker when he sympathizes with the weavers who protest against the injustice of wages that are at or below subsistence level.

One of the principal achievements of the novel is that Mason and Dixon condemn slaveholders and Indian haters, and they work to help slaves. Such actions based on equivalences among Indians, slaves, and workers are possible because Mason and Dixon do not reproduce the accepted judgments of their time. Such dissenting positions avoid being anachronistic because, like many others in our own time and in theirs, Mason and Dixon are capable of seeing ethically in ways that are not limited by their positions — whether as Anglican astronomer and baker's son, or as well-educated Quaker surveyor from Northern England. Perhaps Pynchon identifies General Wolfe and the country Justices of the Peace with a Britain that is hierarchical, imperialistic, and oppressive, while, because of their contact with the early American landscape, he allows Mason and Dixon an access to other perspectives, an openness to other possibilities that he associates with the early days of America. For Pynchon, Dixon, and especially Mason, become Americans.

Whatever the reasons for the differences between the two cases, Pynchon succeeds in re-envisioning the history of the weavers' strike: he vividly animates the earlier historical moment, providing a sense of its active political questions and conjunctures, and the choices individuals can make. Yet the one-dimensional stereotyping of Wolfe and the J.P.s qualifies his success. In these instances, Pynchon does not quite attain the sympathetic understanding of the position of slaves and Native Americans achieved by Mason and Dixon in the rest of the novel, or the questioning of their own act in drawing the Line. Still, the work challenges readers in its own time similarly to question and attempt to step outside our own political judgments and social arrangements.

Notes

[1] Stroud was known in the eighteenth century as "a sort of capital of the clothing villages" in southwest England. The phrase, from Bishop Pococke in 1757, is quoted in Esther Lowndes Moir, "Gentlemen Clothiers: A Study of the Organization of the Gloucestershire Cloth Industry 1750–1835," 225–66, 227.

[2] Here and in what follows, I am indebted to Moir's account of both the clothing industry in the southwest of England and of the events surrounding the strike of October–November 1756.

[3] Journal of the House of Commons, March 1756, 37, p. 503; quoted in Moir, "Gentlemen Clothiers," 246.

[4] See Moir, 264; see also Brian Bailey, *The Luddite Rebellion* (New York: New York UP, 1998), 1–15.

[5] For the population of Stroud at this time, see *Victorian County History, Gloucester*, vol. 3, 100.

[6] In the first paragraphs of "Is It O.K. to Be a Luddite?" Pynchon offers a largely accurate account of the Luddites in the second decade of the nineteenth century, noting that in the previous century, textile workers did not break looms out of hostility to machinery as such, and that the looms were not new, but had been in use for more than a hundred years. He sees the earlier breaking of looms in the eighteenth century as a labor action, which he ascribes to a feeling that the machines were taking work away from the weavers. However, he then goes on, in the principal part of the essay, to discuss a series of figures (he calls them "Bad-asses") whom he considers to be heirs of the Luddites and to stand opposed to the use of machinery. This part of his argument is unfortunate and not consistent with the first part. The presentation of the weavers' strike in *Mason & Dixon* accords with the understanding of the workers in the first part of this article.

[7] On the neutrality of the national government in disputes between workers and manufacturers at least through midcentury, see Hobsbawm, "Machine Breakers," 66.

[8] In a novel that is concerned with the ethical status and treatment of animals, it is noteworthy that Pynchon adds a fourth group to those already named: the inoffensive and defenseless animals whom he imagines Wolfe's troops slaughtering for target practice. It is not coincidental that the name of the commanding officer of the bloody soldiers in the novel is the same as that of the predator who also kills defenseless wild and domestic animals. Pynchon makes Wolfe's name meaningful in his narrative, as though he were writing a fable.

[9] Ironically, in the second half of the eighteenth century, Stroud was well-known as the source of the British soldiers' coats: "the scarlet cloth of Stroud clothed the armies of England" (Moir 232).

[10] For a classic portrayal of the physically frail but iron-willed Wolfe, see Francis Parkman's *Montcalm and Wolfe*. See also the discussion of the continuing impact of Benjamin West's *Death of Wolfe* in Simon Schama's *Dead Certainties, Unwar-*

ranted Speculations. A hagiographic tone pervades most of the scores of books and chapters in the literature on Wolfe.

[11] Pynchon's project thus shares much with the efforts of Michel Foucault, who has been accused of being historically inaccurate, but whose works nonetheless often pointed to a larger historical narrative that had not previously been recognized.

[12] Pynchon also has Mason's American interlocutor, who knows about Wolfe's presence in Stroud, assert that Wolfe was a "nasty little man" who "hated Americans, by the way,— 'Contemptible cowardly dogs who fall down dead in their own Shit,' I believe was the way he phras'd it. . . ." (407). Pynchon seeks to protray Wolfe as the embodiment of British military, imperial, and aristocratic arrogance, obtuseness, and injustice. On Wolfe, see, in addition to Beckles Willson's *Life and Letters of James Wolfe,* John Clarence Webster, *Wolfiana: A Potpourri of Facts and Fantasies Culled from Literature Relating to the Life of James Wolfe;* Robin Reilly, *The Rest to Fortune: The Life of Major-General James Wolfe;* Duncan William Grinnel-Milne, *Mad, Is He? The Character and Achievement of James Wolfe;* and Stuart Reid, *Wolfe: The Career of James Wolfe from Culloden to Quebec.*

[13] Mason serves as the focal point through whom the accounts of Wolfe and his soldiers are presented. However, the passages in question, mostly in free indirect discourse (407, 500–501), are given without any distancing of the narrative voice from Mason and his memories. Similarly, although Wicks Cherrycoke supposedly recounts the entire narrative, there is no indication of Cherrycoke's voice or presence in these passages. The representation of the acts of Wolfe and his soldiers is not framed in any way that would undercut or call it into question.

Works Cited

Adam, Ian, and Helen Tiffin, eds. *Past the Last Post: Theorizing Post-Colonialism and Post-Modernism.* New York & London: Harvester Wheatsheaf, 1991.

Adorno, Theodor W., and Max Horkheimer. *Dialectic of Enlightenment.* Trans. John Cumming. New York: Continuum, 1972.

Althusser, Louis. "Ideology and Ideological State Apparatuses." *Lenin and Philosophy and Other Essays.* Trans. Ben Brewster. New York: Monthly Review Press, 1971. 127–88.

Anderson, Benedict. *Imagined Communities: Reflections on the Origin and Spread of Nationalism.* London: Verso, 1991.

Andrews, Kenneth R. *Trade, Plunder, and Settlement: Maritime Enterprise and the Genesis of the British Empire, 1480–1630.* New York: Cambridge UP, 1984.

Ashcroft, Bill, Gareth Griffith, and Helen Tiffin, eds. *The Empire Writes Back: Theory and Practice in Post-Colonial Literatures.* London & New York Routledge, 1989.

Attridge, Derek. "Expecting the Unexpected in Coetzee's *Master of Petersburg* and Derrida's Recent Writings." *Applying: To Derrida.* Ed. John Brannigan, Ruth Robbins, and Julian Wolfreys. London: Macmillan, 1996. 21–40.

———. "Innovation, Literature, Ethics: Relating to the Other." *PMLA* 114 (1999): 20–31.

Auden, W. H. *The Enchafèd Flood: or, The Romantic Iconography of the Sea.* London: Faber & Faber, 1951.

Baker, Jeffrey S. "A Democratic Pynchon: Counterculture, Counterforce and Participatory Democracy." *Pynchon Notes* 32–33 (Spring-Fall 1993): 99–131.

———. "Plucking the American Albatross." In *Pynchon and Mason & Dixon,* edited by Brooke Horvath and Irving Malin. Newark and London: U of Delaware P; Associated UP, 2000. 167–88.

Balibar, Etienne. "The Nation Form: History and Ideology." Trans. Chris Turner. *Race, Nation, Class: Ambiguous Identities,* edited by Etienne Balibar and Immanuel Wallerstein. London: Verso, 1991. 86–106.

Ball, John Clement. *Satire and the Postcolonial Novel: V. S. Naipaul, Chinua Achebe, Salman Rushdie.* London: Routledge, 2003.

Baringer, Sandra Kay. "The Metanarrative of Suspicion: Surveillance and Control in Late Twentieth Century America." Doctoral Dissertation. U of California, Riverside, 1999.

Baym, Nina. "Melodramas of Beset Manhood: New Theories of American Fiction Exclude Women Authors." In *The New Feminist Criticism: Essays on Women, Literature and Theory,* edited by Elaine Showalter. New York: Pantheon Books, 1985. 63–80.

Bennett, Norman R. *Africa and Europe: From Roman Times to the Present.* New York: Holmes and Meier, 1975.

Bercovitch, Sacvan. *The American Jeremiad.* Madison: U of Wisconsin P, 1978.

———. *The Rites of Assent.* New York, London: Routledge, 1993.

Berkeley, George. "Verses on the Prospect of Planting Arts and Learning in America." *The Works of George Berkeley, Bishop of Cloyne.* 2nd ed. Edited by A. A. Luce and T. E. Jesson. London: Thomas Nelson and Sons Ltd. 1955. 7: 370–73.

Berressem, Hanjo. *Pynchon's Poetics: Interfacing Theory and Text.* Urbana: U of Illinois P, 1994.

Bersani, L. "Pynchon, Paranoia and Literature." *Representations* 25 (1989): 99–118.

Berubé, Michael. *Marginal Forces/Cultural Centers.* Ithaca: Cornell UP, 1992.

Bhabha, Homi K. "DissemiNation: Time, Narrative, and the Margins of the Modern Nation." In *Nation and Narration,* edited by Homi K. Bhabha. London: Routledge, 1990. 291–322.

The Bible. KJV.

Bidney, David. "The Idea of the Savage in North American Ethnohistory." *The American Enlightenment,* edited by Frank Shuffelton. Rochester: U of Rochester P, 1993. 97–102.

Black, Joel D. "Probing the Post-Romantic Paleontology: Thomas Pynchon's *Gravity's Rainbow.*" *Boundary* 2.8 (1980): 229–54.

Bloom, Harold. "Introduction." In *Thomas Pynchon,* edited by Harold Bloom. Modern Critical Views. New Haven: Chelsea House, 1986: 1–9.

Boehmer, Elleke. *Colonial & Postcolonial Literature: Migrant Metaphors.* Oxford & New York: Oxford UP, 1995.

Bondanella, Peter. *Umberto Eco and the Open Text: Semiotics, Fiction, Popular Culture.* New York: Cambridge UP, 1997.

Booth, Sally Smith. *Hung, Strung, & Potted: A History of Eating in Colonial America*. New York: Clarkson N. Potter, 1971.

Botsford, Jay Barrett. *English Society in the Eighteenth Century: As Influenced from Oversea*. New York: Octagon, 1965.

Bourdieu, Pierre. *The Logic of Practice* and *Outline of a Theory of Practice*. Trans. Richard Nice. Cambridge; New York: Cambridge UP, 1977.

Bowden, James. *Pennsylvania and New Jersey*. Vol. 2. *The History of the Society of Friends in America*. London: W. & F. G. Cash, 1854.

Boyle, T. Coraghessan. "The Great Divide: Thomas Pynchon's Novel Features Two Historical Figures Who Were Sent to America to Settle a Dispute." Review of *Mason & Dixon*. *New York Times Book Review* 18 May 1997, 9.

Boym, Svetlana. *The Future of Nostalgia*. New York: Basic Books, 2002.

Bramah, Edward. *Tea & Coffee: A Modern View of Three Hundred Years of Tradition*. London: Hutchison of London, 1972.

Braudy, Leo. "Providence, Paranoia, and the Novel." *English Language Notes* 48 (1981): 619–37.

Brydon, Diana, and Helen Tiffin. *Decolonising Fictions*. Sydney, Mundelstrup & Hebden Bridge: Dangeroo Press, 1993.

Burke, Kenneth. *A Grammar of Motives*. Berkeley: U of California P, 1945.

Burns, Christy L. "Postmodern Historiography: Politics and the Parallactic Method in Thomas Pynchon's *Mason & Dixon*." *Postmodern Culture* 14.1 (September 2003). 1 June 2004. http://muse.jhu.edu/journals/postmodern_culture/toc/pmc14.1.html.

Calvin, John. "Of the Lord's Supper, and the Benefits Conferred By It." *Institutes of the Christian Religion* IV:17. Trans. by Henry Beveridge. 6 April 1999. *Institute of Practical Bible Education*. 16 April 2005. http://www.iclnet.org/pub/resources/text/ipb-e/ipbe-home.html.

Campbell, Gwyn. "The Origins and Development of Coffee Production in Réunion and Madagascar, 1711–1972." In *The Global Coffee Economy in Africa, Asia, and Latin America, 1500–1989*. Edited by William Gervase Clarence-Smith and Steven Topik. New York: Cambridge UP, 2003. 67–99.

Clerc, Charles. *Mason & Dixon & Pynchon*. Lanham, New York, Oxford: UP of America, 2000.

Collado Rodríquez, Francisco. "Trespassing Limits: Pynchon's Irony and the Law of the Excluded Middle." *Oklahoma City University Law Review* 24 (1999): 471–503.

Cooper, Peter L. *Signs and Symptoms: Thomas Pynchon and the Contemporary World*. Berkeley: U of California P, 1983.

Cope, Thomas D. "A Mountain in Perthshire." *Pennsylvania History* 21.7 (July 1954): 231.

———. "Collecting Source Material about Charles Mason and Jeremiah Dixon." *Proceedings of the American Philosophical Society* 92.2 (May 1948): 111–14.

———. "First Scientific Expedition of Mason and Dixon." *Pennsylvania History* 12.1 (January 1945): 24–33.

———. "The Stargazers' Stone," *Pennsylvania History* 6:4 (October, 1939): 205–20.

Cowart, David. "The Luddite Vision: *Mason & Dixon.*" *American Literature* 71.2 (June 1999): 341–63.

Crouzet, François. *A History of the European Economy, 1000–2000.* Charlottesville: UP of Virginia, 2001.

Delaney, Bill. "An In-Depth Look At Opus Dei: A Conservative Catholic Group." *CNN Live This Morning* transcript, 8 May 2001. http://www.cnn.com/TRANSCRIPTS/0105/18/ltm.10.html.

Deleuze, Gilles. *Difference and Repetition.* Trans. Paul Patton. New York: Columbia UP, 1994.

Deloria, Philip J. *Playing Indian.* New Haven: Yale UP, 1998.

De Man, Paul. "The Rhetoric of Temporality." In *Blindness and Insight: Essays in the Rhetoric of Contemporary Criticism.* 2nd ed. London: Routledge, 1983. 187–228.

Dewey, Joseph. "The Sound of One Man Mapping: Wicks Cherrycoke and the Eastern (Re)solution." In In *Pynchon and Mason & Dixon,* edited by Brooke Horvath and Irving Malin. Newark and London: U of Delaware P; Associated UP, 2000. 112–31.

"dispensation." *Oxford English Dictionary Online.* 2005. Oxford UP. 1/31/2001 16 April 2005. http://www.oed.com.

Donne, John. "The First Anniversarie: An Anatomie of the World." Project Gutenberg Renascence Editions. Project Gutenberg Consortia Center. Accessed 20 June 2005. http://www.worldebooklibrary.com/ebooks/renascence_editions/donne2.html.

Duyfhuizen, Bernard. Review of *Mason & Dixon. The News and Observer.* Raleigh, NC. 4 May 1997: G4.

Eco, Umberto. *Foucault's Pendulum.* Trans. William Weaver. San Diego: Harcourt Brace Jovanovich, 1989.

———. *The Island of the Day Before.* Trans. William Weaver. New York: Harcourt Brace Jovanovich, 1995.

———. *The Open Work*. Trans. Anna Cancogni. London: Hutchinson Radius, 1989.

———. *Postscript to the Name of the Rose*. Trans. William Weaver. New York: Harcourt Brace Jovanovich, 1984.

Fabian, Johannes. *Time and the Other: How Anthropology Makes its Object*. New York: Columbia UP, 1983.

Feder, Lillian. *Madness in Literature*. Princeton: Princeton UP, 1980.

Fernando, M. R. "Coffee Cultivation in Java, 1830–1917." In *The Global Coffee Economy in Africa, Asia, and Latin America, 1500–1989*, edited by William Gervase Clarence-Smith and Steven Topik. New York: Cambridge UP, 2003. 157–72.

Foreman, David. "Historical Documents Relating to *Mason & Dixon*." In *Pynchon and Mason & Dixon*, edited by Brooke Horvath and Irving Malin. Newark and London: U of Delaware P; Associated UP, 2000. 143–65.

Foucault, Michel. *Madness and Civilization: A History of Insanity in the Age of Reason*. 1961. Trans. Richard Howard. London: Tavistock, 1967.

———. *Madness and Civilization: A History of Insanity in the Age of Reason*. Trans. Richard Howard. London: Routledge, 1989.

———. *The Order of Things: An Archaeology of Human Sciences*. New York: Pantheon, 1971.

———. "Qu'est ce que les Lumières?" *Dits et écrits, 1954–1988*. Edited by Daniel Defert et Francois Ewald. Vol. 4. Paris: Gallimard, 1994. 562–77.

Fournier, Marcel. *De la Nouvelle-Angleterre à la Nouvelle-France*. Société Généalogique Canadienne-Français. 1992.

"Glossary." *Bivar Inovative Packaging & Assembly Solutions*. 2002–3. Bivar, Inc. 16 April 2005. http://www.bivar.com.

Gilchrist, Ebenezer. *The Use of Sea Voyages in Medicine*. London: T. Cadell, 1771.

Grange, Kathleen M. "The Ship Symbol as a Key to Former Theories of the Emotions." *Bulletin of the History of Medicine* 36 (1962): 512–23.

Grinnel-Milne, Duncan William. *Mad, Is He? The Character and Achievement of James Wolfe*. London: Bodley Head, 1963.

Guzlowski, John Z. "No More Sea Changes: Hawkes, Pynchon, Gaddis, and Barth." *Critique* 23. 2 (1981): 48–60.

Hartman, Saidiya V. *Scenes of Subjection: Terror, Slavery, and Self-Making in Nineteenth-Century America*. New York: Oxford UP, 1997.

Hegel, G. W. F. *The Phenomenology of Spirit*. Trans. A. V. Miller. Oxford: Oxford UP, 1977.

Heindel, R. H. "An Early episode in the Career of Mason and Dixon." *Pennsylvania History* 6.1 (Jan 1939): 20–24.

Hescher, A. "Postmodern Paranoia and Thomas Pynchon, Forms of Discourse in American Literature: The Opening of Constellations of Binary Metaphors in *Gravity's Rainbow*." *Arbeiten Aus Anglistik und Amerikanistik* 22.1 (1997): 53–68.

Hinds, Elizabeth Jane Wall. "Sari, Sorry, and the Vortex of History: Calendar Reform, Anachronism, and Language Change in *Mason & Dixon*." *American Literary History* 12.1–2 (2000): 187–215.

Hipkiss, Robert A. *The American Absurd: Pynchon, Vonnegut, and Barth.* National University Publications. Port Washington, NY: Associated Faculty Press, 1982.

Hite, Molly. *Ideas of Order in the Novels of Thomas Pynchon.* Columbus: Ohio State UP, 1983.

Hobsbawm, E. J. "The Machine Breakers," *Past and Present* 1 (1952), 57–70.

Hofstadter, Richard. *The Paranoid Style in American Politics, and Other Essay.* New York: Alfred Knopf, 1965.

Hohmann, Charles. *Thomas Pynchon's Gravity's Rainbow: A Study of Its Conceptual Structure and of Rilke's Influence.* New York: Peter Lang, 1986.

Hollis, H. P. "Jeremiah Dixon and his Brother." *Journal of the British Astronomy Association* 44.8 (June 1934): 294–99.

Horvath, Brooke, and Irving Malin, eds. *Pynchon and Mason & Dixon.* Newark and London: U of Delaware P; Associated UP, 2000.

Hume, Kathryn. *Pynchon's Mythography: An Approach to Gravity's Rainbow.* Carbondale: Southern Illinois UP, 1987.

Hutcheon, Linda. *A Poetics of Postmodern Fiction: History, Theory, Fiction.* New York: Routledge, 1988.

Irving, Washington. "Traits of Indian Character." *The Sketch Book.* New York: Putnam, 1849.

Jackson, Stanley W. *Melancholia and Depression: From Hippocratic Times to Modern Times.* New Haven: Yale UP, 1986.

Jacobs, Sir Harry H. *A History of the Colonization of Africa by Alien Races.* Cambridge: Cambridge UP, 1930.

Jameson, Fredric. "Cognitive Mapping." *Marxism and the Interpretation of Culture,* edited by Cary Nelson and Lawrence Grossberg. Urbana: U of Illinois P, 1988. 347–60.

———. *Postmodernism, or, the Cultural Logic of Late Capitalism.* Durham: Duke UP, 1992.

————. "Regarding Postmodernism: A Conversation with Fredric Jameson." In *Postmodernism/Jameson/Critique*, edited by Douglas Kellner. Washington, DC: Maisonneuve Press, 1989. 43–74.

Jarvis, Brian. *Postmodern Cartographies: The Geopolitical Imagination in Contemporary American Culture*. London: Pluto, 1998.

"Jenkin, Robert." *Hyperarts Pynchon Page: Mason & Dixon*. Tim Ware, Curator. 16 April 2005. http://www.hyperarts.com/pynchon/mason-dixon/alpha/j.html.

Johnson, John. "Towards the Schizo-Text: Paranoia as Semiotic Regime in *The Crying of Lot 49*." In *New Essays on* The Crying of Lot 49. 47–78.

Kant, Immanuel. "An Answer to the Question: 'What is Enlightenment?'" *Kant's Political Writings*, edited by H. Reiss. Cambridge: Cambridge UP, 1970. 54–60.

————. *Critique of Judgment*. Trans. Werner S. Pluhar. Indianapolis: Hackett Publishing Company, 1987.

Kaplan, Amy. "The Tenacious Grasp of American Exceptionalism: A Response to Djelal Kadir." *Comparative American Studies* 2 (2004): 153–60.

Keesey, Douglas. "*Mason & Dixon* on the Line: A Reception Study." *Pynchon Notes* 36–39 (1995–96 [1998]): 165–78.

Kelly, Robert. "Castaway." *New York Times Book Review*. 22 Oct 1997: 7–9.

Kiely, Robert. "Being Serious in the 'Sixties: Madness, Meaning and Metaphor in *One Flew Over the Cuckoo's Nest* and *The Crying of Lot 49*." *Hebrew University Studies in Literature and the Arts* 12.2 (1984): 215–37.

Klarreich, Erica. "Discovery of Coupled Oscillation Put 17th-Century Scientist Ahead of His Time." SIAM News 35.8 (October 2002): 1–3. http://www/siam.org/ siamnews/10–02/oscillation.pdf.

Klibansky, Raymond, Erwin Panofsky, and Fritz Saxl. *Saturn and Melancholy: Studies in the History of Natural Philosophy, Religion and Art*. London: Thomas Nelson, 1964.

Kolesch, D. "A Creative Paranoia Against Televized History: A Loss of History and Recollection in Thomas Pynchon's *The Crying of Lot 49*." *Arbeiten Aus Anglistik und Amerikanistik* 20. 2 (1995): 275–305.

Krafft, John M. "'And How Far-Fallen': Puritan Themes in *Gravity's Rainbow*." *Critique* 18.3 (1977): 55–73.

Kuhn, Thomas. *The Structure of Scientific Revolutions*. 3rd ed. Chicago: U of Chicago P, 1996.

Labrador, David. "From Instantaneous to Eternal." *Scientific American* 287.3 (2002): 56–57.

Laclau, Ernesto, and Chantal Mouffe. *Hegemony and Socialist Strategy: Towards a Radical Democratic Politics.* New York: Verso, 1985.

Laing, R. D. *The Divided Self: An Existential Study in Sanity and Madness.* 1960. Middlesex, England: Penguin Books, 1971.

———. *The Politics of Experience and The Bird of Paradise.* 1967. Middlesex: Penguin, 1981.

Lalo, Alexei. "Bely and Pynchon: Anatomists of History." *Pynchon Notes* 44–45 (Spring-Fall 1999): 35–50.

Latrobe, John H. B. *The History of Mason and Dixon's Line.* Philadelphia: Press of The Historical Society of Pennsylvania, 1855.

Lay, Benjamin. *All slave-keepers that keep the innocent in bondage, apostates pretending to lay claim to the pure & holy Christian religion; of what congregation so ever; but especially in their ministers, by whose example the filthy leprosy and apostacy is spread far and near; it is a notorious sin, which many of the true Friends of Christ, and his pure truth, called Quakers, has been for many years, and still are concern'd to write and bear testimony against; as a practice so gross & hurtful to religion, and destructive to government, beyond what words can set forth, or can be declared of by men or angels, and yet lived in by ministers and magistrates in America. The leaders of the people cause them to err. / Written for a general service, by him that truly and sincerely desires the present and eternal welfare and happiness of all mankind, all the world over, of all colours, and nations, as his own soul.* Philadelphia: printed by Benjamin Franklin for the author, 1738.

Lefever, Susan. *The Stargazers: Story of Mason and Dixon, an Historical Biographical Novel.* York: Printing Press, 1986.

Liebman, Sheldon W. "Still Crazy After All these Years: Madness in Modern Fiction." *Midwest Quarterly* 34.4 (1993): 398–415.

Logan, William. "Pynchon in the Poetic." *Southern Review* 83 (1998): 424–37.

Lukács, György. *The Historical Novel.* Trans. Hannah and Stanley Mitchell. London: Merlin, 1965.

Lupack, B. T. *Insanity as Redemption in Contemporary American Fiction: Inmates Running the Asylum.* Gainesville: UP of Florida, 1995.

Lynch, Kevin. *The Image of the City.* Cambridge: Technology Press, 1960.

Lyotard, Jean-François. *The Differend: Phrases in Dispute.* Trans. Georges Van Den Abbeele. Minneapolis: U of Minnesota P, 1988.

———. *The Postmodern Condition: A Report on Knowledge.* Trans. Geoff Bennington and Brian Massumi. Minneapolis: U of Minnesota P, 1984.

Mackey, L. "Paranoia, Pynchon and Preterition." *Sub-Stance* 30 (1981): 16–30.

Marietta, Jack D. *The Reformation of American Quakerism, 1748–1783.* Philadelphia: U of Pennsylvania P, 1984.

Marx, Karl, and Friedrich Engels. *The Marx-Engels Reader.* 2nd ed. Edited by Robert C. Tucker. NY: Norton, 1978.

Mason, A. Hughlett. Preface to *The Journal of Charles Mason and Jeremiah Dixon.* Philadelphia: Memoirs of the American Philosophical Society 76 (1969). vii.

Mason, Charles, and Jeremiah Dixon. "Astronomical Observations, made in the Forks of the River Brandiwine in Pennsylvania, for determining the going of a Clock sent thither by the Royal Society, in order to find the Difference of Gravity between the Royal Observatory at Greenwich, and the Place where the Clock was set up in Pennsylvania: To which are added, an Observation of the End of an Eclipse of the Moon, and some Immersions of Jupiter's First Satellite observed at the Same Place in Pennsylvania." *Philosophical Transactions of the Royal Society of London,* 58 (1768): 329–35.

———. *The Journal of Charles Mason and Jeremiah Dixon.* Introduction by A. Hughlett Mason. Philadelphia: Memoirs of the American Philosophical Society 76 (1969).

———. "Latitude of the Observatory at the Cape of Good Hope." *Philosophical Transactions of the Royal Society of London,* 52 (1762): 395.

———. "Observations for determining the Length of a Degree of Latitude, in the Provinces of Maryland and Pennsylvania, in North America." *Philosophical Transactions of the Royal Society of London,* 58 (1768): 274–328.

———. "Observations made at the Cape of Good Hope." *Philosophical Transactions of the Royal Society of London,* 52 (1762): 378–94.

Mattessich, Stefan. "Telluric Texts, Implicate Spaces." *Postmodern Culture* 8.1 (1997). Par. 1–18. 16 April 2005. http://muse.jhu.edu/journals/postmodern_culture.

McHale, Brian. "Mason & Dixon in the Zone, or a Brief Poetics of Pynchon-Space." In *Pynchon and Mason & Dixon,* edited by Brooke Horvath and Irving Malin. Newark and London: U of Delaware P; Associated UP, 2000. 43–62.

McHugh, Patrick. "Cultural Politics, Postmodernism, and White Guys: Affect in *Gravity's Rainbow.*" *College Literature* 28.2 (Spring 2001): 1–28.

McIntosh, Elaine N. *American Food Habits in Historical Perspective.* Westport: Praeger, 1995.

McNickle, D'Arcy. *Native American Tribalism: Indian Survival and Renewals.* New York, Oxford and London: Oxford UP for the Institute for Race Relations, 1973.

Mellor, Timothy. *Empire of Conspiracy: The Culture of Paranoia in Postwar America*. Ithaca: Cornell UP, 2000.

Melville, Herman. *Moby-Dick*. 1851. New York: W. W. Norton, 1967.

Melvin, Richard L. *New England Outpost: War and Society in Colonial Deerfield*, New York: W. W. Norton, 1989.

Milton, John. *Paradise Lost*. 1667. Edited by Alistair Fowler. London: Longman, 1990.

Moir, Esther Lowndes. "Gentlemen Clothiers: A Study of the Organization of the Gloucestershire Cloth Industry 1750–1835." *Gloucester Studies*, edited by H. P. R. Finburg. Leicester: The UP, 1957. 225–66.

Moody, Rick. "Surveyors of the Enlightenment." *Atlantic Monthly* 280.1 (July 1997): 106–10.

Moore, Thomas. *The Style of Connectedness: Gravity's Rainbow and Thomas Pynchon*. Columbia: U of Missouri P, 1987.

Moseley, Benjamin. *A Treatise Concerning the Properties and Effects of Coffee*. Philadelphia: Samuel H. Smith, 1796.

Nicolson, Marjorie Hope. *Mountain Gloom and Mountain Glory: The Development of the Aesthetics of the Infinite*. 1959. New York: Norton, 1963.

O' Donnell, Patrick. "Introduction." *New Essays on* The Crying of Lot 49, edited by Patrick O' Donnell. Cambridge: Cambridge UP, 1991. 1–20.

———. *Latent Destinies: Cultural Paranoia and Contemporary U.S. Narrative*. Durham: Duke UP, 2001.

Oliver, Edward Fitch, ed. *The Diary of William Pynchon of Salem: A Picture of Salem Life, Social and Political, a Century Ago*. Boston & New York: Houghton Mifflin & Co., 1890.

Olsen, Kirsten. *Daily Life in 18th Century England*. Westport, CT: Greenwood Press, 1999.

Pagano, David Frank. "Haunting from the Future: Time, Ghosts, and the Apocalypse of Modernity in Pynchon, Poe, and Romero." Dissertation. University of California, Irvine, 1999.

Palmeri, Frank. "Other than Postmodern? Foucault, Pynchon, Hybridity, Ethics." *Postmodern Culture* 12.1 (2001): 39 pars. 2 December 2002.

Parkman, Francis. *Montcalm and Wolfe*. New York: Da Capo, 1995.

Parsons, William T. *The Pennsylvania Dutch: A Persistent Minority*. Boston: Twayne, 1976.

Pendergrast, Mark. *Uncommon Grounds: The History of Coffee and How it Transformed Our World*. New York: Basic Books, 1999.

Philalethes. *The Case as it now Stands between the Clothiers, Weavers, and Other Manufacturers. . . .*1739.

Poirier, Richard. "The Importance of Thomas Pynchon." *Twentieth Century Literature* 21.2 (1975): 151–62.

Poole, Robert. "'Give Us Our Eleven Days!': Calendar Reform in Eighteenth-Century England." *Past and Present: A Journal of Historical Studies* 149 (November 1995): 95–139.

Pynchon, Thomas. *The Crying of Lot 49*. Philadelphia: Lippincott, 1996.

—. "The Deadly Sins/Sloth: Nearer, My Couch, to Thee." *New York Times Book Review*. 6 June 1993: 3; 57. 15 April 2005. http://www.nytimes.com/books/97/05/18.

—. *Gravity's Rainbow*. 1973. Rpt. New York: Bantam, 1974.

—. "The Heart's Eternal Vow." *The New York Times* On The Web. 15 April 2005. http://www.nytimes.com/books/97/05/18/reviews/pynchon-cholera.html.

—. "Is It O.K. to Be a Luddite?" *The New York Times* On The Web. 28 Oct 1984. 15 April 2005. http://www.nytimes.com/books/97/05/18/reviews/pynchon-luddite.html.

—. "A Journey Into The Mind of Watts." *The New York Times Magazine* 12 June 1966: 34–36; 80–83.

—. *Mason & Dixon*. New York: Henry Holt, 1997.

—. *Vineland*. Boston and London: Little, Brown and Co, 1990.

Pynchon, William. *The Diary of William Pynchon of Salem, 1723–1789*. Boston: Massachusetts Historical Society.

Raffa, Guy. "Walking and Swimming with Umberto Eco." *MLN* 113.1 (1998): 164–85.

Reid, Stuart. *Wolfe: The Career of James Wolfe from Culloden to Quebec*. Rockville Centre, NY: Sarpedon, 2000.

Reilly, Robin. *The Rest to Fortune: The Life of Major-General James Wolfe*. London: Cassell, 1960.

Ricciardi, Alessia. "Lightness and Gravity: Calvino, Pynchon, and Postmodernity." *MLN* 114.5 (1999): 1062–1077.

Richardson, A. E. *Georgian England: A Survey of Social Life, Trades, Industries and Art from 1700 to 1820*. Edinburgh: Darien Press, 1931.

Robinson, H. W. "Charles Mason's Ancestry." *Proceedings of the American Philosophical Society*. 93.2 (May 1949): 135.

—. "Jeremiah Dixon (1733–1779). A Biographical Note." *Proceedings of the American Philosophical Society*. 94.3 (June 1950): 272.

Ross, Andrew, ed. *Universal Abandon?: The Politics of Postmodernism*. Minneapolis: U of Minnesota P, 1988.

Schama, Simon. *Dead Certainties, Unwarranted Speculations.* New York: Knopf, 1991.

Schaub, Thomas H. "Plot, Ideology, and Compassion in *Mason & Dixon.*" In *Pynchon and Mason & Dixon,* edited by Brooke Horvath and Irving Malin. Newark and London: U of Delaware P; Associated UP, 2000. 189–202.

Schmidt, Peter. "Line, Vortex, and Mound: On First Reading Thomas Pynchon's *Mason & Dixon.*" *Thomas Pynchon's Mason & Dixon.* 11 Nov 1999. http://www. swarthmore.edu/Humanities/pschmid1/essays pynchon/mason.html.

Scott, Ridley. *Blade Runner.* Warner Brothers, 1982.

Scott Coe, Justin. "Haunting and Hunting: Bodily Resurrection and the Occupation of History in Thomas Pynchon's *Mason & Dixon. Reconstruction: Studies in Contemporary Culture* 2.1 (Winter 2002). 3 December 2002.

Seed, David. "Mapping the Course of Empire in the New World." In *Pynchon and Mason & Dixon,* edited by Brooke Horvath and Irving Malin. Newark and London: U of Delaware P; Associated UP, 2000. 84–99.

Semmes, John Edward. *John H. Latrobe and His Times, 1803–1891.* Baltimore: The Norman, 1917.

Siegel, Mark. Rev. of *Mason & Dixon,* by Thomas Pynchon. *Journal of Popular Culture* 31.4 (Spring 1998): 176–77.

Simons, Jon. "Postmodern Paranoia? Pynchon and Jameson." *Paragraph* 23. 2 (2000): 207–21.

Slade, Joseph W. "Thomas Pynchon, Postindustrial Humanist." *Technology and Culture* 23 (Jan 1982): 53–72.

Sobel, Dava. *Longitude: The True Story of a Lone Genius Who Solved the Greatest Scientific Problem of His Time.* New York: Penguin Books, 1995.

Soderlund, Jean R. *Quakers and Slavery: A Divided Spirit.* Princeton: Princeton UP, 1985.

Spivak, Gayatri Chakravorty. "Can the Subaltern Speak?" *Marxism and the Interpretation of Culture,* edited by Cary Nelson and Lawrence Grossberg. Urbana: U of Illinois P, 1988. 271–313.

Stein, Roger B. "Seascape and the American Imagination: The Puritan Seventeenth Century." *Early American Literature* 7 (1972): 17–37.

Stephanson, Anders. *Manifest Destiny: American Expansion and the Empire of Right.* New York: Hill and Wang, 1995.

Stephenson, Anders. "Regarding Postmodernism: A Conversation with Fredric Jameson." *Postmodernism/Jameson/Critique,* edited by Douglas Kellner. Washington, DC: Maisonneuve Press, 1989. 43–74.

Strandberg, Victor. "Dimming the Enlightenment: Thomas Pynchon's *Mason & Dixon*." In *Pynchon and Mason & Dixon*, edited by Brooke Horvath and Irving Malin. Newark and London: U of Delaware P; Associated UP, 2000. 100–111.

Szasz, Thomas. *Insanity: The Idea and its Consequences.* New York: John Wiley, 1987.

Tanner, Tony. *City of Words: American Fiction 1950–1970.* New York: Harper & Row, 1971.

Thompson, E. P. "The Moral Economy of the English Crowd in the Eighteenth Century." *Past and Present* 50 (1971): 77–108.

Topik, Steven and William Gervase Clarence-Smith. "Introduction" to *The Global Coffee Economy in Africa, Asia, and Latin America, 1500–1989.* 1–20.

Tryon, Thomas. *Friendly advcie [sic] to the gentlemen-planters of the East and West Indies: in three parts . . . / by Philotheos Physiologus [I] A brief treatise of the most principal fruits and herbs that grow in the East and West Indies, giving an account of their respective vertues both for food and physick, and what planet and sign they are under, together with some directions for the preservation of health and life in those hot climates — [I]I. The complaints of the negro-slaves against the hard usages and barbarous cruelties inflicted upon them — [I]II. A discourse in way of dialogue, between an Ethiopian or negro-slave, and a Christian that was his master in America.* André Sowle: London, 1684.

Valenstein, Elliot S. *Great and Desperate Cures: The Rise and Decline of Psychosurgery and Other Radical Treatments for Mental Illness.* New York: Basic Books, 1986.

Vaughn, Alden T., and Edward W. Clark, eds. *Puritans Among the Indians: Accounts of Captivity and Redemption, 1676–1724.* Cambridge and London: The Belknap Press of Harvard UP, 1981.

Velcic, Vlatka. "Postmodern and Postcolonial Portrayals of Colonial History: Contemporary Novels About the Eighteenth Century." *Tennessee Philological Bulletin* 38 (2001): 41–48.

Venturi, Franco. *Utopia and Reform in the Enlightenment.* Cambridge: Cambridge UP, 1971.

Victorian County History, Gloucester. Vol. 3.

Webster, John Clarence. *Wolfiana: A Potpourri of Facts and Fantasies Culled from Literature Relating to the Life of James Wolfe.* New Brunswick: Shediac, 1927.

Weisenburger, Steven. *A Gravity's Rainbow Companion. Sources & Contexts.* Athens: U of Georgia P, 1988.

Weld, C. R. *History of the Royal Society* 2. London, 1848: 11–17.

Wharton, Donald B. "The Colonial Era." *America and the Sea: A Literary History.* Edited by Haskell Springer. Athens: U of Georgia P, 1995. 32–45.

———. "The Revolutionary and Federal Periods." *America and the Sea: A Literary History,* edited by Haskell Springer. Athens: U of Georgia P, 1995. 46–63.

White, Hayden. *The Content of the Form: Narrative Discourse and Historical Representation.* Baltimore: John Hopkins, 1987.

Willson, Beckles. *The Life and Letters of James Wolfe.* New York: Dodd, Mead & Co., 1909.

Wood, Michael. "Pynchon's *Mason & Dixon.*" *Raritan* 17.4 (1998): 120–30.

Yeats, William Butler. *Selected Poems and Plays.* Edited by M. L. Rosenthal. New York: Collins, 1980.

Contributors

COLIN A. CLARKE is an assistant professor of English at Suffolk County Community College. His publications include articles on Robert Lowell, Sylvia Plath, and Anne Sexton.

IAN COPESTAKE is a lecturer at the Institut für England- und Amerikastudien at the Johann Wolfgang Goethe Universität, Frankfurt. He is editor of the following books: *American Postmodernity: Essays on the Recent Fiction of Thomas Pynchon*, and *Rigor of Beauty: Essays in Commemoration of William Carlos Williams*.

PEDRO GARCÍA-CARO received his Ph.D. in 2004 from King's College, University of London with a thesis entitled "Dismantling the Nation: History as Satire in the Narratives of Thomas Pynchon and Carlos Fuentes." He has published on Peter Ackroyd and Pérez-Reverte, and has recently translated "The Fever" by Wallace Shawn into Spanish. He has taught Spanish and Latin American literatures at Oxford and MIT, and currently at the University of Oregon.

ELIZABETH JANE WALL HINDS is professor and chair of the English department at SUNY Brockport in upstate New York. She is author of *Private Property: Charles Brockden Brown's Gendered Economics of Virtue* (U of Delaware P, 1997), and articles on Brown, Pynchon, Olaudah Equiano, and topics in popular culture.

MITCHUM HUEHLS is an assistant professor of English at College Misericordia. He is currently working on a book manuscript that addresses formal approaches to the textual performance of temporality in the last three decades of twentieth-century American literature. Focusing on intersections between form and culture, articles on William Carlos Williams's "Kora in Hell" and Harryette Mullen's "Muse & Drudge" have appeared recently in *Paideuma* and *Contemporary Literature*, respectively.

DENNIS LENSING is adjunct faculty in the Liberal Studies Division of Huston-Tillotson College, an historically black college in Austin, Texas. He is presently a Ph.D. candidate in English Literature at the University of New Mexico, researching and writing his dissertation on postwar American fiction and the construction of a new consumerist ethic. His essay "Pariah among Pariahs: Images of the IV Drug User in the Context of AIDS" appeared in the Fall 2002 issue of *Americana: The Journal of*

American Popular Culture, 1900–Present, and he won the South Central Modern Language Association's 2001 Gender Studies Award for his essay "Hymen as Hydra in *Fanny Hill.*"

FRANK PALMERI is professor of English at the University of Miami, where he teaches eighteenth- and nineteenth-century literature and literary theory. He is the author of *Satire in Narrative* (1990) and *Satire, History, Novel: Narrative Forms, 1665–1815* (2003). On Pynchon he has written "'Neither Literally nor as Metaphor': Pynchon's *The Crying of Lot 49* and the Structure of Scientific Revolutions" (*ELH*, 1987), and "Other than Postmodern: Foucault, Pynchon, Hybridity, Ethics" (*Postmodern Culture,* 2001).

JUSTIN M. SCOTT COE is a Ph.D. student at Claremont Graduate University. His major emphasis is Early American literature, and his dissertation is on covenant theology and its influence on American political thought. He received his M.A. in Anglo-American Literary Relations at University College London.

BRIAN THILL is a Ph.D. candidate in English and instructor in the Humanities Core Curriculum, at the University of California, Irvine, where he is completing his dissertation on the aesthetics of American anti-fascism. He has received numerous fellowships, including the Sally Casanova Pre-Doctoral Fellowship and the Jacob K. Javits Fellowship. He has recently presented papers on Ernest Hemingway, James Joyce, and George Schuyler.

Index

Eco, Umberto, 22, 126, 129–33, 136, 137, 138–41, 142
Eco, Umberto, works by: *The Island of the Day Before*, 22, 125, 126, 129–33, 136, 139, 140; *The Name of the Rose*, 129; *Postscript to the Name of the Rose*, 126
Elect, the, 161, 162
election (Calvinist), 171. *See also* religion
eleven days, 10, 41, 160–63
Eliza Fields, 12–13, 39, 134
Emerson, William, 6, 10–11, 12, 20, 25–26, 28, 33–34, 35, 36, 43 n. 4
empathy, 51, 52, 68
Enlightenment, the, 5, 9–10, 11, 17, 22, 49, 54, 64, 73, 103, 108–10, 112, 118, 122 n. 13, 141, 159, 164, 183
entropy, 4
epiphany of complicity, 75 n. 4
Ethelmer, 13, 39
Eucharist, 82, 93, 95, 149, 156, 158, 160, 162, 163
evil, 11, 63, 65, 66, 70, 83, 114, 119, 140, 156, 157, 181
exceptionalism, 21, 102–3, 106
expansionism (westward), 21, 102, 106, 113–14, 118. *See also* Indian Removal; westward expansion

fantasy, 18, 71–73, 74, 97, 152, 156, 162, 183
fate, 10, 81, 154. *See also* destiny
Feder, Lillian, 177, 178–79
feng shui, 12, 31, 141, 148
food, 20, 21, 62, 77–86, 91–98, 160, 189, 193, 196; *ketjap*, 77, 78, 79, 80, 81, 85; mutton, 77, 79, 92; sandwich, 21, 92–94, 95, 96, 98, 160, 163
food riot, 97, 160

Foreman, David, 18, 50
Foucault, Michel, 111, 112, 122 n. 13, 129, 130, 177, 184 n. 5, 198 n. 11
Fox, George, 59–60, 75 n. 3
frames, narrative, 13, 20, 33, 34, 38, 39, 44 n. 7, 45 n. 12
Franklin, Benjamin, 6, 7, 11, 88, 122 n. 18, 134, 150
Freud, Sigmund, 167 n. 5, 177–78
frontier, 21, 78, 84, 87, 89, 91, 94, 95, 97, 98 n. 10, 111, 161
fusion (cooking), 94–95, 96, 97
future, 15, 17, 19, 23, 26, 31, 35, 37, 38, 39, 41, 42, 45 nn. 13, 14, 46 n. 17, 97, 107, 114, 119, 142, 148, 154, 162–63, 164, 179, 182, 191
futurity, 19, 22, 37, 38, 148, 161

gallows, 157
Garcia Marquez, Gabriel, 147, 165
genocide, 67, 101, 165
The Ghastly Fop, 8, 13, 39–40
ghosts, 6, 45 n. 13, 154, 161. *See also* phantoms
Gibbon, Edward, 11
global market, 20–21, 49, 51, 52, 56, 75
globalization, 20, 78
Gloucestershire, 23, 122 n. 15, 185, 187, 189, 190, 193, 197 n. 1
gluttony, 53, 63, 64, 65
gnosis, 162, 168 n. 13
Gnosticism, 168 n. 13
The Great Gatsby, 175
Griffiths, Gareth, 77, 86
Guattari, Felix, 167 n. 5

Harrison, John, 10, 127–28, 129, 135, 136, 137, 142 n. 2
Hartman, Saidiya, 51–52

resurrection, 22, 147–48, 149,
151, 153, 163, 164–65, 168 n.
13
Revolution, American, 22, 58, 78,
89, 94, 97, 106, 112, 113, 118,
119, 123 n. 30
Ross, Andrew, 141
Royal Society, 6, 7, 8, 11, 77, 85,
104, 123 n. 28, 125, 128, 136,
150, 153, 160, 161, 165

salvation (religious), 81–82, 93,
95, 98, 108, 131, 151, 162,
168 n. 13
science, 5, 8, 9, 44 n. 9, 89, 103,
107, 119, 129, 130–32, 134,
137, 148, 149, 152, 153, 155,
165, 175
Scotland, 150, 160, 163
Scott Coe, Justin, 19, 22
segregation, 81
sex, 157; fetishistic, 157;
ritualistic, 156; with/to
produce slaves, 72, 79, 118,
156
Shropshire, 189
sin, 63, 66, 74, 112, 116, 128,
161
Sino-Jesuit (Chinese-Jesuit)
conspiracy, 12
slave labor, 57, 61, 62–63, 72–73,
98, 118. See also labor; slavery
slavery, 4, 5, 14, 16, 20, 21, 23,
49–56, 57–61, 63, 64, 66, 68–
69, 70, 71–74, 80, 81, 82, 84,
87, 90, 97, 98, 104, 116, 117–
18, 141, 155, 156, 157–58,
176, 181, 186; and Quakers,
59–61, 64, 75 n. 1. See also
slave labor
sloth, 63, 64, 65–67, 69, 72, 73,
74
Sobel, Dava, 128, 130, 131, 137
social activism, 49, 51, 52, 55, 57,
67, 71, 75 n. 1

South Africa, 7, 8, 50, 72, 85,
119, 125, 134, 141, 150,
153, 155, 156, 157–58, 186 .
See also Cape Town
space, 4–5, 17, 20, 22, 25, 28–
29, 31, 32–33, 35, 36, 40–41,
51, 57, 92, 102, 106, 107, 112,
114, 120, 121, 127, 137–39,
149, 150, 153–54, 156, 159,
160, 161, 163, 179, 180
St. Helena, 39, 40, 68, 82–84,
85, 86, 90, 92, 97, 110, 118,
133, 154, 155, 157, 167 n. 8,
176, 181
Starbucks, 12, 21, 88, 89, 97
Stephanson, Anders, 113, 121
Stroud, 23, 185, 186, 187, 188,
189, 190, 193, 197 nn. 1, 5, 9,
12
subjunctive, 15, 41, 42, 71, 73,
74, 110, 113–14, 116, 120–21,
123 n. 22, 149
sublime, the, 44 n. 8, 171
sugar, 4, 56; and colonialism, 64,
66, 85–86, 97; and slavery, 20,
57–58, 87, 90, 97. See also
cotton; tobacco
surveying (land), 25, 28, 30, 36,
37, 38, 39, 40, 45 n. 15, 56,
88, 150
Symmes' Hole, 4. See also hollow
earth
Szasz, Thomas, 177–78

teleology, 102, 142
Tenebrae, 13, 39
Them (from Gravity's Rainbow),
195
Thompson, E. P., 189–90
Thoreau, Henry David, 175
Tiffin, Helen, 77, 86, 94, 98 n. 1
time (chronology), 3–4, 5, 7, 9–
11, 12, 13–15, 17, 20, 25–42,
43 n. 5, 44 n. 6, 46 n. 16, 51,
112, 114, 127, 128, 136, 137,